Devon and Exeter
in the
Civil War

Eugene A. Andriette

Assistant Professor of History
University of Louisville Kentucky   USA

Devon and Exeter
in the
Civil War

david & charles : newton abbot

ISBN 0 7153 5256 3

Set in 10/12 point Baskerville
and printed in Great Britain
by W J Holman Limited Dawlish
for David & Charles (Publishers) Limited
South Devon House Newton Abbot Devon

Contents

List of Illustrations

Plates

*These plates are reproduced by permission of
The National Portrait Gallery, London
That of the Prince of Wales by gracious permission of
Her Majesty the Queen*

In the Text

Introduction

In thinking of the English civil wars of the 1640s most people generally call to mind the names Naseby and Marston Moor, Cromwell and Rupert, London and Oxford. Few indeed venture to think in terms of Great Torrington and Barnstaple, Seymour and Chudleigh, Plymouth and Exeter. But even in a cursory survey of the civil war period in the West Country, these last are names which spring prominently to the fore. Once this study has run its course, these persons and places connected with the first Civil War in the County of Devon, and in the City and County of Exeter, will perhaps once again possess the stature granted to them by their contemporaries. The first objective in these chapters is to present as fully as possible the story of what happened in the counties of Devon and Exeter during this period and thus to show that the region was of outstanding importance to both Cavalier and Roundhead. The second is to explain why events occurred as they did and to evaluate their significance in the Civil War as a whole.

The basic contention of this study is that no great issue in the history of any country can be completely understood until its manifestations at the local level have been assessed. The first Civil War especially falls within the category of subjects which have been studied and developed by outstanding historians, but too often from a national and central viewpoint. This work attempts to place the emphasis on those who were tragically caught up in the dilemma of the times, to side with King or Parliament, to join brother or cousin, to rebel or to remain loyal. In other words, it is an approach which attempts to add depth to the overall picture. There will be no attempt made, however, to re-examine the deep-seated causes of the civil strife, nor even to reconstruct the events which brought major segments of the English community into conflict with one another, conflict which could be resolved only by force of arms. Rather, given the framework of parliamentary privilege and royal prerogative, Puritan striving as opposed to Laudian reform, traditional constitutional practice versus attempted innovation, the task here is to portray Devon's role in a wartime period of enormous tension.

One of the dangers involved in a project of this kind is the possibility of placing too much emphasis on the importance of one county over another, of one place over another; ie, of so narrowing the scope of one's view as to obscure the often integral relationship of Devon and Exeter with other counties in the West Country, particularly with regard to Cornwall in the west, and Somerset, Wiltshire and Dorset in the north and east. The danger exists, also, of forgetting that the Civil War was a national phenomenon, only a part of which took place in Devon. Thus, Devon and Exeter were not islands unto themselves in this era of civil strife, and to read into the following activities of 1640-6 such an exaggerated emphasis would be a mistake—although isolated county identity will be seen to play a vital role.

While scholars have concentrated their attention on the more populous regions or where more famous battles took place, this area of England, long outstanding for its contribution to the political and economic life of the nation, has been neglected. Miss Mary Coate's work mentions events in Devon and Exeter as they affected her study of Cornwall during the Interregnum, as does Arthur R. Bayley in his study of Dorset in this period. John R. Powell has examined the naval aspect of the war in the West in his book *The Navy in the English Civil War*. But only Richard W. Cotton, in *Barnstaple and the Northern Part of Devonshire during the Great Civil War, 1642-1646*, and R. N. Worth in his articles on Plymouth during this period, have devoted themselves in a significant manner to Devonshire, and both writers completed their work before 1900.

Nor do these works make use of the Quarter Sessions records, Dartmouth Papers, and other documents kept in the Devon County Record Office and the Exeter City Record Office. The availability of a large body of Seymour papers, which escaped the notice of the Historical Manuscripts Commission, has significantly contributed to this study. In addition we have, for the period of parliamentary control in Exeter, Dartmouth, and Plymouth, full and complete accounts of every penny spent on defence by the local authorities. Unfortunately, no such collection of records is to be found for the period of royalist control in the area, and the lack of correspondence, and especially the absence of royalist county committee records, has imposed a severe limitation upon the scope of this study. It appears that defeat in 1646 brought about a widespread destruction of official and private royalist papers by those attempting to spare themselves future losses because of past political indiscretions. On the other hand, the businesslike habits of many parliamentarians, most of whom expected full payment for their efforts in support of Parliament, resulted in their keeping complete accounts of their wartime expenses.

An attempt was made to examine all aspects of life in the counties of Devon and Exeter with the object of obtaining as full and complete a picture as possible. Because of the nature of available materials, however, the political and socio-economic events of these years have not emerged with the same degree of clarity as have the military affairs. For the military side of the story a greater abundance of material survives.

The reader should understand that whenever the word 'Devon' or 'Devonshire' occurs in the text, the reference is to the administrative county which surrounds, but does not include, the then City and County of Exeter. Exeter was a distinct political and economic entity, while at the same time serving as the county town of Devon.

For the sake of clarity and continuity of style, spelling and punctuation have been modernized, and abbreviations spelled out in full. Dates are rendered according to the old style calendar so far as the day and month are concerned, but the year is given according to the new style, beginning on 1 January rather than on 25 March.

Prologue

. . . there be within the province XXXVIII market towns besides the city of Exeter of which XI be incorporated. The number of parks be very much impaired and of many remain not above or about XX, besides the two forests of Dartmoor and part of Exmoor, which some times was replenished with red deer, but now the game is very small and little regarded. And as for waters no one particular province in this land is more or better stored than is this county, for of rills, brooks, lakes, and springs, the number is as it were infinite or very hard to be numbered. And these by reason they do fall into great streams and rivers they do make them very great and some of them to be navigable; as namely, Exe, Dart, Plym, Tamar, Taw. In these rivers is great abundance of sundry . . . fish; . . . .

As for the country itself it is very strongly seated, . . . if the loyalty, faith, and obedience due unto the sovereign be yielded. It is not then very safe begotten nor invaded. For on the north and south sides it is . . . hedged with . . . British seas and on the west it bords . . . upon the river Tamar which is now the . . . [boundry] between the two provinces of Devon and Cornwall; . . . only the East part lyeth open upon the main land . . . ; and these marches being also full of vales, hills, rocks, and stone is very safely to be made strong and fortified against the invasion of any enemy if the disloyalties of the subjects do not cause the contrary.

The whole province and country within these boundries is in greatness the second to the greatest in this land and is altogether or for the most part wild, full of wastes, heaths, and moors, uphill and downhill among the rocks and stones . . . , long, craggy, and very painful for man or horse to travail as all strangers travelling the same can witness it. . . . And therefore so much the less passable for the enemy with his troops and impediments of war. The soil itself which was full of craggy hills and altogether full of stones and plains which were full of heaths and sedges and the valleys which were altogether full of briars and brambles are by mans travail and industry . . . become fertile and fruitful and do yield great varieties and plenties and plenty of herbs, fruits, and corn for the ease of man and goodly feeding and pasture for beasts of the field, great abundance of all kinds of fruits. . . . Great store of cattle both for necessity and for pleasure. The abundance of fowl both wild and tame, and of sea fish and of the like variety and abundance as in no other country [ie, county] the like freshwater fish and of all other things which . . . if severally to be set down requireth a greater volume. And likewise [in] the belly of the earth there be found and digged sundry rich mines, some of gold and silver, some of tin and lead, some of iron and other metals. . . .

And if I might speak without offense I dare avouch that which one writeth of generally of this land. That England may better live of self without any other nation then any other nation without it. And even so also this little corner of this land can live better of itself without the rest of the land than all the residue can live without it.[1]

See note on page 188

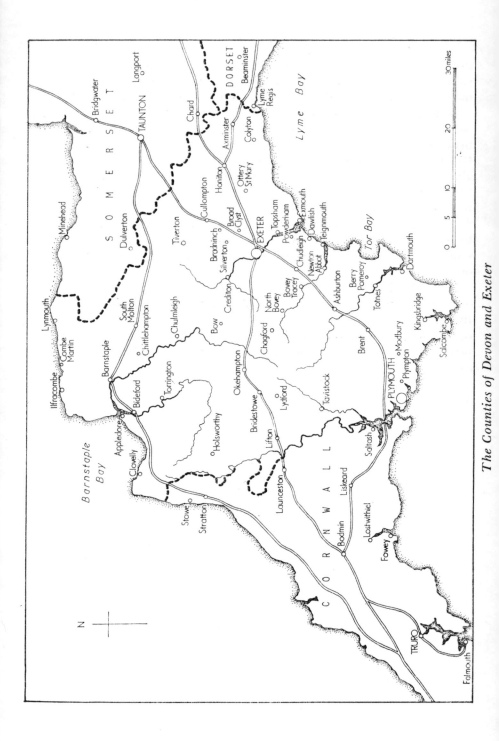

The Counties of Devon and Exeter

I

Structure of the County and City by 1640

Stripped of its chauvinism and outrageous sixteenth-century pride, this description of the County of Devon in 1599 by John Vowell alias Hooker provides a brief sketch of the prosperous and pleasing, but rugged and wild county as it could be seen on the eve of the first Civil War. In geographic terms Devon was the third largest county in England, after Yorkshire and Lincolnshire. From north to south the county extended, at its furthest point, almost seventy-five miles, and from east to west almost seventy-three miles. Within this area, divided into more than 450 parishes, lived approximately 40,000 families, totalling about 227,000 inhabitants. In terms of wealth and population, seventeenth-century Devon was regarded as among the top two or three counties in the kingdom, with the thriving commercial centre of Exeter functioning as the county town.[2]

Exeter itself was looked upon as one of the principal cities in England throughout the sixteenth and seventeenth centuries, having obtained county status as early as 1537. As the largest urban centre in Devon, Exeter (population between 9,000 and 10,500 people) dominated the area in its role as the commercial, administrative, ecclesiastical, and social hub of the county, consistently maintaining its place as fourth or fifth in wealth and size amongst the cities of the realm.[3] Following Exeter in urban importance came the maritime community of Plymouth with a population of between 8,000 and 9,000 people.[4] After Plymouth, ranked the boroughs of Totnes, Tiverton, Barnstaple, and Bideford, smaller in population and importance. As the reign of Charles I proceeded, all of these centres of commercial industry felt the effects of varied economic forces.

In the wider sector of the rural economy this period witnessed an expansion of the enclosure movement which reduced the amount of waste land in the county and incorporated this acreage for purposes of increased tillage and more extensive sheep-raising. The limited amount of evidence that survives, primarily with regard to increased tax returns from rural parishes, higher sums paid for extension of farm leases, and greater rural stability than in previous years, all points to a period of expanding prosperity for the freehold farmers and minor gentry who were numerically predominant in the Devon countryside. This was the era of 'high farming' in Devon, when the region was reputed the 'best-farmed county in England.'[5]

As Hooker pointed out, it was hard work and consistent effort that had turned the rugged landscape into the garden-spot of the West. And while average farm size appears to have been on the increase, the possession of freehold leases was becoming evermore diversified, spreading economic strength amongst a larger number of people.[6] According to Sir William Pole's survey of early seventeenth-century Devon, there were six aristocratic families which owned land in the county, but only the Earls of Bedford and Bath seem to have maintained homes there.[7] The majority of the county was thus in the hands of resident gentry, yeomen, and tenant farmers who drew a more or less satisfactory income from their lands.

In addition to its agricultural pursuits, industrial Devon was fully occupied along other lines of endeavour. Although Hooker did not stress it, by the time he began to write in such glowing terms of the county's mineral resources, the mining of silver, lead, copper, and especially of tin, was of minor significance. Hooker pointed to the 'great quantity' of silver that Mr Adrian Gilbert was reputed to have dug out around Combe Martin in recent years, to say nothing of the valuable and ancient tin production which dated from before the time of Edward I. But Devon tin mining had seen its heyday in the first half of the sixteenth century, and by the year 1640 the county was producing only some 15,000 hundredweight a year. On the eve of the Civil War tin 'had ceased to be of much consequence in the economy of Devon . . .' And at the same time, the iron mines near Ashburton and Brent in South Devon were replacing those in the foothills around Exmoor.[8]

A major secondary industry, and of far greater importance than mining, was the flourishing Devon fishing industry. Bordering both the Atlantic Ocean and the English Channel, Devonians had ready access to the adventure and profit which a maritime tradition had long since taught them to enjoy and develop. In the north Clovelly and Lynmouth were particularly well-known for their catches of fine herring, while on the south coast especially there had developed the pilchard trade with Plymouth as the major exporting centre, but with Dartmouth, Teignmouth, and Dawlish deeply involved.[9] By the mid-seventeenth century the prosperity of many West Country ports was based almost exclusively on the the famous Newfoundland cod fisheries, an industrial pursuit which annually involved many tons of shipping and thousands of men.[10] Dartmouth, Barnstaple, Plymouth, Bideford, and other such places drew their life-blood from the fishing trade. Dartmouth especially prospered as numerous maritime interests came to settle in this coastal town to take advantage of an enterprise which functioned without severe governmental interference or restrictions, and which permitted a good deal of local initiative and control. Mercantile interests around the country invested money in this very lucrative industry, and the ships engaged in the fishing trade sailing from Dartmouth were often owned by people from far afield.[11]

In surprising contrast to its dominant position in other aspects of Devon commerce, Exeter was not particularly involved in the Newfoundland fishing industry.[12] Rather, this county town gained pre-eminence through its close and profitable connection with the woollen cloth trade which provided the staple industry for the entire nation. Given its ideal location, Exeter was at the heart of one of the two significant West Country woollen industrial areas, that comprising all of Devon and west Somerset. Within this area goods, from the Totnes-Ashburton district were exported through Dartmouth, and the products from the vicinity of Tavistock moved through Plymouth harbour. But most of the woollen goods produced in the three major districts of west Somerset, the Exeter valley, and north Devon, found their way through Exeter and its subsidiary ports to the markets of Europe.[13]

The important cloth industry within the counties of Devon and Exeter had gained prominence particularly as a result of the widespread trade in the material known as the 'Devonshire kersey', or

B

more often, the 'Devon dozen'. During the 1620s Exeter, Tiverton, Crediton, and Cullompton had comprised the heart of this kersey manufacturing area.[14] The ensuing decades found Exeter taking up the production of the so-called 'New Drapery', leaving Tiverton especially to continue the production of the kerseys for which it was nationally known.[15] Thus, by the time Charles I came to the throne Exeter was widely known for its cloth market (supplied from an extensive tributary district) and for 'its cloth finishing industry and exporting trade', while the smaller towns retained a reputation for skill in craftsmanship.[16]

During the period immediately preceding the civil wars Exeter's economy, and that of Devon, functioned on a relatively simple process of exchange or barter. Exeter was the 'distribution centre for a prosperous regional economy' which kept the place humming with commercial life as it supplied the goods and services for the whole area.[17] While West Country cloths made up the largest part of export trade to France and Spain, and later to northern European markets, these countries in return sent to Exeter, for shipment throughout the region, large quantities of canvas and linen, along with wines, corn, salt, and a host of other items.[18]

As was the case in Exeter, most urban centers in Devon, whether inland industrial communities or coastal maritime and trading centers, all came within the control of wealthy and powerful merchant oligarchies which dominated both industrial and commercial activities, as well as municipal government itself. In Exeter the commercial policy of the port was controlled by the Company of Merchants of Exeter Trading to France, under whose authority fell all those trading with that country. Made up as it was of some of the wealthiest men of the community, the French Company easily came to dominate the city government as well.[19]

A similar situation existed with regard to Dartmouth. Although no formal trading guild or company was established there, the Mayor and Corporation, composed of the most outstanding and wealthy citizens, came to control the fishing industry and to regulate that trade, never failing to use municipal powers to increase this vital sector of the town's economy.[20] Again, in Barnstaple, the mayor, aldermen, and twenty-two capital burgesses who made up the municipal corporation—all stout and prosperous merchants who held office almost on a hereditary basis—ruled the lives of the 4,000 inhabitants within that community, as the same time controlling the economic policy and activities of the municipality.[21] The same situation occurred in other urban centres where the municipal authorities, constituting self-perpetuating bodies, tended to be composed of the most substantial members of the community.[22] These men were generally of the wealthy mercantile class who, often allied with the neighbouring landowners, used governmental authority to promote their own and the community's economic ends.

But while mercantile control might dominate in urban centres, no such situation existed where countywide government was concerned. In this area of jurisdiction, where justices of the peace were appointed to administer and adjudicate individually around the countryside, and preside as a group in the Quarter Sessions; where a lord lieutenant and his deputies were authorised to see to the security of the county; and where a sheriff enforced royal, statutory, and local decisions, it was the landed gentry which dominated. It was from this same gentry class that county representatives to Parliament, and many of the burgesses of the towns, were selected.

The position of lord lieutenant of the counties of Devon and Exeter, usually given to the same person, represented the major instrument of aristocratic control within the region. This prominent official, generally a member of the Russell family during these years, would select his deputy lieutenants from amongst the leading gentry families of the county or leading citizens of the towns.[23] It was this group of men, together with the more numerous JPs, who ran the affairs of the county of Devon at large, and whose influence was most often felt in local jurisprudence, legislation, and society. On the other hand, it was the mayor and recorder, together with a select list of corporation aldermen and burgesses, who received appointments as deputy lieutenants and JPs for the individual boroughs, and for Exeter itself. Within their own sphere the municipal authorities were generally supreme, although forced to compromise in instances of local parliamentary elections, or when major issues arose.

Although the mercantile interests were extremely influential politically within the local community, their social position was not so secure. Hooker placed merchants in the category just below that of noblemen and gentlemen, describing these leading urban dwellers as industrious people attaining great wealth especially through overseas activities. This money was then put to good use in making more money, and also 'in purchasing of land and by little and little they do creep and seek to be gentlemen'.[24] Hooker did not object to the notion of class mobility, but would much rather have witnessed their advancement in society as a result of other factors than the mere acquisition of money. But money was one commodity which they certainly did have, if Stephens' figures concerning Exeter merchants are correct.[25] Wealth was not enough to secure for the merchant oligarchy of Exeter the complete social acceptance which they so much desired. Within the urban community they had no social superiors save for the episcopal hierarchy. But without the 'intangible but all-important prestige of birth' they could never be regarded in the county at large as anything other than 'parvenus'.[26] This social inferiority existed notwithstanding the fact that within their areas of jurisdiction—as JPs, DLs, commissioners—these 'merchant magistrates' exercised the same legal authority as their better-bred colleagues in the country.

Over the years certain merchant families continued to remain dominant in their communities to such an extent that they came to regard their position in urban society as equivalent to that of the gentry in rural society.[27] Given legal and political status as well, these oligarchic groups in Devon and Exeter came to be awarded something akin to social equality by those county families who found it expedient to work closely, and often intermarry, with those newly arrived who could bring an infusion of economic vitality into long established lines. Numerous examples exist of this process of intermarriage which gave urban mercantile families enhanced position in the county by connection with gentry families, at the same time securing for the better-bred a financial impetus which often meant a new lease on life.[28] In this way a good working relationship developed between leading families in town and country which provided for mutual acceptance if not complete social equality.[29]

Influential though the merchant class might be, Hooker, for one, was much more impressed with the governing class of the countryside, the gentry. Within the category of 'gentlemen', he includes all those 'noble men, knights, and esquires' who by reason of birth and past family achievement have attainted a special position in society. It has been noted that Devon did not boast a large number of resident aristocrats. Instead, she prided herself on her numerous gentry class, composed of men '. . . very civil, courteous, gentle, affable, and of good virtue, temperate and modest in all their gestures and no more seemly than moderate in their apparall, without any sumptuousness, pride or excess. . . .'[30] In other words, a gentry who worked and played hard, and did not waste time, money or energy. Whether or not this was in fact the case, in the final analysis it was this 'squirarchy' which controlled Devon. In fact, the Devon countryside 'swarmed' with greater and lesser members of this squirarchy. In the more remote hills and vales many families of minor gentry, resident there for centuries, maintained themselves on their 'barton' or home farm, while often owning some six to ten other tenements which they leased out on the basis of three lives. Income from this type of estate usually ranged between £50 and £100 a year with which they could support themselves in a rough kind of gentility.[31] Numerically this class of minor gentry, and those just above them in the social scale, constituted a dominant segment of the Devon squirarchy.

A step up from these minor gentry were the 'lesser squires', men who enjoyed incomes of £100 to £200 a year which came largely from their barton farm, and from holdings in neighbouring parishes. This range of gentry generally had obtained the lordship of one or more manors, in addition to the ownership of divers surrounding farms,[32] and were often the younger sons of old families. As younger sons, they had been forced to look elsewhere for subsistence. Some turned to the law,[33] others to the Church, to commerce,[34] or to marriage to find incomes for themselves—and quite often to establish their own families of landed gentry in the process.[35]

Composing the elite of Devon gentry were such families as the Courtenays of Powderham Castle, the Seymours of Berry Pomeroy, the Drakes of Buckland, Prideaux of Netherton, and the Chudleighs of Ashton. This was the group from which the knights of the shire, burgesses representing the towns, sheriffs of the county, and other regional officials were selected. This top group of more than fifty families had close and intimate ties with the few aristocratic families resident in the county, and with leading gentry in neighbouring counties.

This elite dominated a society which extended through the ranks of those who were landowners to include the yeomanry of the country who:

> . . . consisteth of farmers, husbandmen, and freeholders which be men of a free nature and of good conditions and do live of such grounds and land as which they do hold freely . . . for a rent or of some of their own freeholds, being at the least of a clear value by the year of £10.[36]

By the end of the sixteenth century, Hoskins estimated that at least one-fifth of the Devon rural tenantry consisted of such free tenants.[37] Many of these people operated good-sized farms that afforded them a substantial living: '. . . for his fine being once paid he liveth as merrily as doth his Land Lord and giveth himself for the most part to such virtuous conditions and qualities as doth the gentleman. . . .'[38]

The so-called 'occupiers' of land, owning very little, if any, property themselves, constituted the other four-fifths of the rural tenantry. Some were occupiers by customary tenure, others by copyhold, others by lease for a specific number of years.[39] But these people were generally little better off than the numerous class of farm labourers who worked for the larger landowners and who, in the early sixteenth century had made up at least one-third of the entire Devon rural population. Proportionately as large in the following century, this labouring class relied for its comfort on accommodation and food provided by the farmer-employer. With food, drink, and other items provided, wages were correspondingly low. Thus, in a period of rising prices and low wages, the seventeenth-century farm labourer was particularly hard hit.[40]

Hoskins' description of the rural Devon existence in Stuart times is worthy of repetition:

> The typical farmer of Stuart times lived in an isolated farmstead, some distance from his neighbour. . . His farmhouse, barns, and stables had probably all been rebuilt since 1580, and the buildings of his medieval predecessors swept away. He lived in the midst of his enclosed fields, arable and pasture, though his pasture was tending to become more important. In the higher parishes of mid- and west-Devon, extensive tracts of rough heath and moor separated him from his neighbours, and made social intercourse next to impossible for several months of the year. There were, however, more favoured parts, like the Vale of Exeter, the Torbay region, and the South Hams, where villages were more common, and where there was little isolating 'waste'. Here life was a more sociable business.[41]

The economic and social structure of Devon was consistently being changed as both the merchant class and the yeomanry, together with members of the minor and lesser gentry, strove to better their condition in life or to secure for themselves and their posterity a more advanced and secure position. It is significant that the sole exception to this statement—excluding the relatively few aristocratic and ecclesiastical members of the county population—are the gentry elite, or 'local governor' class, as Thomas Barnes refers to them. This rank of fifty to sixty families was well-satisfied with their socio-economic and political status within the county, given their social position which permitted them to dominate county life. These people were not consciously seeking advancement; those below them were.

Notes to this chapter are on page 188

2
Years of Growing Discontent
1625-40

Why were Devon and Exeter susceptible to civil conflict by 1640? What were the series of events which irritated and antagonised the populace and created opposition in these counties, opposition which could be built upon and enlarged by a daring leadership? When examining the years immediately preceding the first Civil War, historians tend to over-exaggerate the actions of the royal government and to pass over completely the mischief caused by natural and uncontrolled events. Not only did unusual and irregular taxation and borrowing harass the people of Devon, but the strains of poor harvests, plague, inflation, and unemployment added substantially to the distress caused by actions of arbitrary government. To the infringement of conscience and the slighting of principle occasioned by a zealous episcopacy must be added the fear of piracy, the dread of popery, the dearth due to over-population, the dislocation of internal and external trade. For in studying the two counties during this period one must complement the imprudence of Buckingham, the enthusiasm of Laud, the rigour of Strafford, and the poor judgement of Charles, with a local examination of impressment and billeting of troops, the scourge of infectious diseases, the reforming spirit of county puritans, and the crisis of the woollen cloth trade.[1]

In the spring of 1625 Charles I came to rule a nation being visited by the dread plague which would return again and again before the great visitation of 1665. Along with many other areas in Devonshire, the plague struck in Crediton, Ashburton, Dartmouth, and Okehampton, severely disrupting normal life and bowing neither to wealth nor rank.[2] Exeter was hit particularly hard in the autumn of that year and remained affected until January 1626.[3] During 1626 Ashburton alone suffered 464 dead, while the estimated death toll for Exeter was as high as 2,300 people.[4] Although the area was not completely freed from the infection until July 1628, the first two years of the new reign were by far the worst, with a decline in the severity of the scourge coming toward the end of 1626. The usual method of dealing with this epidemic was to attempt to confine the disease-stricken locality, hoping in this way to keep the infection from spreading to other sections of the community. Weekly rates were levied and collected from adjacent hundreds in order to provide support for the growing number of people forcibly shut up within the infected districts. During the 1625-6 period the heavy burden of these rates, and the widespread nature of the disease, was reflected in the increased number of communities calling upon their neighbours for support. From the general rates Tiverton received £100 a week, Totnes, Ashburton, Buckland, and North Bovey £150 a week between them, and so it went, as primitive methods continued to be applied to this wild contagion.[5] Plymouth seems to have been fortunate enough to have escaped the plague during most of 1625. But by the year's end the disease was raging there also, widely thought to have been introduced by the numerous soldiers forcibly quartered in the town and surrounding countryside.[6]

Intent on an aggressive and glorious foreign policy, the youthful monarch, coached by the Duke of Buckingham, began an immediate build-up of forces in the Plymouth area soon after his accession to the throne. By the end of July 1625, some 6,000 men were reputedly billeted there, waiting for the royal command.[7] At the end of September, Charles and his entire Court arrived in the West Country to inspect his forces and to give the order which was to launch them on the ill-fated Cadiz expedition.[8] In less than three months this army, beaten and disease-ridden, was back in Plymouth carrying with it the infection which so frightened the townspeople that they refused to support the troops whenever they could.[9] Rather than disperse this motley crew, the government ordered the deputy lieutenants of the county to retain the troops in the Plymouth area in order that they might be available for future use. As a consequence, Devon was to be plagued with the billeting of these men for many months to come. Throughout 1626 the local commissioners appointed to see to the maintenance of this army continually plied the Privy Council with requests for money, clothes, and supplies with which to implement their task and somewhat lighten the burden heaped upon the people of the county. But although they lacked funds to support the army, they did not lack energy to plead constantly for the removal of the troops to other counties, as plague and infection followed the soldiers into all the parishes that they occupied.[10]

By late June 1626 conditions had become so intolerable that the commissioners ordered the remaining troops to move to Plympton. Such action, however, only increased the fears which the subsequently unprotected borough felt, as rumours spread of an imminent Spanish invasion. It seemed that Plymouth could live neither with nor without the soldiers who, short of proper food, clothing, and pay, were becoming ever more unruly and disorderly.[11] On 6 July a message from the deputy governor of the fort at Plymouth brought news that the Spanish had landed and urgently demanded the return of the soldiers. The invasion did not materialise, nor were the troops granted a very warm welcome upon their return. But in reporting this alarm to the Privy Council, the commissioners could only repeat their former request, that sufficient money be sent down so that the troops might be paid off and withdrawn from the county.[12] None knew better than the members of the King's Council that such sums of money were not to be had. But few knew better than the desperate commissioners that the disgruntled and heavily burdened county could not continue with this formidable nuisance and expense. For not only were the surrounding parishes taxed for support of sick families in time of plague, but they also had to bear the brunt of maintaining the unwanted soldiers in the form of a countywide 'special rate'.[13]

The Council decided to ease Plymouth's burden in November 1627 by sending a number of newly recruited troops (reinforcements for the Isle of Ré expedition) to Exeter for billeting. A letter of 4 November instructed the 'Commissioners for the well ordering and billetting of soldiers at Plymouth' to send a reasonable number to the county town where they were to be 'received and entertained . . . in the same manner as they are in other towns of that county'.[14] Of the 2,000 new recruits, 106 were eventually sent to Exeter, and proved themselves expensive guests, costing the city £102 2s 3d (£102.11) from 6 November to 23 December.[15] Not satisfied with this situation, the Council sent word that these soldiers were to be moved closer to Plymouth, and that the charge for their maintenance should continue to be met by the citizens of Exeter at the cost of 3s 6d (17½p) per week per man, for 100 soldiers.[16] The inhabitants of Exeter were delighted to be rid of this band of men, but were not very happy at the continued imposition.

As the months passed without any real relief for the county, many of the local magnates, deputy lieutenants, commissioners, and justices of the peace were put under heavy local pressure to petition the court and Council for release from this intolerable obligation. Along with the rest, Sir John Chichester was entreated to submit to the lord lieutenant that at least the horse contingent scheduled for Shaugh Prior (a moorland parish) might not be encamped there as proposed because of the extraordinary expense which such action would entail and the shortage of provisions. Sir George Chudleigh, for another, had so spent himself in attempts to get the soldiers removed from Devon soil, on one occasion going to London to put the county's case before the Council, that he was granted £100 for his pains by the Quarter Sessions.[17] If these 'local governors' had been required only to represent their fellows to the national authority, they would have counted themselves lucky. But at the same time that the deputy lieutenants were acting as commissioners for the army, they were (in their capacity as JPs) also responsible for the continuous judicial and administrative functions of local government. As their tasks became more difficult the value of their locally prestigeous positions deteriorated in their own eyes, and in the eyes of the people.[18]

The continuous representations to the Council by the local magnates and officials were either ignored or given little attention. If maintenance charges for soldiers were becoming unbearable in particular areas, then the commissioners were instructed 'to levy the pay of the soldiers on the county at 4s 8d (23½p) per week per man', and thus distribute the burden more evenly. All sums thus raised were to be eventually repaid, 'but their way of repaying it was by raising forced loans in the county for that purpose'.[19] Some £9,300 were actually collected for this charge in 1627, but that amount fell far short of the total cost of billeting thousands of men over a two-year period. An anonymous Devonian gave voice to the feelings of many of his countrymen when he wrote in 1627:

What, say the people, will his Majesty make war without provision of treasure, or must our county bear the charge for all England? Is it

> not enough that we undergo the trouble of the insolent soldiers in
> our houses, their robberies, and other misdemeanours, but that we
> must maintain them, too, at our own cost?[20]

Comments of this nature mounted into a flood of complaint which
had already been given voice by West Country MPs in the unsuccessful parliaments of 1625 and 1626, to which was finally
added the voice of the Earl of Bedford, Lord Lieutenant for
Devon and Exeter. Following his petition to the Council in
November 1627,

> . . . for the easing of that County . . . from the great burthen which
> it hath and doth sustain, by the billetting of soldiers, in regard that
> the Town of Plymouth, hath borne the place of rendezvous for those
> supplies and recruits, that were levied for the reinforcing of his
> Majesty's army while it was in the Isle of Ré. . . ,

it was ordered on 21 November that the royal army be removed
from the two counties. Eight days later, the commissioners were
finally given instructions for the immediate withdrawal of troops
into the neighbouring counties.[21]

It would appear, however, that winter conditions, lack of supplies, and deficiency of funds for transportation, delayed the
execution of this order for some months. Not only did the soldiers
not leave, but late November and early December witnessed
'. . . diverse outrages and disorders that have been lately committed
in the City and County of Exeter by the soldiers that are billetted
in those parts. . .' On 17 December the Council wrote again to the
commissioners and reiterated their previous order demanding the
removal of the troops from that county, at the same time admon-
ishing them to take good care that no further mischief take
place.[22] It was not until March 1628 that Devonians finally saw
the last of the thousands of unruly men which an ambitious and
foolish foreign policy had fostered on them.[23] The initial joy at
the accession of a new monarch had by this time become heavily
tempered by the natural dread of plague and the man-made horror of war. Plymouth in particular, and Devon in general, had
suffered severely from infection and disorder, taxation and impressment, all arising from Charles' ill-considered and ill-advised
expeditions against Spain and France.[24] But the years 1625-8 were
a mere foretaste of exactions to come.

Forced loans had previously been raised in the county to provide some of the funds necessary to keep the army together. These

loans, and the free gift of 1626 which had preceded them, were the fruits of the 'new councils' which Charles had warned a recalcitrant House of Commons that he would be forced to follow if they did not supply the money needed to carry out the government's aggressive foreign policy. What he could not get from their representatives, the king proceeded to extract from the freeholders of each county on the strength of his own prerogative authority.[25] With the grant of only two subsidies from his first parliament,[26] the king returned to an old Elizabethan device of requiring so-called Privy Seal loans, or outright contributions from his wealthier subjects, in return for the promise of eventual repayment issued under the Privy Seal.[27] There appears to have been little opposition from Devon to this particular attempt to raise money, probably because only a small number of people were directly affected.

The king's policies were becoming so expensive, however, that no such contributions could be expected to satisfy the royal needs. Thus, on 7 July 1626 the JPs were told to demand of their countrymen the free gift to the Crown of the proposed amount to have been granted by the second parliament of Charles I.[28] The remarkable failure of this expedient to raise money caused the government to give up such efforts for a voluntary contribution by late autumn. In its place came the more lucrative, but decidedly more dangerous, program of forced loans. The extant records of those who refused or were unable to pay the sums demanded in Exeter during 1626-7 show the extent of government pressure to obtain every penny. For in a city of its size, very few indeed took this opportunity to oppose the government's wishes, and none who did so was of importance in the community.[29] By a commission dated 11 October 1626 the king authorised the mayor and aldermen of the city to raise the loan which he indicated was to enable him to continue fighting in Germany and to aid his uncle, the King of Denmark.[30] Similar instructions were sent to the other commissioners for loans appointed in the county of Devon.

Early response from Devon and Exeter with regard to these loans would appear to have been very favourable as is witnessed by a letter to the commissioners at Exeter in May 1627. While giving thanks to these gentlemen for their past efforts, the lords of the Council urged them to push on with the work of collecting loan money from those areas in arrears, and send it to London as soon as possible, together with the names of those who continued to refuse payment. On the same date, however, the Privy Council sent the Exeter commissioners a second letter in which the lords complained of the slowness with which the loan was being collected in Devon, and demanded a full account be made by 15 July.[31] Receipt of this last message caused the commissioners a good deal of alarm, and in their anxiety they wrote to Sir George Chudleigh, county treasurer for collection of the loan money. Presumably speaking from long experience with the mysteries of central bureaucracy, Chudleigh wrote reassuringly on 17 August that the second letter had probably never been meant for the Exeter authorities. In any case, he instructed them to order their collectors to pay the second installment of the loan to him, as they had done previously. Chudleigh was willing to accept full responsibility for this action, particularly as most of the money had already been assigned to him and his fellow commissioners for the maintenance of the army still quartered in Devon. Sir George's reasonable handling of the matter appears to have been acceptable to the government as nothing further is heard of it until the end of October.[32]

The collection of loan money was successful in Exeter and, generally speaking, throughout Devon. As mentioned above, some £9,300 was collected in 1627, most of which was devoted to the upkeep of the army then billeted on the county. Thus far in the reign of Charles I Devon and Exeter had seen little of the fruits expected from so young and vigorous a monarch. To be sure, the king could not be held responsible for the spread of the plague— except in so far as his ill-fated expeditions had contributed to the unhealthy condition of the soldiers—nor could he be blamed for the depressed economic conditions within the county, the growth of poverty, the shortage of food, or the increase of vagrants along the Devonshire roads. By the end of 1627, however, blame for illegal taxation, coercive measures of government, foolhardy foreign adventures and economic wars could be and was, placed at the royal doorstep, although at this point the Duke of Buckingham received the brunt of the criticism. At the same time, the economic hardships and commercial dislocation within the county made payment of forced loans particularly loathsome. While the plague and press-gangs had taken their toll of available manpower from the clothing and shipping industries, the very wars for which these men and supplies were collected did infinite damage to

Devon's economy. Exeter in particular had long relied almost exclusively on a French and, to a lesser extent, Spanish market for her cloth; and the commercial war which ensued between these countries and England during the 1620s made that city sharply aware of the danger of reliance on a limited market.[33]

When in 1626, and again in 1627, the lords of the Council asked that Exeter provide and maintain two ships for the fleet being outfitted for the war, the Chamber minced no words in protesting vehemently against such an exceptional burden in such difficult times. In rehearsing all of the afflictions they had suffered since the king's coronation, the city authorities pointed to the heavy losses due to piracy,[34] plague, impressment, forced loans, and unreliable foreign markets. The Privy Council's demand for the following year (1628) that Devon contribute £17,475 to the outfitting of a fleet brought such violent protest that not even threats could bring acquiescence.[35] In defence of the Council, however, it should be stated that money collected for the outfitting of a fleet of any description was bound to help West Country shipping against the perennial evil of piracy. Throughout the reigns of James I and his son, shipowners from Exeter, Dartmouth, Plymouth, and other Devon ports repeatedly petitioned the Crown for aid in efforts to suppress the piracy which took an ever-increasing toll of men, ships, and goods.[36] 'Dutch, French, Spanish, Portuguese, and most feared of all, the fierce, dark-skinned, turbanned rovers from Sallee and Algiers swarmed in the Channel', and made commerce risky at best.[37] But if the trade was hazardous, all concerned knew that it was also profitable.

The profits gained from foreign trade made the fortunes of many men in the West Country, and not least of all in Devon and Exeter. To improve conditions of trade during this period, these same men repeatedly petitioned the government for naval protection which the financially embarrassed Stuarts were never able to provide in sufficient measure. But while the protests continued regarding the suffering sustained by his Majesty's loyal subjects in their honest endeavours, few of these worthy gentlemen were ever willing to devote much individual efforts or support to suppressing the pirates.[38] On the several occasions on which the merchants took the initiative, it was never enough to recruit the funds or ships necessary for a sustained expedition.[39] It therefore became quite obvious, as atrocities at sea and on land continued,[40] that only government action could curb this expensive nuisance. Royal inability to get along with a succession of parliaments, however, and the decision to rule without recourse to that body, only made it more difficult for the king to obtain funds with which to finance the needed vessels. The unwillingness of the West Country ship-owners and merchants to contribute to the suppression of piracy in the 1620s, along with national resistance to ship money in the 1630s, further complicated the matter.[41]

With parliament no longer available to receive petitions after 1629, the mercantile interests turned to the king and Council in order to obtain naval protection. In the autumn of that year Nicholas Spicer of Exeter was authorised by the city chamber to represent their case at Whitehall. Spicer did so by contacting as many friends in London as he could to aid in his petition to the secretary of state, and he appears to have been at least moderately successful in his efforts, as one ship was promised to cruise the Torbay area.[42] One ship was hardly enough to suppress piracy in western waters, and in 1630 the Exeter Corporation again petitioned for further protection. Not satisfied with the results of these efforts, an attempt was made to obtain permission for a general tax on West Country merchants to raise money for the outfitting of private ships.[43] Although this petition was approved, communal action on the part of the mercantile interests had not been successful by 1632.

In February of that year, at the urging of such merchants as John Delbridge of Barnstaple,[44] a general meeting was held in Exeter of representatives from Plymouth, Barnstaple, Dartmouth, and Exeter, in addition to Weymouth and Melcombe Regis. This group drew up resolutions which set forth the grievances suffered by them and their colleagues in the loss of ships, goods, and men due to the aggressive activities of the Moors. It was further decided that a petition representing the general feeling of West Country merchants should be immediately dispatched to the capital, along with an agent from each community represented, in order to stress the need for government action.[45] John Clement of Plymouth was one of the men selected to carry this petition to the Privy Council. From his letters of May 1633—well over a year after the original meeting—the slow process of obtaining aid from a financially impoverished government becomes apparent.[46] The lords of the Council, although long since convinced of the desirability of further naval protection for foreign trade, were not at all willing to commit themselves unless given assurances of financial support from the merchants, and towns, then petitioning. Since the western agents had no authority to commit and bind their fellows, the Privy Council refused to take action until they knew exactly from where the money was to come.[47] Although letters and petitions to the Council continued, only half-hearted efforts were made by merchants and council to remedy the situation.[48] It was not until 1638-9 that greater efforts appear to have achieved a measure of success. By that time some Turkish captives had been redeemed by force of arms, and additional royal ships assigned to coastal patrol.[49]

More effective protection for foreign trade was not solely the result of popular pressure. The government was ready throughout this period to co-operate wherever possible—ie, where resources permitted—to aid in the suppression of piracy. What made Devon petitions more fruitful in the mid-1630s than earlier was the growing ability of the government after 1634 to outfit and maintain a respectable fleet. And, of course, the method by which the money for such a cause was raised was through the infamous ship money writs, a scheme of extra-parliamentary taxation which hit Devon and Exeter as hard as any county in England. Having often been subjected to the burden of supplying ship money in the past,[50] it is probable that the arrival of the 1634 writ came as an unpleasant but not unfamiliar demand to the inhabitants of the two counties.[51] Although the nation was then at peace, some Devonians paid this irregular tax in the hope that the money thus collected would be applied to a fleet which could gain control of the coastal waters bordering their county, and thereby keep the sea avenues open.[52] But however much this justification might work for coastal communities, and indeed the Devon ports seem to have contributed without strong protest, there was no such enthusiasm exhibited among a number of inland towns where opposition was vehement against this new assessment.[53] Many Devonians, along with people throughout the realm, became ever more unwilling to submit to a tax which was traditionally felt to be the responsibility of the maritime communities alone, since they were considered to be more directly affected and would be more likely to profit.[54]

The Devon commissioners for the assessment of ship money

c

presumably agreed that this application of the tax was a burdensome innovation, and fifteen of them signed a petition to the Council requesting that the inland communities named be not required to pay. The lords of the Council were of a different opinion. They ordered the five leading commissioners to present themselves to explain their action in opposing the collection of ship money.[55] Four of them did appear at Whitehall on 1 March 1635, but received only a mild reprimand, '. . . it being punishment enough to them to have travelled 400 miles to so small purpose.'[56] Having successfully crushed the limited initial opposition to ship money, the Privy Council then went on to demand from the county an assessment of £9,000 in order to outfit a 900 ton ship for the royal service.[57] Presumably the rough lesson recently administered aided the commissioners to assess, and induced the inhabitants to pay, what was demanded of them by the 1635 writ. No further serious opposition was heard beyond the normal complaints which would be natural in an age when any form of taxation was despised, even more so when granted without parliamentary sanction. A third writ for the collection of ship money, that of 1636, brought more ominous sounds of opposition.[58] Increasing the burden of taxes for so ostensibly narrow a purpose tended to widen the government's unpopularity at a time when it could least afford it. Only in the town of Okehampton does there appear to have been little tension over the tax, for in the period 1636-9 the inhabitants paid their assessment of £30 with little dissent. Not so with most of the county.[59]

With the issuance of the 1636 ship money writ some of the more determined and courageous amongst the government's opponents in Devon began to take a more rigid stand. The widowed Lady Joan Drake refused to contribute and in this was strongly supported by her brother, Sir Richard Strode. It was their brother, William, who was still in the Tower, the last of the nine MPs imprisoned in 1629. To these Devonians, royal success at extraparliamentary taxation meant the continued imprisonment of their relative.[60] Their refusal to pay, coupled with the growing storm of protest over an imposition no longer regarded as temporary, might eventually lead a financially bankrupt monarch to recall parliament and to release William Strode. Mr Dennis Rolle of Bicton, Sheriff of Devon in 1636-7, was the first sheriff to feel the repercussions of this hostile attitude. During his year in office he forcefully complained to the Privy Council of the difficulties with which he and his subordinates were faced in raising the amount of money assessed for the county. His agents were continuously confronted with threatening looks, gestures, and scurrilous words, while numerous ratepayers forced him to resort to the distress of goods in order to collect the required sums. Notwithstanding the difficulties involved, however, Rolle seems to have finally succeeded in collecting most of what was assessed in Devon and Exeter.[61] His successors were not so fortunate.

Ship money became the cause célèbre in 1637 and, as elsewhere in England, attention in Devon was focused on the trial of John Hampden. It was only natural that during the course of the trial, since the legality of ship money was being questioned, the people of Devon increased their opposition to efforts to collect the tax. The sheriff of Devon for 1637-8, Thomas Wise, was forced to call the mayors of the various towns, and Exeter, to a special meeting held at Okehampton on 26 October 1637.[62] Presumably, since the topic to be discussed was ship money, the sheriff hoped to exhort the municipal authorities to greater activity in collecting what had been assessed on their communities. Mr Wise does not seem to have been very successful. By May 1638 almost a third of the total county assessment of £9,000 was still uncollected, and as late as December 1639 Wise was still attempting to make good the arrears, explaining to the Council the numerous obstacles confronting him in his efforts to tax a people determined not to pay.[63] By this late date, his subordinate officials, upon whom the greater share of the work rested, had had enough of the contempt and abuse of their neighbours and were no longer making any serious attempts to carry out their task. At the same time some of the officials were found to be corrupt. One man in the parish of Cheriton Fitzpaine was removed for having extorted more than was required from the taxpayers. Others were found to have pocketed what they had collected. Thus, the inability and 'remissness' of the constables was complained of by both Sheriffs John Pole and Wise.[64]

The increasing difficulty in raising ship money was felt by all local officials. In August 1639 the mayor and ex-mayor of Totnes reminded the Privy Council of their valiant efforts to collect arrears due, but claimed that they could do nothing in the face of mass opposition.[65] The same situation was true in Exeter, as indicated by the pleas of the mayor and sheriff for more time in which to bring in their arrears.[66] At the same time, they did send up lists of those who had refused payment.[67] Sheriff Sir Nicholas Martyn was quite serious when he wrote the council: 'Did their Lordships know the difficulty and opposition I have had in collecting this little sum, as they may account it, £792.7.5 (£792.37) I believe they would acknowledge it the greatest they have ever received'.[68]

The severity of the ship money controversy in Devon and Exeter during the 1630s should not, however, conceal the fact that these counties were facing additional problems no less severe. It seems probable that, despite the heavy losses as a result of the plague in the repeated visitations, Devonshire was having a very real problem with overpopulation, especially as seen in the growth of a 'propertyless wage-earning class'. In everyday terms, this was reflected in the limited amount of available resources in relation to the growing number of people making demands on those resources. The increased population looking for land to cultivate and jobs to occupy led inevitably to 'low wages, unemployment and underemployment, poverty, bad housing, insecurity, and emigration to New England'.[69] While a certain number of wealthy merchants and clothiers were able to found new county families on the basis of mercantile fortunes recently acquired, a larger element of the population was being driven to desperate action for want of available opportunity. The Quarter Sessions' records for this period clearly point to the increased concern of the JPs with the poor, the unemployed, and the vagrant. The roads of the county were becoming crowded with beggars and indigent poor, augmented by the recently arrived 'wandering Irish'.[70] A severe shortage of grain in 1630 tended to magnify the problem facing the JPs, and steps were taken to satisfy the basic food demands of the people and at the same time clamp down on alehouses, 'disorderly assemblies, and riotous meetings' where the unemployed and the wayward might cause all kinds of trouble.[71]

While some Devonians took to the roads in search of employment or adventure, the more sturdy folk betook themselves beyond the seas in the hope of establishing a more secure future.[72] There was no severe oppression forcing several thousand Devonians to leave their county during the 1620s and 1630s, but many personal factors promoted the desire for advancement.[73] As R. D. Brown has commented: Devonians '. . . were not harried out of the land; they chose to go'.[74] It was the natural thing for many to do after having heard for years of the adventures of Raleigh, Drake, and Gilbert, seen the profits from overseas fisheries and trade, and become susceptible to the tales of abundant land in New England. Although members of the yeoman class provided the backbone of this emigration, younger sons of gentry families invariably appear amongst the lists, along with fishermen, husbandmen, and labourers who found personal misfortune and hard times at home good reasons for leaving England.[75]

Those who had emigrated from Devon by 1640 had left behind them an economy suffering from external limitations and internal dislocations. The 1630s saw the resurgence of piracy, the continued commercial warfare between France and England, as well as the internal reorganisation of the staple cloth trade, with new cloths being produced and different strains of wool being used. Although Exeter trade experienced a slow revival from 1632-8, (largely because of the shift in emphasis from French to Spanish and Dutch markets) unemployment grew at such an alarming rate that the Privy Council actively intervened to encourage work projects for those craftsmen adversely affected.[76] On the one side quarrels with France led to the confiscation of Devonshire goods in an ever more restricted staple market. On the other hand, increased taxation from a financially embarrased government limited the amount of foreign goods the local market could absorb.[77] For in addition to the burden of ship money laid on the counties since 1625, Devon had also borne its share of the increased purveyance due to the king, as well as the extraordinary imposition of fees for knighthood; the recurring expenses for the ransoming of Turkish captives; the cost of a relief for plague-infected areas, and the load sustained in the billeting of soldiers.[78]

In analysing economic recession in his city, the mayor of Exeter in 1639 pointed both to the fall in local demand for imported goods, and to the decline in the sale of Devon cloths to London merchants for export.[79] At the same time, the Devon JPs in Michaelmas Quarter Sessions (1639) rehearsed for the Privy Council the evils wrought upon the county by the recently acquired Exeter patent granting control of the worsted combers within that city, much to the dislocation of the general serge industry.[80] A situation had thus arisen in which traditional control of industry was increasing the problem of unemployment and dampening the necessary home market which Exeter badly needed. Further, while different cloths were being introduced to meet the demands of a new northern European market, the limitation of the local wool supply was severely inhibiting the capacity for economic recovery, and creating a situation made worse by the attempted regulation of the essential wool combers craft.[81]

So much for social and economic dislocation. What of the religious convictions of this county, commonly described as a 'puritan stronghold'?[82] Fierce opposition between the so-called puritans and more orthodox Anglicans had no place within the conservative Devon community of 1625-30, and although efforts were made to bring reform into the Church of England, it was done on a purely personal basis and with little disturbance.[83] In this fashion a great deal seems to have been accomplished to expand the control and influence of puritanism within the established structure of the Church. The advent of William Laud to the See of London, and then Canterbury, however, brought into ecclesiastical and political prominence a man willing to implement fully the Stuart policy of 'No Bishop, no King'. For with this one decisive promotion, and the subsequent innovations which came to be embodied in the Laudian program of reform from above, the moderate puritan movement in Devon of reform from below became automatically ranged on the side of political opposition.[84] As Laud came to enforce conformity with the use of such instruments as the Court of High Commission, and as royal secular power came to be identified with this increasingly hated ecclesiastical tyranny, many conscientious Devonians found themselves in opposition to archbishop and to king. They took up the cause of the subject's liberty in parliament and in parish in order to protect and maintain what they felt to be absolutely essential to their spiritual existence.

The widespread nature of Devon puritanism becomes evident when one examines the lists of those who were brought before the Court of High Commission, questioned as to their views, and pressed to conform to the Anglican dispensation. These people came from all sections of the county and from all walks of life, tanners as well as JPs, clerks as well as gentry, vicars together with husbandmen. But what is particularly striking is their common rural background, and the apparent shortsightedness of the High Commission in missing an opportunity to investigate those from urban centers.[85] For little good did it do the church or state to breathe thunder at Sir Peter Prideaux, Edmund Fortescue of Fallapit, William Lange vicar of Bradworthy, Roger Beere rector of Morchard Bishop, John Beare tanner of Bovey Tracey, and the many others from the countryside, while the puritans of Plymouth, Tavistock, and Bideford were left to continue their reforming activities unimpeded.[86]

The continuous process by which private gentlemen bought up impropriations of tithes and advowsons in order quietly to introduce and pay reform-minded clerics, lecturers and preachers in Devon communities, can be seen at Bideford where the godly William Bartlett was appointed lecturer for the town.[87] In the predominantly puritan community of nearby Barnstaple, fear of creeping Romanism made the inhabitants more than ready to pay the large salary of £50 per annum for three years to keep Benjamin Cox on as weekly lecturer, notwithstanding the Laudian persuasion of the vicar and neighbouring divines.[88] The influence of the Earl of Bedford in the development of the puritan movement in Devon was also significant. Nowhere was this more keenly felt than in the market borough of Tavistock, in the heart of the county lands owned by the Russell family. Here, as elsewhere, the slow process of personal conversion and ecclesiastical reform was pushed forward, '... onwards and upwards toward the heights of godliness undreamed of in the bad old days of popery', as sympathetic preachers were employed to help look after the state of private morality.[89]

Efforts on the part of the heavily puritan population of Plymouth to obtain sufficient preaching to their liking were frustrated as early as 1631 when royal interference rejected the appointment of Thomas Ford of Brixton as lecturer, and in 1632 denied the vicarage to Alexander Grosse. Although Grosse was retained as an occasional lecturer, pressure for more reform-minded preaching continued. It was apparently as a result of these setbacks that the town petitioned the Crown in 1634 for authority to establish a second church in Plymouth. In 1641 royal and parliamentary approval were obtained for the erection of what became Charles Church, a new parish with the right of advowson in the hands of the puritan Plymouth Corporation.[90]

It was apparently only in Exeter that the growth of puritan influence came into direct conflict with government authorities, and then only on the eve of the Short Parliament. There, as elsewhere in Devon, the puritan movement had gained in strength and influence through the gradual process of infiltration by men of quiet determination who were allowed to proceed within an atmosphere of episcopal tolerance.[91] In this city Alderman Ignatius Jourdain was the 'Arch-puritan' figure, and a man to be reckoned with. It was this official who had remained to administer the city government when most of his colleagues had fled the 1625 plague, and it was he who led the local opposition to royal intentions to stamp out the 'seditious practices' of a rebellious Scotland.[92] The first measure of public opposition on the part of the puritan aldermen of Exeter came with '. . . their irreverent carriage with their hats on in the Cathedral Church of Exeter at such times as his Majesty's proclamation touching the seditious practices of some of Scotland was read, the rest of the congregation being uncovered'.[93] Jourdain and his fellows had been consistently fearful of the Laudian innovations, and could feel nothing but sympathy for the revulsion of their northern brethren at the introduction of similar policies in Scotland. They were certainly not going to join in a war against their co-religionists. At the moment that Jourdain, Thomas Crossing, and Mayor James Tucker replaced their hats for the reading of the royal proclamation there began in that city the internal division which would split the community.[94] Soon after this incident the Exeter Corporation came firmly within the puritan grasp. Elections held to fill three vacancies within the governing chamber saw 'exceptional influences' employed to return men favourable to the puritan party. With the consequent majority provided, these gentlemen were able to consolidate their position and eventually bring over to the side of Parliament the resources of one of the leading communities in the West Country.[95]

The reaction in Devon to the news of the Scots' rebellion was not at all favourable to the government. In many areas it was downright hostile. When subsequently called upon to join with the forces being collected to march north, many remembered their own manifold grievances against the state and refused their aid. Thus, delay and opposition were the order of the day, and the mutinous nature of the troops clearly foreshadowed the military chaos which was soon to follow.[96] The men of north Devon were particularly energetic in expressing their opposition to a war apparently aimed at suppressing fellow Protestants in order to set up Romish bishops and ceremony.[97] Having marched only as far as Wellington in Somerset on their way to the north (July 1640), men of Captain Gibson's company mutinied against their officers, and savagely killed one of them, a reputed Roman Catholic by the name of Lieutenant Compton Evers.[98] Fear and hatred of the papist threat which Laud's innovations had come to represent, combined with years of accumulated frustrations and grievances, found their escape in barbarous cruelty and mutinous riot.[99]

An anonymous document found among the Buller Papers probably gives best expression to the strong West Country sentiment against the royal call-up of the militia to suppress the Scots rebellion:

> I see not how we should trouble ourselves to bring them to their duty and stir great work and engines to crush a flea which may for all our endeavours slip from us. Bishops put out by a general consent cannot be set up again unless guarded like castles or shaped into so many rocks that are not easily removed out of their place.

This much was common sense, but the rest was ominous indeed for the future:

> Though our king be gracious and just: others after him may not [be]: therefore things must be so settled that when kings shall not be well minded they may not do much hurt.[100]

The 'flea' which this writer thought so harmless, and not tending at all to the harm of the English nation, proved to be more than the government could crush. As a direct consequence of the nation's lack of concern, the so-called Short Parliament of April-May 1640 was called into being, bringing to an end the 'personal rule' of Charles I, and foreshadowing the settlement of government in England wherein kings could not 'do much hurt'.

Notes to this chapter are on page 190

3
Devon on the Eve of Conflict
november 1640-august 1642

Distance from the scene of action, however, makes an enormous difference in the effect of news. Whilst excitement was often at fever-heat
in London, the tranquility of life in the West was disturbed only by
religious bickerings, as to true doctrine, the righteousness of sports on
Sunday, and, above all, as to the proper position of the altar in parish
churches. Seeing that there was no such thing as religious liberty, and
that no one proposed there should be, the animosity aroused on these
matters was intensely bitter; but such a dislocation of society as is
implied by civil war was certainly not expected at this time.[1]

As thorough-going as might be the local disagreements on matters
of conscience,[2] few Devonians approved the atmosphere of civil
strife as it rapidly developed during the period from November
1640 to August 1642. Most people were in favour of reform in
church and state, and it was with this in mind that Devon voters
had selected various MPs in the autumn elections. Opponents of
the government had been busy in Devonshire throughout the
summer of 1640 organising pressure for a new parliament so as to
have numerous grievances redressed.[3] One result of this activity
was the petition drawn up at the Devon assizes and delivered to
the Council on 12 September.[4]

Once the new parliament had assembled the representatives
from Devon wasted no time in rehearsing the numerous complaints of their constituents.[5] An extensive list of grievances
ranged from the threat of piracy, poor economic conditions, and
mismanagement of the stannaries, to the more widely held complaints regarding ship money, illegal collection of tunnage and
poundage, arbitrary authority, and the growing threat of Laudianism.[6] But while the maladministration of the stannaries, and
the fear of popish conspiracies could be handled by parliamentary

action, much more revolutionary techniques would be required to overhaul the abuses resulting from 'thorough' and Laudianism.[7] As far as most Devonians were concerned it was still the petition for redress of grievances, directed to king and parliament, that would solve their problems. This was the traditional role of the suppliant subject bringing forth his complaints to the ancient authority which had always been the fount of justice and mercy. During the period of Charles' personal rule the inhabitants of Devon and Exeter had constantly forwarded requests for aid to the Council in hope of protection against pirates or for economic support, as was again witnessed in the petition of September 1640. With the calling of the November parliament, the floodgates were again opened for all those complaints which had not been settled during the Short Parliament, but which would be pressed this time with added determination.

Many of the same gentlemen who had drawn up the September petition in Devon signed their names to a statement of grievances introduced into the House on 11 November 1640. This petition set forth 'the sum of the general grievances of this Kingdom . . .', but particularly emphasised the misbehaviour of Mr Coryton, MP, in his capacity as Vice-Warden of the Stannaries.[8] As in September, the local authority attached to the names Acland, Chudleigh, Prideaux, Rolle, Hele, and Fortescue attested to the bipartisan nature of the support given by leading figures of the county to the need for reform in a wide area of activity.[9] Those who stood for substance, power, and wealth in the community recognised the necessity to rectify past abuses, regardless of the side they were to assume once war had broken out.

The contents of several petitions from Devon and Exeter within the next several months following the return of parliament are unknown, but the fact that they continued to seek redress supports the notion that the people of this area were not slow to take advantage of the opportunities available to rectify abuses. The 12 December petition from the Corporation of Okehampton was presumably concerned with the matter of reinfranchisement as it was referred to the Committee for Privileges for consideration.[10] In late January (30th) 1641 came a complaint from Exeter and London merchants with regard to two ships that had been recently taken by 'Dunkirkers' and whose recapture was desired.[11] It was not until March that the House decided to take action to rid the nation of this persistent threat, and even then it was a decision to debate the advisability of sending six vessels to guard the western trade.[12] Local sentiment in the county was further expressed in 1641 petitions (undated) from Tavistock and Plymouth to the justices sitting in Quarter Sessions at Exeter. The corporation of Tavistock was particularly concerned with the decline in the cloth trade in their area, for which they blamed 'the dread of the Turks at sea, and of popish plots at home; . . .'. The inhabitants recognised the efforts recently made by the Commons to remedy the situation, but felt strongly that little could be permanently effected in the face of 'the votes of the popish Lords and Bishops in the Upper House; . . .'.[13] It was hoped, therefore, that an address from the county authorities directed to the king might help matters. The corporation and inhabitants of Plymouth complained as strongly about their declining fishing industry for which they also blamed the 'Turks'. Their petition to the Quarter Sessions made further mention of the 'tyranny of the Irish rebels, who are encouraged by certain popish and ill-affected lords and bishops'.[14] The people of both communities thus added their voices to the growing demand in Devon that something be done externally with regard to pirates and Irish rebels, and internally with regard to disaffected and pro-Roman clerics and peers at whose doors were heaped the troubles and grievances of the whole country.

But Tavistock and Plymouth were by no means the only areas in Devon that urged county action in presenting their grievances to king and parliament. The corporation and inhabitants of Totnes represented the difficulties in the textile trade then plaguing their town as a result of the 'intolerable taxes' enacted by 'the granting of Letters Patent to several companies . . .'.[15] They stressed their fear of the actions of the popish peers and clergy, but not to the same degree as in the petition which the justices received from the people of Dartmouth and its environs. The mercantile population of Dartmouth, as much as the people of Plymouth, were greatly disturbed over the decline of trade resulting from increased piratical activity, rebellion in Ireland, and 'still more to the dread entertained of a popish rising'. They feared for the safety of their county and country until such time as king and parliament would consent to the 'removal of the popish lords and Bishops from the Upper House'.[16] The volume of protest thus continued to mount as various sections of the county reported to the local magistrates the effects of their increasingly difficult economic conditions, and supplied an explanation which appealed to popular imagination and superstition.

The JPs were more than sympathetic to the petitions and complaints pouring in on them which tended only to reinforce their own previously stated convictions and suspicions. As a result of this agitation, a petition was drawn up in the name of 'the Baronets, Justices, and Gentlemen of the County of Devon at their General Sessions' and presented to the House of Commons on 24 January 1642, and to the House of Lords on the following day.[17] This moderate document presented the complaints of Devonians concerning the decline of trade (attributed to pirates, rebellion in Ireland, and 'London distractions'), the increased immigration of refugee Protestants from Ireland, and the threat of invasion from Irish rebels as well as from 'Popish Plots'. 'And all this they do with so much probability conjecture to proceed from the practices of the Popish Lords, and their constant adherents in most of their votes, the Prelates in the House of Peers, . . .'.[18] The closing plea of this petition was for greater cooperation between king and parliament during this period of growing political distrust and misunderstanding. The hope of avoiding a critical confrontation was eloquently expressed by the JPs: 'And by the mercy of God . . . , Prerogative and Privilege will kiss each other, when His Majesty shall think it his greatest Honor to grant your just Privilege, and you acknowledge it your best Privilege to enjoy the benefit and glory of his due and princely Prerogative'.[19]

While the Devonshire authorities were preparing their petition, the officials of Exeter were working on a statement of their own. Within a week following Charles' dramatic invasion of the House of Commons, the Exeter Chamber met to consider the various petitions which had been presented to them '. . . by many of the commons and inhabitants of this City expressing several dangers apprehended by them to the decay of their trades occasioned by the disturbances in London, and oppositions by bishops and popish lords in parliament . . .'.[20] Four aldermen of the chamber were selected to prepare the petition based on the documents presented by the citizens, and two of their number were asked to deliver it immediately to Westminster.

On 25 January the House of Lords thus received representations from the city and county of Exeter at the same time as those from the county of Devon.[21] As in the statement received from Devonshire, the Exeter city fathers lamented the decline in the trade and manufacturing of their city, 'as also the distresses of our Brethren in Ireland', all of which was once again attributed to the disruptive influence of the 'Bishops and Popish party', as well as to 'the distractions in the City of London, which, . . . are occasioned by the infringing of the Rights and Privileges of Parliament, and the just liberty of the Subject'.[22] The Exeter petition went on to request what soon became the recurring parliamentary theme:

> . . . That the true Protestant Religion may be still preserved, the Rights and Privileges of Parliament maintained, and the just Liberties of the subject supported; and that the Popish party may be disarmed, which (notwithstanding the former Laws and Orders) have been neglected; and that the Kingdom may be put into a posture of defence, and the Forts and places of strength may be committed to the hands of trusty persons; and that the power of voting in Parliament may be taken from the Bishops and Popish Lords, and also the said distresses of our afflicted Brethren in Ireland may thoroughly be taken to heart, and speedily remedied.[23]

Thus, the rationalisation for revolution was being formed by the people of a provincial capital who were immediately disturbed by declining demand for serges and perpetuanas, and over unusual behaviour in London. They did not really understand what this position would lead to, but implicitly placed their faith in parliament to set it all right once again. And certainly nothing could more strongly reaffirm this trust and support of parliament than the overwhelming response of the county to the Protestation of 1641 'against all Popery' which all males over the age of eighteen were required to sign.[24] As this universal affirmation suggests, more than fifty years after the defeat of the Spanish armada popery was still the demon and quite capable of deeply stirring a normally peaceful people.

Particularly evident among the complaints issuing from Devon during this period, and tending only to compound the decay in trade and commerce,[25] was this growing fear of the spread of popery as a consequence of the Irish rebellion and massacre of 1641. Already suspicious of Laudian reforms as popishly inclined, and aware of the arming of certain Roman Catholics in their midst, Englishmen looked upon the upheaval in Ireland as an additional proof of the universal conspiracy against Protestant England directed from abroad by the pope, and aided from within by the bishops and popish peers. Devon, of course, was not alone in raising the cry against this dreaded attack on country and religion. But Devon was closer to Ireland than most other English counties, and the natural recipient of Protestant refugees fleeing from that country to find safety with friends and relatives in the West Country.[26] Unlike the inhabitants of more remote counties, Devonians could point to the great influx of refugees during the last months of 1641 and into the new year, and to the subsequent burden to the county which relief for these people represented. Large sums appear to have been collected in Devon and Exeter in response to the original Act for Contribution for Ireland.[27] This law left it to the Committee of the House for the Contribution-money to determine the sums to be given directly to the refugees in Devon and in Ireland, as well as what money was to be spent on military necessities in maintaining the English army in Ireland.[28] At the same time the House saw to it that the county storehouse in Devon was replenished with additional barrels of gunpowder, for by March 1642 the double purpose existed of strengthening their political position within the county, and preparing for rumoured invasions from Ireland and elsewhere.[29]

The threat of subversion from Irish Catholics flooding into the country during these disturbed times seemed real enough to the House of Commons. On 29 January 1642, in an attempt to stop the flow of men and material into rebellious areas of Ireland, and to halt the movement of Irish papists into England, the House declared:

> And whereas also, divers poor people, men, women, and children, of the Irish nation, and Papists, are lately come in great numbers out of Ireland into Cornwall, Devon, and other parts of this Kingdom; where they have been and are very disorderly; and much terrify the inhabitants where they come; and due care is not taken, in all places, for the suppressing and punishing of them: The Lords and Commons, . . . , do hereby further order and require all officers before mentioned, that they put the laws in due execution against such wandering Irish Papists before expressed; and that they cause them to be forthwith conveyed back into that Kingdom.[30]

The people of the West Country were becoming increasingly frightened by this unprecedented influx of foreigners. Local authorities took severe precautions to check on the illegal passage of goods and men in and out of Ireland from Devon ports, and to question suspicious travellers.[31] Along with a number of others, Edmund Fortescue was thanked by the House on two separate occasions for his diligence in preventing Irish officers, men, and supplies from reaching their destinations.[32]

On 19 March 1642 an act to reduce Ireland received the royal assent whereby subscriptions volunteered for the suppression of the Irish rebellion would be guaranteed by, and repaid in, confiscated Irish lands. As a result of this act, and of the three others following which amended and extended it, Exeter alone contributed some £15,728.10.0 (£15,728·50) before 29 April 1643, while the Corporation of Dartmouth, led by its MPs, underwrote the sum of £2,668.7.6 (£2,668·37½).[33] The adventurers' papers indicate that people from all walks of Devon life, and from varying shades of political opinion, were united in this desire to contribute toward the suppression of the Irish rebellion. Their aim was to halt what they regarded as an attack upon Protestantism, against family and friends in Ireland, and against the best interests of their country. The fact that business and commercial interests were suffering by this insurrection can be seen from the large number of merchants, small businessmen, and craftsmen who were amongst the most forward of those donating toward the reducing of Ireland. At the same time these people must haves been affected by the heavy emotional and financial burden of providing for the refugees flooding into their county, relating tales of horror and massacre wherever they went. A very active fear developed that a papist victory in Ireland would threaten the sea-bound county as one of the earliest victims of invasion. Thus, investment in Irish suppression could bring protection, and possibly even profit from Irish lands as well as increased commercial opportunities.

This appeal of investment in foreign lands must have been a major consideration for those who contributed. In a society dominated by the notion of landed gentility, where estates provided substance and respectability in an era of land shortage, the possibility of obtaining property in nearby Ireland was attractive. One must note particularly the preponderance of people from urban centres who rushed to contribute as opposed to the much smaller number of landed gentry or squires. And, as one might suspect, it was those from port towns such as Dartmouth, Bideford, Barnstaple, and Exeter who invested heavily where their interests were

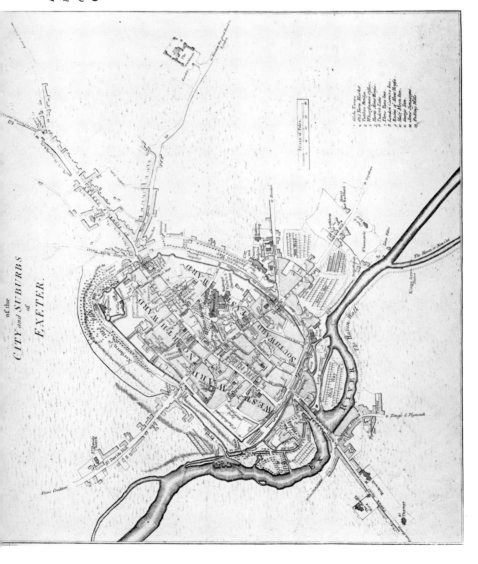

Exeter and Vicinity in the Seventeenth and Eighteenth Centuries

Charles I

so directly involved, while the people of Totnes, Tiverton, Torrington, and such places did not contribute nearly as much as their wealth might have suggested.

At the same time as a network of family relationships tied together the people of Devon with the Irish Protestants, the same kind of family and business contacts kept the people of the West Country in touch with events at Westminster and throughout the country. Privately circulated newsletters and correspondence, although slow in delivery, held together a society unused to frequent travel and disinclined to regular meetings over long distances and rough terrain. John Willoughby of Payhembury was one such gentleman who maintained a steady flow of communication with far-flung relatives, and especially with his daughter Bridget and her husband John Turberville in London. It was from their letters, and those of his nephew William Davy, that Willoughby received news of the Scots' invasion during August and September 1640, of Strafford's imprisonment in the Tower for treason, of the ejection of the monopolists from the House of Commons, as well as Windebank's commitment, and of the numerous other events which brought the country to the eve of civil war.[34] Some Devonians, then, were surprisingly well-informed as to what was happening in the rest of England, and in the struggle between parliament and crown to adjust grievances and to reform church and state. John Bampfield at Poltimore was excited by the news he was receiving, as he wrote to Edward Seymour:

> The news of these times are so excellent that he deserves not to breathe this British air who prayeth not God heartily for them, and is not in himself very well pleased with them, hence you may perceive how acceptable your missives are, and yet not so much for the novelty, as that you deign sometimes to remember your country friend. For ever be this Parliament renowned for so great achievements, for we dream now of nothing more than of a golden age. How cheerfully and how easily do we go under a just burthen, though weighty, though we gall and wince under an unjust one, be it never so light. It is the nature of freedom, or the freedom of our nature, that so pleaseth.[35]

Rumours were widespread, however, and the trustworthiness of one's information obviously depended upon the reliability of the correspondent's intelligence and contacts. Amias Bampfield's letter to Willoughby of 17 March 1641 makes clear the universal nature of unsubstantiated rumour in this period of tension, and general desire for reliable information. Turberville wrote: 'Worthy

D

Sir I do believe you have more news in the country than we have here in London. But yours is at the second hand, and therefore I have sent you those pamphlets here enclosed of the first edition. How the times are, every man knows, what the times will be, no man knows'.[36]

It was certainly true that most MPs by mid-1641 were unaware of the direction in which their revolutionary activities were taking them. With Laud imprisoned, Strafford executed, prerogative courts abolished, the church in turmoil, and the state turned upside down, just what would happen next was anyone's guess. But without a doubt the parliamentary leaders could see clearly enough that the traditional pattern of government must be altered, and worked in that direction. Of necessity, they attempted to build up a party of sufficient strength in both parliament and country to support the changes which would inevitably come about. Davy wrote to his uncle on 1 July 1641: 'Sir I have inclosed sent you two speeches, *to prepare your thoughts* [author's italics] for that change which is like to be'.[37] He went on to relate a number of changes which parliament was then forcing on the king, with more to follow. It is certainly too much to say that Davy, or the leaders of parliament for that matter, had a definite programme for which they were aiming; but determination for a revised form of government certainly did exist, and the country had to be convinced of its necessity as well as did the rest of the House. With this in mind, the circulation of pamphlets and letters throughout the countryside became more widespread.

Each newsletter, pamphlet, and private letter during the spring months of 1642 must have brought with it into Devon additional threats of constitutional crisis and civil conflict. Those Willoughby received certainly tended in that direction as he obtained further word of the king's separation from his parliament, of the confrontation at Hull, the withdrawal of the peers and officials from Westminster to York, and of the steady build-up of arms, men, and money on each side. Davy spoke for many of the people of the country when he wrote: 'I hope, under colour of preserving the King's prerogative, we shall not destroy one another, whilst we all protest on all sides to make the King glorious, and the kingdom happy. We have all protested to maintain the King and privilege of Parliament, and we cannot better perform our vows than by keeping peace between them'.[38] This was precisely the opinion expressed by the collective body of Devon JPs in special sessions in July 1642 when they drew up two petitions, addressed to king and parliament respectively, in an unsuccessful attempt to mediate between these two ancient authorities before the final confrontation. The content of these petitions constitute about the only concrete expressions of opinion arising from the county during this very difficult period of denunciation and crisis. Otherwise, only a limited amount of unrest within the county can be detected, such as the refusal of some Devonians to pay martial rates for the maintenance of the royal armies, or of others to pay rates for repairs to parish churches.[39]

In April 1642 two Devon divines were recommended by the county MPs as suitable to be consulted with regard to the 'matter of the church', giving partial expression to the widespread dissatisfaction in the county to the existing Laudian persuasion.[40] On 19 May 'An information was given [in the House of Commons], of words spoken by Henry Davie against the Parliament', and Mr Peard was ordered to instruct the JPs near Barnstaple to look into the matter.[41] By 25 June the people of the county were becoming more divided in their opinion as between king and parliament, some now attacking the Commons for their 'new tricks and new Laws' and especially for their being 'all puritans, for the protestants were all gone away from them to the king. . .'[42] Thus, signs of division did exist, and it is safe to assume that much more numerous were the Devonians who spoke out privately against the 'evil councillors' surrounding the king, or about the 'Roundheaded apprentices' causing trouble in the capital. Few, however, could have been found who would have had a good word to say in favour of a fratricidal war of which there was general fear and lively repugnance. It was to avert this threat that the Devon JPs merged their differences long enough to address to king and parliament their hope for peace and mutual understanding already mentioned.[43] But as Hamilton put it: 'Read by the light of subsequent events . . . [these petitions] sound like a woeful cry of peace when there was no peace'.[44]

Exactly how reluctant the county of Devon was in promoting civil conflict can be seen in the petitions of 12 July 1642, and in the later unsuccessful efforts between February and April 1643 to make Devon and Cornwall a neutral zone. An address sent to the parliament, and read in the Lords on 16 August 1642, requested that 'in this time of dangerous distraction' the two houses bring themselves to a reconciliation with the king. The petition goes on: 'Two acts we chiefly pray for: one of forgiveness, another of forgetfulness'.[45] In their address to the king the full dilemma of the people of Devon, and of England, was exposed:

> Your Majesty commands our obedience to the commission of array, whilst both houses of Parliament adjudge us to [be] betrayers of our liberty and property if we do so. They persuade submission to the militia, whilst your Majesty proclaims it unlawful and derogatory to your prerogative; how unhappily are we here made judges in apparent contraries; in how hard a condition are we whilst a two-fold obedience, like twins in the womb strive to be born, to both we cannot chose but look upon the privileges of Parliament with a natural affection; from our fathers' loins we derive a touch that leads us thither as the needle to the loadstone. We desire to preserve them because the death of liberty without that support is inevitable.[46]

Their petition, then, was for a reunion of affection between crown and parliament which would 'close up the present breaches of this distracted [country] and the other bleeding kingdom of Ireland ..', and avoid the fratricidal war breaking out upon them.[47]

Notwithstanding sincere and serious efforts, these petitions could not have had much effect. It was too late for the course of events to be altered. Troops were already being marshalled, arms collected, and supporters sought. With the proclamation of the Militia Ordinance, parliament had declared its sovereign authority within the state and was actively setting about to maintain it. The royal Commission of Array was the response of a monarch attempting now to regain his sovereignty from rebellious subjects through the force of arms. With such forces at work, little could be done by the peace-loving people of Exeter and Devon. They were being dragged into a conflict which they as yet did not view as their own cause, and for which there was much reluctance.

Notes to this chapter are on page 195

4
Parliamentary Control of Devon
august-september 1642

The first Civil War has traditionally been dated from 22 August 1642 when Charles I formally raised his standard at Nottingham Castle and called upon his loyal subjects to come to his aid. A very good case can be made for setting the opening date as early as the siege of Hull, if not indeed back to 2 January when Charles invaded the House of Commons in search of Five Members. As far as the counties of Devon and Exeter were concerned, however, the Civil War began with the attempt of the Marquis of Hertford to put into effect the commission of array.

Immediately upon its reconvening on 11 January the House of Commons had issued instructions to the counties that the local militia and trained bands were to be organised for purposes of defence.[1] Regularly thereafter local authorities took steps to see to it that their regional forces were prepared in terms of training and arms for the test of strength which appeared likely in the growing political crisis facing them.[2] At the same time parliament ordered the Protestation oath taken by all adults in the nation. And, as in each county the militia was the responsibility of the lord lieutenant, the Commons attempted to secure the appointment of men favourably disposed toward the parliament. In the case of Devon and Exeter, this meant retaining the Earl of Bedford in that office as a man of proven support for the aims and ambitions of the popular cause.[3]

For several months following the attempted arrest of the Five Members the critical struggle between king and parliament was focused on their respective efforts to gain control of the country forces as the only vestige of military strength in the nation.[4] As early as February parliament had pressed upon the king their demand for control of the militia in the form of the Militia Bill which, once rejected, became law as an 'ordinance', issued without royal consent.[5]

Within a fortnight (4 June) the parliament was exhorting the deputy-lieutenants to execute assiduously the conditions of the Militia Ordinance and to be present in person on the dates appointed 'for the training, mustering, and exercising of the inhabitants of the said counties'.[6] That same day Sir John Bampfield was ordered to remain in Devon to see to it that the ordinance was indeed carried out in that county. This first declaration of parliamentary sovereignty appears to have been agreeable to the majority of the nation as by mid-June 'most of the counties' had accepted it.[7] On 20 June Sir John Northcote was sent down to assist Bampfield. 1 July was the date finally decided upon as suitable for putting the Militia Ordinance into execution in Devon and Exeter.[8] Three days later the Commons ordered that Sir George Chudleigh, Sir Peter Prideaux, Northcote, and Bampfield 'shall be the persons employed by this House, for the advancing the Propositions in the county of Devon, for the raising of Horse, or subscribing for Money or plate'.[9] To all intents and purposes the Devon Parliamentary Committee was formed and in operation some weeks before the king officially opened the Civil War. Charles responded to this challenge by issuing commissions of array to loyal subjects who were authorised to establish their authority over the militia, and with a proclamation to enjoin the country to disregard those officials not appointed by him.[10] With these antagonistic credentials each side attempted to gain the popular support of the people within their counties against the illegal invasion of the constitution—of which each accused the opposite side.[11] Therefore, 'with so much difference of opinion, it was open to the individual to take the side which was best fitted to his own judgment or convenience'.[12]

On 19 July the Commission of Array for Devonshire was issued to Henry Bouchier, Earl of Bath, Edward Viscount Chichester, and twenty-six other gentlemen, knights, and baronets of the county who, in the ensuing struggle, represented the core of royalist support there. These men were ordered to organise, arm, and train the county forces for purposes of defence against external or internal enemies of the kingdom. Equipped with this authority the Earl of Bath, in the company of the Marquis of Hertford, travelled into the West Country to begin the effective organisation of royalist control of Devon.[13]

News of the commissions of array granted to gentlemen through-out the countryside, and to leading Devonians in particular, stir-red up a great deal of animosity among the people of the county against another example of a new and unusual instrument of oppression on the part of the king and his ministers.[14] Its appear-ance was used by the opposition to reinforce their claim that it was the king who was in fact the aggressor in raising troops to threaten and enslave the representative body of the nation as assembled in the Parliament at Westminster. Not understanding a device which was new and uncertain in precedent, the purpose of the commission 'was misrepresented, and rumour grew upon rumour until alarum and apprehension became general'.[15] The uncertainties to which this document gave rise, coming as they did on top of the growing tensions of the time, the move of the king to York, and the attempt on Hull, were reflected in the renewal of petitions addressed to men of prominence and authority. On 9 August an Inquest Jury held at the Exeter Assizes appealed dir-ectly to the Earl of Bath as a man of 'eminency and known interest in his Majesty's favour', to use his good offices toward an 'accom-modation between his Majesty and Parliament; and that war, the greatest and worst of evils, be not conceived and chosen for a means to heal our distempers, rather than a Parliament, the cheap-est and best remedy'.[16] This was only the first of several petitions which resulted from the meetings of the Assizes that week. On 12 August the Grand Inquest for the county presented an overwhelm-ing vote of confidence to three of the county's MPs; ie, Bampfield, Northcote, and Rolle, 'to congratulate those faithful services which you have performed in Parliament for us...', and to re-quest that they continue their efforts to end civil strife in the country.[17] These MPs were at that moment in Devon implement-ing the Militia Ordinance, organising the county's defences, and recruiting funds and supporters for the parliamentary cause.

While consistently repeating their desire for a peaceful settle-ment of the constitutional crisis, the Devon JPs (nineteen of whom signed the petition addressed to the MPs) clearly show their pre-disposition toward a parliamentary solution of the nation's prob-lems; ie, the king working through parliament in the traditional pattern to reform the grievances and evils besetting the nation.

Their conviction that a solution could be obtained only by working with and through parliament was clearly set forth in the address made to Sir Robert Foster, Judge of Assize on the Western Circuit, also on 12 August. Among the grievances listed by the Grand Inquest functioning 'as the representative body of this County . . .', these leading Devonians declared 'That his Majesty's yet estranging from his greatest Council the Parliament, is a grievance of grievances'. The Inquest Jury went on to speak of the commission of array as 'a matter of extreme grievance and terror to us all' and, in addition, '. . . that the war actually begun in other parts of this kingdom, and fearfully preparing here is a grievance tending to the dissolution of the ancient government of this kingdom'.[18]

The county's representatives may have avoided placing blame or overtly taking sides as yet, but it seems certain that the majority would, when ultimately pressed, give full support to the popular cause. That they had completely accepted parliament's authority and jurisdiction over themselves and the local militia is clear. That they considered the king to be in the wrong by removing himself from his parliament is also evident. That they were greatly concerned with the increasingly violent turn of events in general, and the commission of array in particular, is also apparent. Without much doubt, then, the majority of these leading county figures who signed and gave evidence at the August Assizes were controlling the county, under the guidance of Chudleigh, Rolle, Prideaux, and Bampfield, for parliament, and were taking steps to secure this control in both civil and military spheres.

Although Sir Robert Foster reported everything to be fairly quiet in the counties when he visited them during August,[19] the parliamentary agents were busy martialling their forces as is evidenced by the order sent to Captain Robert Bennett of Hexworthy to muster his men at Great Torrington by 22 August. This, presumably, was not the only such order sent out.[20] The royalist attempt to stop this rendezvous was completely unsuccessful, as the militia was by this time securely within the control of the parliamentary agents in Devon, and the commission of array was being wholly ignored.[21] From the outset, then, the parliamentary supporters appear to have gained control of the institutions of county authority, including the magistracy and lieutenancy. By this means the executive machinery, as administered by the Quarter Sessions, and the militia, under the jurisdiction of the lord lieutenant and his deputies, were secured for parliament. The third, and weakest, branch of county government, the office of sheriff, was held by Richard Culme of Canonsleigh, a man sympathetic to the royalist cause. The inability of that official to maintain control of the county for the Crown was evident by the very nature of his office. His only instrument of power was the posse comitatus, and that was to prove totally ineffective in Devon. In addition, since the sheriff could work only through the unpaid constables of each hundred, he was apt to find little in the way of eager support for an authority which was becoming increasingly unpopular and for a cause which was gaining disrepute as the aggressor and initiator of civil strife.

Along with other petitions that month, Sir Robert Foster received an address signed by thirty-two constables from the various hundreds in Devonshire. These minor officials called Sir Robert's attention to the ominous commission of array which had recently been granted to the Earl of Bath, as well as the declarations of parliament regarding such commissions. The constables requested that the statements of parliament 'may now openly be read in Court that so your petitioners and the rest of the County may know the Law therein and accordingly shape their obedience...'.[22] It is apparent, therefore, that the county was well infused with a distrust of royal motives and that the general feeling was one of apprehension at the threat of innovations such as that of the commission.[23] Foster, however, carefully avoided making any pronouncement with regard to either the commission or the ordinance, but rather impressed upon the sheriffs of the western counties the necessity of working 'to preserve the peace'.[24]

The Earl of Bath retaliated against the aspersions of the parliamentarian propagandists on 13 August by publishing the commission which had been granted to him and his colleagues to take immediate and effective control of the county's militia, and to obtain the co-operation of the local authorities in the execution thereof, notwithstanding any other authority to the contrary.[25] At the same time the Earl issued a statement to the county promising that he had 'undertaken nothing contrary to the Lawes of this Kingdom, nor prejudicial, or hurtful, to any that shall observe it'. He assured the people that he had received no authority to levy taxes and impositions on the county as had been rumoured, but instead to provide whatever protection was needed to secure the public safety.[26] This declaration was quickly answered by an anonymous author who briefly set forth the various arguments to show that the illegally constituted commission of array was interfering with the due execution of the Militia Ordinance and, as a consequence, bringing on the unrest and tension within the nation which threatened to 'embroil this Kingdom, that the rebellion may prevail in Ireland'.[27] During the first part of August the parliamentarians seem to have encountered little difficulty in carrying out their plans to control the Devon militia; the latter part of the month, however, brought them more trouble.[28]

Clearly, soft words and fair promises were not sufficient to convince a suspicious people of the legal and legitimate purposes of the royal commission. Notwithstanding general and widespread resentment and opposition, the commissioners continued their efforts to bring the local military units within their own control, hoping to outdistance similar efforts by the opposition. The Earl of Bath was particularly optimistic that his efforts in Devon would be as successful as those of the royalists in Cornwall.[29] Relying over-much on the Bouchier name and landholdings in the county, Bath did not carefully consider the nature of his opponents, their talent and organising ability,[30] the strength and widespread nature of popular feeling, and the determination with which he was being opposed. The loyalty of the Cornish to their local leaders and squires was not to be found in the more independently-minded and larger county of Devon. As the royal representative in the county, the Earl of Bath was the centre of activity from the moment he returned from York. It was to his home at Tawstock, about two miles from Barnstaple, that 'divers knights and gentlemen daily resorted' for purposes of discussion and instruction so as to put their commission into execution. Amongst the enthusiasts listed, who were collecting arms and deeply in league with the Earl, were men from a number of well-known local families, all of 'great worth' especially in the eastern part of the county, and in the north, with supposedly wide-ranging authority amongst the local tenantry. In south Devon, however, there was little royalist activity reported.[31]

The larger landowners of north Devon appear to have been particularly energetic in late August to get the commission into execution and the militia into sufficient shape to withstand the forthcoming crisis. Edward Viscount Chichester, Sir Hugh Pollard of King's Nympton, Arthur Basset of Heanton Court, and John Gifford of Brightley all joined in to stir up royalist sentiment amongst their tenants and to convince the inhabitants in their areas of the legality and justice of the royal cause.[32] Impressive as was this array of local magnates, it would appear that an even larger group of potentially royalist sympathisers, especially amongst the lesser gentry, would have nothing to do with these war-like activities. The 'Array-men', as they were called, were looked upon, '. . . as the first instigators of a breach of the peace'.[33] Thus, limited in number and generally suspected or actively disliked, the commissioners worked against great odds to fulfill their mission.

That the distrust of the king's commission was widely felt among all elements of Devon society is shown by the various attempts made by the commissioners to execute their charge. Shortly following the original publication of their commission, Mr Ashford and Sheriff Culme attempted to have it read in Cullompton where the constable, Walter Challis, and the inhabitants of the community turned out in force to withstand this supposedly illegal action. In the presence of John Acland, John Willoughby, and Peter Sainthill's son-in-law, Ashford tried to force Challis into accepting the commission and the warrants which would have halted a militia muster scheduled for that week. The solid opposition of the parish defeated any possibility of success that Ashford might have expected as a result of the presence of so many worthy gentry.[34] What was of greater concern to the parishioners of Cullompton was the appearance of the Earl of Bath, together with a body of cavaliers, to reinforce Ashford's stand. To protect themselves, the townsmen were busy exercising their trained band, throwing up chains, repairing walls, and seeing to their arms. But more insidious than Bath's activities were those carried on by Peter Sainthill at his home in Bradninch, outside Exeter. It was reported that he was slowly gathering both arms and supplies under his roof, meeting and intriguing with various gentlemen of the neighbourhood, and attempting to take control of the community magazine. At the same time that they were looking to their own defence, the men of Honiton, Ottery, as at Cullompton, were preparing to send off forces within the week under Colonel Prideaux's command to aid the parliamentary cause at Sherborne against the forces accompanying the Marquis of Hertford.[35] What evidence there is would seem to support the impression that the parliamentary supporters in Devon felt sufficiently confident of their control of the county in August to send troops outside Devon.

On 29 August Charles issued under the Privy Signet at his court at Nottingham instructions to his commissioners of array to raise whatever troops they could for his immediate support against the rebellion of the 'Earl of Essex, and his confederates', and others attempting to institute the illegal Militia Ordinance. While specifically empowered to suppress violence and disorder in their respective districts, the commissioners were to place whatever troops they could muster under the command of the Marquis of Hertford who, on 2 August, had been commissioned 'General of our forces in the Western parts', and was at that moment active in raising royalist support in Somerset.[36]

Only in a few instances, however, were these instructions, or earlier attempts, successful. Humphrey Cudamore, constable of Witheridge Hundred, had willingly sent out warrants to restrain the appearance of the trained bands under the authority of the Militia Ordinance. For his troubles, Cudamore was ordered to be arrested by command of the House of Commons in order to be questioned as a 'Delinquent'. And although a royal warrant had gone out to Arthur Basset to replace Sir Samuel Rolle as Colonel of the regiment in north Devon, Rolle was able to inform the House that with the assistance of his fellow MPs then in the county, and with the sympathetic co-operation of the DLs, the Devon militia was well in hand, as was the civilian control of the area.[37] This widespread initial support for the parliamentary cause in Devon was clearly brought home to the Earl of Bath during his abortive attempt to read his commission in the northern community of South Molton. On Tuesday, 13 September, the earl, in company with a substantial group of country gentlemen, entered the borough only to be confronted by a motley array of citizens in arms who were:

> in a great rage with the Mayor and his company, for giving licence that they should enter, and swore that if they did attempt anything there, or read their Commission of Array, they would beat them all down and kill them, if they were all hanged for it.[38]

An eye-witness to this confrontation claimed that upwards of 1,000 people gathered in the market-place, arming themselves:

. . . some with Muskets loaden, some with Halberts and Black Bills, some with Clubs, some with Pikes, some with dung Evells, some with great Poles, one I saw which had heat the calke of a sive [scythe] and beat him out right and set him into a long staffe. The women had filled all the steps of the Cross with great stones and got up and sat on them, swearing, if they did come there, they would brain them. One thing, which is worth the noting, a woman which is a Butcher's wife, came running with her lapful of Ramshorns for to throw at them.[39]

The menacing appearance of this howling mob dissuaded the royalists from any public announcements that day. The earl and his retinue were forced to withdraw from the town, obviously hoping for greater success elsewhere.

The universal support for the parliamentary cause exhibited in South Molton appears to have given additional impetus to the activities of other parliamentary sympathisers in the northern part of the country, an area of potentially strong royalist influence. While Barnstaple and other communities fortified themselves, the parliamentary agents Chudleigh, Bampfield, and Northcote were doing their best to organise units, recruit supplies, plate, and men for the companies grouping under the command of the Earl of Bedford, then at Taunton.[40] These last efforts were apparently not too successful, but this probably arose from a natural disinclination of the people to move outside their own county, or to become active participants in the conflict which Bedford's activities represented.[41] Sir Hugh Pollard's letter of 25 September addressed to the Earl of Bath is the first extant reference notifying Devonians of the Marquis of Hertford's withdrawal from Somerset, and the fact 'that most of his troops are marched into Cornwall'.[42] Within weeks these same royalists, reinforced by Cornish volunteers, would be returning to Devon to begin the task of recapturing the county for the king.

In the meantime, the parliamentarians had things all their own way in Devonshire. On 28 September the Earl of Bath was peaceably arrested by Captain Dewett and his troop of horse detached from Bedford's forces in Somerset. As early as 15 August Bath had signified his break with parliament by rejecting a summons to return to his place in the Lords, excusing his non-attendance on the grounds of the 'interruptions and menaces and affronts by people in London and Westminster' to which he had been subjected in the earlier sessions. On 23 August his arrest had been ordered by the House of Lords, but the warrant could not be executed for over a month.[43] During that time Bath and his followers had done what they could to stir up support for the royalist cause in north Devon, and it would appear that they initially had a certain amount of co-operation from the gentry. These efforts were bound to fail at first, especially when the major instrument of execution, the commission of array, was so popularly suspect. This was particularly true when the traditional structure of authority, working through the lord lieutenant and his deputies, could point to the more acceptable authority of the parliament, grounded as it was on universal sympathy, respect, and near-reverence.

This is not to say, however, that royalist supporters would be entirely lacking in Devon. The majority of the county gentry were ultimately to take the king's side in this struggle. It did mean that in August and September of 1642, although the MPs had been forced to decide and take sides in the halls of Westminster, the people of Devon (and especially the gentry) had not generally done so, and would continue to refrain from committing themselves until absolutely driven to it by the course of events. At the same time, the county as a whole felt no contradiction in universally opposing the commission of array with the same spirit that they had opposed ship money, tunnage and poundage, or any of the other royal innovations. Although they protested individually and collectively against the approach of civil strife, few could actually bring themselves to the realisation that civil war was already a reality and not just a possible danger.

Certain communities and individuals had long since made up their minds as to which side they would support. The Corporations of Plymouth, Barnstaple, Dartmouth, and Exeter had given repeated assurances to the parliament of their loyal support.[44] Along with the other maritime and industrial communities, these urban areas had suffered most directly as a result of the royal maladministration of the past twenty years, and were largely inhabited by puritan sympathisers who took every possible opportunity to register their opposition to the Stuart regime. But while the larger towns were able to take immediate steps to protect themselves from aggressive forces,[45] and were thus more vocal in their support for the parliament, smaller communities such as Totnes, Tiverton, and Axminster were much more circumspect.

Although favourably disposed toward reform in church and

state, the inhabitants of these boroughs were generally hoping to avoid becoming involved, and therefore went out of their way to antagonise neither side. Rather, as the war progressed, these communities are seen to change formal allegiance whenever a different force moved into their area. This was certainly true of Axminster, Totnes, and a number of other communities that found themselves, unlike Plymouth and Exeter, constantly changing hands with the shifting fortunes of war, and having to contribute to the support of both armies.[46] Okehampton, due to its unique position on the major road crossing central Devon, was particularly susceptible to these fluctuations.

The question as to why certain people came to support the cause they did in the first Civil War is difficult to answer. The rationale behind the decisions of many is probably best summarised by Wedgwood when she wrote:

> Parliament's claim to stand for the liberties of the subject seemed more plausible than the King's protestation that he did so, for his numerous infringements of his subjects' liberty were well-remembered and well-advertised, while those of Parliament had so far affected only a minority. The same was true of the King's assertion that he stood for the true Protestant religion: whatever the purity of his personal faith, he had shown over the last twelve years that he preferred Papists to Puritans and by so doing had brought the Church of England under suspicion with large numbers of his subjects. This was the issue on which a great many earnest Protestant Christians made their choice when it came to war.[47]

It must be made clear, however, that a myriad of reasons and influences existed for the thousands forced to make the distasteful decision between king and parliament. Without doubt, most sensible Englishmen would have preferred to stay out of the war entirely, as many were never convinced that either side was completely right. Devonians, then, were by no means unanimous as to the side they chose to support as the civil war grew in severity and gathered momentum. The aristocratic family of Russell was badly split as the third and fourth earls supported parliament, while John Russell, MP, came out for the king. Other aristocrats with seats in Devon, such as the last Bouchier, Earl of Bath, Edward Viscount Chichester, and John Lord Mohun of Okehampton, all supported the royalist cause. The gentry, the real ruling oligarchy in the county, was badly divided between the minority of leading gentry who favoured parliament, and the majority of local magnates who evenually supported the king. The larger section of minor gentry, heavily tradition-bound, were also inclined toward the king. And while the yeomen and tenants of the countryside, if giving the matter any thought at all, were well-disposed toward the parliament, they went along with the majority of the county who hoped to remain neutral, or at least uninvolved in the conflict.

The strong centres of puritan sympathy, the large towns and boroughs, were probably the strongest areas of support for the parliamentarian cause. Led by the example of Plymouth throughout the war, Exeter, Barnstaple, and Dartmouth were devotedly attached to the popular cause against the religious and secular innovations which the Crown had recently promoted. Exeter, however, does appear to have harboured a strongly royalist minority, more dangerous than that in other areas, which brought constant anxiety to the new parliamentarian governors.[48] Nor could the governors of Dartmouth rest too easily, situated as they were in the strongly royalist South Hams.[49]

Suffice it to say that, as in other parts of the country, families split, connections dissolved, and old friendships were broken. In a county controlled by a widespread and interlocking network of gentry, Devon saw its magnates and leading families break apart and fight one another, while the unwilling yeomen and labourers were impressed into service or otherwise committed to a cause that few among them could understand or care about. Courtenay Pole of Colcombe and Shute stood opposed to his father, Sir John Pole.[50] The Fortescues of south Devon, with their seat at Fallapit in East Allington parish, took the royalist side against their relatives in North Devon, Hugh Fortescue and his son Robert of Filleigh.[51] The Fortescues of Weare Giffard and Filleigh actually did what they could to maintain the appearance of neutrality, although giving freely to the parliamentarian cause. Likewise, the Champernownes of Modbury came out actively in support of the king while the branch at Dartington affected strict neutrality, even though Arthur Champernowne's father-in-law was the zealous royalist, Sir Francis Fulford.[52] The family of Sir Francis Drake, second baronet, was luckier than most. Although the interconnections of marriage and relationship were large and complex, most of the Drake relations fought on the same side; ie, for parliament. Sir Francis was married to Dorothea Pym, daughter of 'King

Henrietta Maria

The Prince of Wales, later Charles II

Pym' and brother to Charles. Among his uncles and cousins and brothers-in-law were numbered Sir George Chudleigh, Sir Samuel Somaster, Sir John Davy of Creedy, Sir John Young of Stedcombe, William Strode, Elizeus Crymes, and the Bampfields.[53] This group represented a formidable network of parliamentarian sympathisers and active supporters who worked forcefully for the popular caused during the opening days of the war. Much the same kind of family network, although not nearly as extensive, was operative among the Champernownes of Modbury, the Fulfords of Fulford, and the Seymours of Berry Pomeroy, all of whom took up the royalist cause. Nor did the few Roman Catholic families in the county hesitate in rallying to the king.

In sum then, it appears that at the outset of civil war the county of Devon was markedly pro-parliamentarian in both town and country, with the leading gentry as the potential strength of the royalist cause. But quickly deprived of leadership with the arrest of the Earl of Bath, this element remained a minority without unity, organisation, or spirit, and was thus susceptible to parliamentary control. Added to these considerations was the universal desire for non-involvement and neutrality. The suspicions aroused by the commission of array and Bath's Declaration did nothing to help unify this dormant force. This lethargic attitude compared unfavourably with the innovating zeal which the parliamentary agents exercised in terms of swift action and strong organisation in gaining control of the county. Taken together, these factors worked to limit royalist activity in Devon until Hopton's invasion at the end of the year. Within this void the parliamentary agents worked upon the natural sympathy and general concern of the masses to secure dominance over the militia, Quarter Sessions, and municipal governing bodies. The growing royalist element, within Devon and in Exeter, was to stir itself before the end of the year in an attempt to regain lost ground, although success would elude them until overwhelming military force could be brought to bear on the parliamentary urban strongholds of the county, and Exeter, Barnstaple, Dartmouth, and the rest—all but Plymouth—could be taken.

Notes to this chapter are on page 197

E

5

Outbreak of Civil Strife:
Royalist Offensive in Devon
august 1642-june 1643

As Englishmen took sides for the approaching struggle, the royalist command took steps to ensure the continued loyalty of the West Country. The Marquis of Hertford, in company with Sir Ralph Hopton, Lord Seymour, and a number of other gentlemen, left Beverly (Yorkshire) for the west in mid-July to put into execution the commission of array recently granted to him by the king. Soon after, on 2 August, Hertford's powers were increased by a further commission appointing him lieutenant-general of the six western counties.[1] Early optimism was not rewarded, however, and the Marquis was unable to recruit the forces and support in Somerset and Wiltshire that had been originally anticipated. By the first week in August he was forced to take shelter in Sherborne Castle in Somerset, where he was besieged by troops under the command of William, Earl of Bedford. Unable to obtain their prize, the parliamentary forces withdrew to Yeovil, thus permitting the royalists to advance to Minehead on the north Somerset coast. With some of the more prominent gentlemen, Hertford retreated into Wales, intending thereby to rejoin the king.[2] Hopton with only 160 horse and dragoons, turned inland and decided to make for Cornwall instead.[3] From Minehead he led his men through South Molton in Devon, and stopped for a rest in the village of Chittlehampton on 24 September before crossing the river Taw some seven miles above Barnstaple.[4] The royalist presence was well-known in north Devon, and Barnstaple had 500 men on alert, ready to withstand imminent attack. Not looking for trouble, the weary cavaliers avoided their opponents and, with the aid of local sympathisers, found their way out of Devon to the relative safety of Stowe, Sir Bevil Grenville's estate on the north Cornish coast, by Sunday, 30 September.[5]

Anticipating their arrival, the parliamentary committee for Cornwall had called out the trained bands and volunteers to rendezvous at Bodmin on 28 September. There was a constant flurry of activity amongst the parliamentarians as they kept close watch on royalist recruitment, and struggled to raise as many men as possible for the defence of the county.[6] The Cornishmen sent off urgent pleas to Sir Samuel Rolle and the Devon committee in the hope of receiving aid from the Devonshire militia, and at the same asked for help from the Earl of Bedford. Rolle offered what advice he could, but warned the Cornish of the difficulties in taking Devon forces out of their own county, no matter how much he and his colleagues might want to help.[7]

In the meantime Hopton and his followers were just as active in raising the county of Cornwall for the king. Sir Ralph had immediately gained the zealous assistance of Sir Bevil Grenville, Sir Nicholas Slanning, John Trevanion, and John Arundell, together with other commissioners of array who quickly helped to raise some 300 men of the posse comitatus.[8] Notwithstanding the confidence of the Cornish parliamentarians in their own strength, supported as they were by the five or six troops of horse which Chudleigh had gathered at Tavistock,[9] Hopton was able to drive all before him, entering Launceston unopposed and forcing the parliamentarians to take refuge within the safe confines of Plymouth.[10] Although Slanning and the others wanted to pursue their quarry into the neighbouring county, the posse would not move outside Cornwall.[11] Local pride and loyalty could easily rally men to protect their property from invasion, but could not get them to move very far from home. The prospects of a march into Devon to recruit from the large number of royalists overawed by the parliamentarian control of the militia, had little attraction for the Cornish volunteers and trained bands. Hopton's forces melted away, and he was forced to rely completely on volunteers for his invasion of Devon.[12]

The crushing success of the royalists in Cornwall led to unprecedented activity both at Westminster and in Devon in an attempt to secure parliamentary control in the West Country. Beginning on 11 October, the Commons issued a series of orders instructing the Devon committee in their preparation for defence against expected invasion. Colonel John Bampfield's regiment, along with those of Sir Samuel Rolle and Sir George Chudleigh, was to be brought up to strength, while the city of Exeter was specifically authorised to use £300 of the public funds for city fortifications and repairs to the castle.[13] The mayor and DLs received full power to put everything in order to withstand royalist aggression, and within a short time a disciplined garrison was on the alert, with some twenty-five pieces of ordnance guarding the walls.[14] Barnstaple, under the guidance of Mr Peard, MP, and Plymouth were also actively engaged in preparations for their defence—generally at their own expense, but with assurances of repayment from public funds.[15]

On 17 October parliament issued instructions which required the DLs and leading parliamentarians to call before them the prominent gentlemen of the county 'to demand what every man will lend, either by the week, month, or in gross, for the defence of the Kingdom'.[16] At the same time, the county was to raise a troop of horse and a body of 100 dragoons, to act as a constant patrol and to be of use wherever needed.[17] This force, as well as all others to be raised within the six western counties, and the Isle of Wight, was put under the command of the Earl of Pembroke.[18] Responding to parliament's orders, warrants were sent out to the leading gentry calling upon them to appear at Exeter on the 21st of the month 'that each man may contribute his advise what he think fittest for the establishment of our defence and peace, . . .'.[19] The warrant sent to John Willoughby of Payhembury was signed by the leading spirits who made up the Devon parliamentary committee.[20] It was this group which was responsible for the normal functioning of the county during the opening days of the civil war, as many of them had been during the period of 'personal rule'. Drawn from the ruling class of county gentry, the committee was now directly responsible to parliament, as these men had once been to the Privy Council. Within their jurisdiction came the military organisation and defence of the shire, and the necessary civilian administration with which to collect men, money, and supplies. The committee's major strength came from its use of well-established institutional procedure in retaining authority in the area, while the king was forced to depend upon newly created machinery to reassert his control. The popular cause thus worked within the framework of tradition and rule of law, and was consistently supervised from above. Royalist agents, on the other hand, had free reign as long as they somehow worked toward a common end, ie, monarchial supremacy.[21] Rolle, Northcote, and others of the Devon committee were not slow in following the example of their defeated Cornish brethren by applying to parliament, once the threat to the county was realised.[22] On 21 October the House of Commons received their letter describing 'the distracted condition of the County', which was soon followed by a petition from the inhabitants of Devon and Cornwall (22 October) requesting supplies of arms and ammunition with which to combat the growing royalist forces. The Commons promised to send down what supplies they could, but were especially eager that all 'well-affected to the King and Parliament' should meanwhile enlist in the forces under the Earl of Bedford, and contribute money and plate wherever possible.[23]

It was obvious from the king's point of view that Western affairs had taken a much more favourable turn than was expected. To facilitate Hopton's task, Charles issued a proclamation from Maidenhead on 9 November offering a full pardon to the citizens of Exeter for their activities in aiding and promoting the rebellion, if they would immediately return to their true allegiance. Chudleigh, Northcote, Rolle, and Martyn, being 'traitors and stirrers of sedition against us', were alone excepted from this generous offer, and were to be arrested on sight.[24] By the same post a commission was sent to Edward Seymour at Berry Pomeroy to raise a regiment of 1,200 volunteers from Devonshire, presumably to aid Hopton in regaining the county for the king.[25] Royal proclamations notwithstanding, the Corporation of Exeter 'with the entire body of the town, . . . [were] resolved to stand for the commonwealth', believing that there was no better way of serving the king 'than in serving his high Court of Parliament'.[26]

Hopton's efforts, however, did not depend on outside aid, and within weeks of the disbanding of the Cornish trained bands, a volunteer army of more than 1,500 foot had taken their place.[27] Their first encounters were skirmishes around Millbrook and Mount Edgcumbe, just across the border in Cornwall, when groups of Plymouth soldiers sallied out on two different occasions to attack the cavaliers stationed there under Major Walter Slingby.[28] Both sides claimed significant victories from these encounters, but little was actually accomplished apart from the capture of a few prisoners and limited equipment. Hopton and Grenville, encouraged by the Devon royalists, decided to lead their forces across the Tamar in early November. The intervention of Colonel Robert Savery with a large parliamentary force, however, prevented Sheriff Culme, and his royalist adherents, from gathering a posse at Tavistock as planned. Savery's occupation of Tavistock placed him between the Cornish army concentrated near Launceston, and the strong cavalier area of the South Hams. Notwithstanding this opposition, Hopton's advance was able to force a parliamentary retreat until Tavistock was taken, and Colonel William Ruthven's men were forced back toward Plymouth.[29] While it appears certain that Hopton's major consideration at this time was to consolidate his position in the West Country, it was widely believed that his true intensions were to march through Devon to rejoin Hertford's forces reportedly moving out of Wales, or to rendezvous with the king near Reading.[30] Not seriously opposed by any parliamentary forces,[31] the Cornish army was able to advance to the very walls of Exeter by Friday, 18 November.[32] Hoping to obtain the surrender of the city without bloodshed, the royalist commanders sent in a message which called upon the corporation to submit immediately to the royal authority. The mayor and corporation overwhelmingly determined to refuse entry to the royalists, and to do all they could to hold Exeter for parliament.[33]

Setting siege to the city, the cavaliers entrenched themselves around Exeter and concentrated their artillery fire on the west side, receiving in return a heavy bombardment from the seven pieces of ordnance which the defenders had mounted there. On Sunday afternoon the parliamentarians surprised the besiegers by a sudden sally out of the city which resulted in fierce hand-to-hand combat. The citizens were forced to return to the safety of the city walls as night approached, but a council of war that night decided to launch a major offensive in order to drive away these 'disturber[s] of the public peace'.[34] Early that Monday morning the mayor personally led the attack on the unsuspecting Cornishmen, moving quietly out of the city's east gate and around to the rear of the enemy lines. Again caught off their guard the royalist army put up a resolute resistance, but this became ever more futile as thousands of the inhabitants poured out of the city, falling on them from every side. Badly dispersed, the Cornishmen retreated, not to 'their lurking-holes in Cornwall' as was originally reported, but only as far as Tavistock, whence they could readily threaten Plymouth and harrass the western part of Devon.[35]

During the weeks following the Cornish retreat from Exeter, the London newsbooks and pamphlets gave full coverage to the violence and destruction supposedly carried out by the cavaliers who were reported as 'plundering without mercy', even to the gates of Exeter.[36] In reality, the Cornishmen concentrated their attention on the advance toward Plymouth and the siege of that vital parliamentarian stronghold. On 29 November Colonel Ruthven sent a contingent of 270 men to attempt a holding action at Plympton. This proved to be impractical with the advance of the much larger royalist force from Tavistock, and the Plymouth men retreated.[37] Two days later (1 December) Ruthven personally led four troop of horse and seventy dragoons back to Plympton to get a better idea of the enemy strength, and of the possibility of stopping their progress. He, too, was forced to return to the safety of the Plymouth fortifications after only a brief brush with the enemy. The royalist army, estimated between 2,500 and 3,000 men, settled in the Plympton area, and thereafter closely threatened the town of Plymouth.[38]

The siege of Plymouth had immediate repercussions at Westminster as well as at the local level. On 5 December, the Commons authorised three regiments of volunteers to be raised in the western counties, one under Ruthven's command and another under Bampfield. At the same time, Dartmouth was ordered to fortify itself, and Lord Robartes was recommended to replace the inactive Pembroke as commander in the West.[39] Despite considerable discussion, little positive action took place to bring relief to the hard-pressed Devon parliamentarians who repeatedly petitioned for aid.[40] But on 6 December the Commons authorised a further levy of 1,000 dragoons in Somerset, Devon, and Cornwall, and the advancement of more than £1,000 for the equipment of this body of men.[41] Parliamentary orders, however, could not stave off the immediate danger that threatened Plymouth. With enemies approaching in strength from without, this parliamentary stronghold suffered from the same kind of internal dissent and friction which troubled Exeter and Dartmouth. The royalist minority, heaviest in south Devon, gave strong voice to their dissatisfaction with the course of events under the pro-parliamentary authorities, especially with a cavalier force so close to give support.[42] The House of Commons had previously been informed, since Hopton's invasion of Cornwall, of the refusal of some wealthy Exeter citizens to contribute to the common defence, and Dartmouth had complained of the same problem.[43] Philip Francis, Mayor of Plymouth, and John Waddon, MP, stressed the difficulty of their situation in a letter to Sir John Yonge on 2 December in which they outlined their 'several charges against Mr Trelawney',[44] who was not present in Plymouth but was considered responsible for widespread royalist activity in the town. Francis and Waddon maintained that Trelawney's influence caused a large number of people to refuse to contribute toward the town's defence. With the Cornish army quartered just three miles away, and unrest within the town walls, the mayor again asked that immediate help be sent into the West.[45]

With the encouraging presence of Hopton's army within their county, the Devon royalists took their first major step toward organising a cavalier force of their own since the ill-fated efforts of the Earl of Bath. Edmund Fortescue, newly selected sheriff of Devon, took advantage of the momentary ascendancy of the Cornishmen to issue a call to the county for the raising of a posse comitatus to rendezvous at Modbury, ten miles west of Dartmouth, on Tuesday, 6 December. On the day appointed 'a great concourse of people' gathered in Modbury in a very festive, but noncombative, mood. Expecting little from such a group, but impressed with the possibilities of a successful attack on Dartmouth, Hopton sent Sir Nicholas Slanning to inform Sir John Berkeley and Colonel Ashburnham of his change of plans. As a result, Cornish horse arrived from the Plympton quarters to guard the approaches to the Modbury gathering, while additional foot soldiers marched directly to Hopton's aid.[46] But before they could arrive the Plymouth men took advantage of the posse's disorganisation to attack and disperse what could have become a formidable opposition. At three o'clock on the morning of Wednesday, 7 December, Colonel Ruthven, with a force of more than 500 horse and dragoons, marched from Plymouth in a northward arch around the Cornishmen stationed at Plympton, and west of those settled at Totnes, and surprised and dispersed the 3,000 cavalier recruits at Modbury.[47] Hopton and Slanning were able to make good their escape undetected. Not so lucky, however, were some of the leading Devon cavaliers who were captured after a brief struggle.[48] Moving swiftly, Ruthven brought his prisoners safely to Dartmouth where he reinforced the garrison and awaited further help from the county and from Westminster.[49] Unable to overtake the parliamentarians, the main body of Cornishmen moved to Totnes, where at least half of their army was quartered.[50] Despite the setback at Modbury, this better trained segment of Hopton's forces ranged widely over southern and central Devon during the next few weeks, with little interference from the parliamentary authorities. Once again houses were freely pillaged, and gentlemen forced to take refuge in nearby towns and cities.[51]

Their colleagues winning such dominance in the south, the royalists of north Devon attempted to organise themselves in support of the king's cause. Reports from Barnstaple and other northern communities during late December told of large groups of gentlemen meeting at the Earl of Bath's Tawstock home, at Sir Hugh Pollard's house, and at the homes of other prominent gentry.[52] Such activity frightened the inhabitants of Barnstaple into renewed efforts for defence, and by the middle of the month recruitment had brought their garrison to over 700 men under the command of Sir Samuel Rolle and Colonel James Chudleigh.[53] What particularly worried the Barnstaple men was the movement during mid-December of almost 500 cavaliers to within ten miles of their town as the royalists under Colonel John Acland took control of Great Torrington and the surrounding area. At the end of the month, when the main body of Hopton's army was again preoccupied with a siege of Exeter, a thousand of the Barnstaple horse and foot attempted to overthrow the royalist control of Torrington, and finally succeeded in driving them out of the town on 3 January.[54]

Encouraged by general reports of the enemy's weakness and by the desire for additional supplies and recruits from eastern Devon, the Cornish leaders decided to make another attempt to capture Exeter.[55] Thus, Alphington, Powderham, and Topsham were taken just before Christmas. But, unable to overcome the difficulty of straddling the river Exe, and not having sufficient forces for a blockade, Hopton could not prevent Ruthven from reinforcing Exeter by Christmas day.[56] Although disrupted by an occasional false alarm, the siege was a quiet one during most of the Christmas week.[57] Time and again Hopton attempted to replace force with reason, hoping to persuade the city fathers by the legality of his cause and commission to return to their true allegiance, and to help bring an end to this 'unnatural war'.[58] The adamant refusal of the city to capitulate led to a final unsuccessful Cornish assault early on New Year's day, 1643, before the royalists finally broke off the siege.[59]

With winter well upon them, the Cornish leaders finally recognised their inability to conquer Devon. Not only had Exeter been strongly reinforced with Plymouth troops, but more parliamentarian forces were on their way into the Southwest under the command of the Earl of Stamford. In addition, failure of optimistic sympathisers to produce much-needed supplies and recruits led to a dangerous level of resentment and ill-discipline in the Cornish ranks. Consequently, by slow stages the royalist army retreated westward by way of Crediton, Bow, Okehampton, and Bridestowe, and finally into Cornwall, facing only slight opposition from Ruthven's troops in the vicinity of Okehampton.[60] Hopton's efforts thus far to regain control of the West for the king, or even to break through to join Charles, had resulted in utter failure outside Cornwall.

On Friday night, 6 January, the Earl of Stamford arrived in Exeter in advance of an army reputed to consist of at least three regiments of foot.[61] Stamford's immediate aim was to join forces with Colonel Ruthven at Plymouth and, with 4,500 troops between them, to pursue and destroy the Cornish army then quartered around Launceston.[62] To ensure local support, the Lords and Commons on 10 January agreed to a set of instructions which directed the Devon DLs to renewed efforts in raising money and troops to suppress the Cornishmen. Devon was allowed £5,000 for this purpose, in addition to the rates levied locally by the constables and overseers of the poor, to ensure eight pence (3p) per day for the pay of the parish-trained recruits.[63]

The time had come for the parliamentarians to strike back. On 13 January county forces under Colonel William Strode gained control of New Bridge, Gunnislake which spanned the Tamar about seven miles from Saltash (Cornwall), and the following day penetrated into Cornwall to join with Ruthven.[64] Ruthven had no intention, however, of waiting to be reinforced by Stamford. The previous week he had carried out a vigorous artillery attack on Saltash, just across the river from Plymouth. Hurriedly reinforced by Colonel Trevanion's regiment and some forces under Captain William Arundell, Saltash had more than held its own until news of Stamford's advance became known. The Cornish commanders were not prepared to withstand the combined parliamentary forces, and subsequently retreated to Liskeard, and then to Lostwithiel.[65] Eager for a confrontation before Stamford arrived, Ruthven (now General) crossed into Cornwall and personally led his Plymouth forces in pursuit of the enemy. This rash action brought him a resounding defeat on 19 January when the Cornishmen, reinforced by the county's trained bands, smashed the invading Devon forces at Braddock Down, a few miles outside Liskeard.[66]

Meanwhile, the Earl of Stamford was wasting his time reassuring himself as to Plymouth's fortifications.[67] He had marched as far as Launceston before receiving word of Ruthven's defeat and, not being as rash as his junior officer, immediately withdrew his troops to Tavistock. As Ruthven still attempted to retain a foothold at Saltash, the Cornish decided to meet this double threat by splitting their forces in order to pursue each of the parliamentary commanders. Hopton, supported by volunteer regiments and trained bands, was able to clear the enemy from Saltash on Sunday, 22 January, and thus restore the country to royalist control.[68] With Saltash secure, the Cornishmen could continue at will their operations against Plymouth, while using Cornwall as a source of supplies and recruits. But although victory in Cornwall gave renewed spirit to the royalist cause nationally, that county was of little use to the king if he did not control its immediate neighbour.[69] Without Devon the royalists could not take advantage of ready access to France and Ireland in order to bring in foreign aid, nor of the great stock of men and supplies which that larger and wealthier county could provide. Hopton's efforts to gain control of the West were so far unsuccessful but he returned immediately to the attack. The parliamentarians on their side had to keep control of Exeter and Plymouth if they desired to hold the county.

Following their reconquest of Saltash, Hopton's forces again marched into Devon and besieged the formidable Plymouth stronghold, recently reinforced by part of Stamford's army.[70] For weeks thereafter the inhabitants of Plymouth remained in a constant state of preparedness, expecting an attack at any moment. Although confident of their ability to resist royalist control so long as they maintained access to the sea, Plymouth became increasingly hemmed in during the last week of January as Berkeley and Ashburnham drew up their forces from Tavistock and took up positions in Plympton, Modbury, and neighbouring communities, and blocked parliamentary access to the east. At the same time, the royalist commanders sent out warrants to raise the county militia and volunteer companies of subjects loyal to the king.[71]

On Sunday, 29 January, the first steps were taken toward a re-establishment of peace when talks got underway for a cessation of hostilities between the forces under Hopton and Stamford. On this occasion, Hopton, Godolphin, and Lord Warwick Mohun met with Francis Buller and the elder Chudleigh at Robert Trelawney's house just outside Plymouth.[72] These first attempts at a negotiated surrender of Plymouth failed completely after only limited discussion, largely due to Hopton's insistence on the restoration of Plymouth's fortifications to royal control.[73] The following day the Cornishmen attempted a direct assault on the town and, being severely repulsed, withdrew their forces into siege positions.[74]

While Hopton was tightening his grip around Plymouth and securing his hold in south Devon, Northcote, Rolle, Bampfield and other leading parliamentarians were raising the county militia in north Devon to march to the aid of their beleaguered colleagues.[75] Reports vary as to the exact number of men collected by the deputy lieutenants and the Devon committee, but it seems certain that several thousand men answered the call to help rescue Plymouth.[76] In order to prevent a parliamentarian rendezvous at Tavistock, Cornish troops from the Plympton quarters marched to Okehampton and beyond to intercept and disperse them.[77] Just after dawn on the morning of 8 February a force of cavalier horse and dragoons led by Berkeley and Ashburnham surprised some 500 of Northcote's troops billeted in the small town of Chagford on the northern edge of Dartmoor.[78] But without the support of infantry, the royalists were soon put on the defensive, and had a difficult time escaping as they attempted to cut their way through the town. It was in this chance encounter at Chagford that the royalist cause suffered the loss of young Sidney Godolphin, of whom Hopton wrote: '. . . he was as perfect, and as absolute [a] piece of virtue as ever our Nation bred'.[79] Having received a rude shock as a result of this hasty action to disperse the north Devon militiamen, Berkeley led his men to the safety of Okehampton where he saw to the decent burial of Godolphin and the regrouping of his forces.[80]

Meanwhile other militiamen continued uninterrupted toward Plymouth by way of Totnes and Kingsbridge.[81] By Monday, 20 February, a parliamentary force of 8,000 men had gathered at Kingsbridge.[82] At a council of war plans were made for an immediate attack upon the two regiments under Slanning and Jack Trevanion which had taken possession of neighbouring Modbury the preceding week and thus dominated the rich South Hams district.[83] Although quickly reinforced by royalist forces near Plymouth, Slanning's troops numbered fewer than 2,000 men. Digging in as best they could, and taking full advantage of the numerous hedgerows, the cavaliers prepared to meet the approaching threat. Shortly after noon on Tuesday, 21 February, the forces moving south from Barnstaple and Bideford, unaware of the entrenchments around Modbury, stumbled against the waiting royalists.[84] Quickly backed up by the main body of their army, the Devonians gave battle with an 'abundance of resolution' against seasoned opposition. Throughout a long afternoon and evening of desperate fighting, the parliamentarians drove the enemy back into the town. Under the mantle of darkness, however, Slanning was able to bring away the majority of his men to Plympton.[85] Considering the great odds against them, the cavaliers could count themselves lucky for having lost only 100 men in the fighting and the same number taken prisoner, in addition to five pieces of ordnance and 1,000 muskets.[86] The Cornish had put up a gallant struggle, and retreated in an orderly fashion to Plympton where they joined the forces under Ashburnham, Berkeley, and Grenville.

While fighting was going on at Modbury, the Plymouth forces under the Earl of Stamford had launched the second phase of the parliamentarian offensive against the two regiments quartered in the northern outskirts of Plymouth, near Stoke.[87] Having received word of the retreat from Modbury and of the necessary evacuation of Plympton, Hopton ordered his forces to raise the siege of Plymouth once again, and to withdraw toward Tavistock.[88] Lord Stamford, with 1,000 men, marched immediately to Modbury to join with the larger body of parliamentarians there, and began preparations for pursuing the cavaliers.[89] But although his forces were spirited men, still excited over their victory at Modbury and the freeing of Plymouth, they were poorly equipped.[90] Fortunately, however, these men were not called upon to fight following the success at Modbury. The widespread desire for peace, together with the need to regroup forces, led to a declaration of truce between the armies of Devon and Cornwall in early March.[91] By 6 March the forces on both sides were being disbanded, and Devonians returned to their normal occupations as the Cornish retreated across the Tamar.[92]

The short truce and twenty days of succeeding 'cessation' which was subsequently arranged, followed the examples of Yorkshire, Cheshire, and Dorset, in attempting a local solution to a national problem, by withdrawing whole geographic areas from the struggle.[93] Having had a taste of the death and destruction caused by civil conflict, many Englishmen were content to swear a plague on both houses and to return to local affairs, at the same time praying that the newly opened Oxford talks between king and parliament would bring about national pacification. Many people in Devon and Cornwall shared this abhorence of an unnatural division which was wrecking the family, financial, and friendly relationships which had held the two counties together for generations. During this period of cessation which was to last until 27 March, nine commissioners from each side met at Mount Edgcumbe house in Cornwall to discuss the conditions for what was originally hoped would be a permanent peace settlement. To witness the sincerity of their intentions, the commissioners swore to a protestation oath which affirmed their desire for peace based on the traditional laws and religion of the realm, and confirmed this measure by taking Holy Communion together. [94]

Agreement on the idea of peace was soon found to be insufficient for a lasting settlement. First the Cornish, and then the Devonians, set forth propositions which were considered essential to any lasting neutrality. Although considerable consensus existed on the desirability of a return to pre-war conditions, neither side completely trusted the other, nor was willing to sacrifice any advantage in terms of fortifications or forces. As early in the discussions as 6 March the commissioners decided that invitations should be sent to Dorset and Somerset to join with them in an attempt to bring peace to the entire south-west of England, mainly by united defence against outside invasion. The date for this general meeting was set for Tuesday, 14 March, at the New Inn in Exeter, but by that time the Cornish and Devon commissioners had reached an impassed as a result of new Cornish proposals.[95] Although permitting negotiations to continue, the leading county factions on each side were far from satisfied with the discussions, and authorities at Oxford and Westminster were anxious to squelch this kind of local initiative wherever it appeared. Zealous elements in each party looked upon this period of cessation as an opportunity not to achieve peace, but to further their own preparations for war, while condemning the enemy for doing the same.[96] The need to play for time probably explains the surprising strength of these new Cornish proposals, and especially Hopton's demand for passage through Devon to join the king.

The royalist high command now recognised that the Cornishmen were unable to take Plymouth, much less the counties of Exeter and Devon, without additional aid. Certainly, it would take the Cornish army a long time to join the king for the intended campaign in southern and eastern England, and until that time London remained safe. Final royalist victory, if it was to come at all, could not be realised without Hopton's army. At the same time, parliament could not afford to lose the large contributions from Devon and Exeter, or permit further divisive activities on the part of the local gentry which might provide a bad example for other areas. The parliamentary cause was under severe strain as it was, and notions of peace without control of the monarch could not be permitted.[97]

The Exeter authorities were most emphatically opposed to any association of neutrality with their neighbours. Although the Exeter committee had to deal with a strong royalist minority, it could still assure the House of Commons of its ability to follow what orders were necessary for the safeguard of the parliamentary cause.[98] The appointment of this loyal stronghold as the place of rendezvous for the western commissioners to discuss a neutralist association thus played into the parliament's hands. On 11 March the Commons decided to send two influential West Country MPs, Anthony Nicoll and Edmund Prideaux, to Exeter in order 'to signify their [ie, parliament's] dislike of the whole business to the several counties, and by all means to break in pieces the agreement, from which they feared such mischiefs would rebound unto them'.[99] By the following Monday (13 March) the two MPs had reached the county town and taken steps to ensure that the meeting scheduled for that Tuesday would never take place within Exeter's walls.[100] The Commons had instructed Nicoll and Prideaux to make it perfectly clear with what profound suspicion and distrust the parliament viewed the recent neutralist negotiations, and to explain to the local committee:

> how derogatory it is to the power and authority of Parliament, that such proceedings should be without their consent and concurrence; and how dangerous to the Kingdom, that two or more counties should by such means be divided from the rest. And you shall declare, that the Parliament is not bound by any such Treaty; . . .[101]

The MPs effectively carried out their orders and destroyed any hope for success which these discussions might have produced.[102] The Devon committee, spurred on by the two MPs, sent up a complete report of the transactions between Devon and Cornwall, but it was not until 17 April that Chudleigh and other members were ready to acknowledge the failure of their peace efforts.[103]

Nicoll and Prideaux had also been ordered to take advantage of the cessation to prepare Devon against possible attack from Cornwall, and at the same time prevent a break-through by the Cornishmen into southern England.[104] By 24 March the MPs could report to the Speaker that although the commissioners were still fruitlessly discussing peace, and had even extended their cessation for a further ten days, preparations were well underway toward the raising of three parliamentary regiments in order to resume the conflict when the truce ended at midnight on 22 April.[105]

In the absence of the gout-stricken Earl of Stamford, Major-General James Chudleigh gathered some 1,500 foot and 200 horse in the area of Okehampton during the last few days of the cessation, and by Friday, 21 April, he was only ten miles from the Cornish headquarters at Launceston. Chudleigh advanced to Lifton on Saturday, and although not reinforced as expected, decided to continue his march toward the poorly defended royalist quarters.[106] Crossing the Tamar at Polston Bridge early on 23 April, just hours after the truce had terminated, Chudleigh's troops met scattered opposition from some of Thomas Basset's men, but moved on quickly toward their main objective, Launceston. Although a Cornish rendezvous was scheduled for that day (Sunday), Bevil Grenville's regiment constituted the bulk of the Cornish forces actually present. Putting up fierce opposition, the outnumbered Cornish slowly retreated, hedge by hedge, from their outer defences on Windmill Hill.[107] After the original shock had been sustained, the Cornish held fast, and were soon reinforced by Godolphin's and Lord Mohun's regiments, as well as by forces under Sir John Berkeley. By seven in the evening Slanning and Trevanion's regiments also came up and made it possible for Hopton's combined troops to launch a counter-offensive which forced the Devonians back across the river.[108] With a less experienced commander, and without much needed reinforcements, the Devon invasion could have become a disastrous rout, and west Devon left completely unprotected. As it was, Chudleigh's small army lost a number of men through desertion before he was able to quarter the main body around Okehampton.[109]

Taking most of Monday to rest and regroup his men, Sir Ralph Hopton made another attempt to move east on 25 April, this time hoping to join forces with the king's army for the spring campaign.[110] That Tuesday some 4,000 foot and 500 horse advanced into Devon, through Lifton, and on to Bridestowe. News of the growing weakness of the parliamentarian army at Okehampton, just five miles away, encouraged the Cornish leaders to attempt in their turn a surprise attack on the enemy's quarters:

> The Army being drawn forth upon the western part of Sourton Down before the night was shut in, was there put on order for a night march, and indeed it appeared upon view the handsomest body of men that had been gotten together in those parts all that war.[111]

But unfortunately for Hopton's fine-looking troops, many of them volunteers and raw recruits, Chudleigh was not going to see his men destroyed without a struggle. Unaware of the Cornish approach until they were less than four miles from his quarters, the major-general quickly consulted with his officers and decided that the safest defence was a swift offensive move, in this case an ambush.[112] Captains Gould, Drake, and Pym, along with Chudleigh and three troop of horse, numbering about 108 men, were thus divided into six groups of eighteen men and scattered around Sourton Down to await the advance of the enemy.[113] The discharge of a trooper's rifle inadvertently warned the Cornish, but by that time their vanguard had moved well on to the down. Led by Drake's group, and making as much noise as possible in order to disguise their numbers, the Devonians attacked from six different directions. As a result: 'The enemy's horse, dragoons, and the van

F

of their foot, were routed at the very first assault: and by the help of them, routed the rest of their army, charging them through to their very ordnance; . . .'.[114] Playing hovoc with the inexperienced and frightened recruits, the parliamentarians were able to disrupt the entire vanguard of Hopton's army, causing many to throw away their weapons and to flee from the field. Reinforcements secured the royalist ordnance and ammunition from serious threat, but could not halt the widespread panic that permeated the entire army.[115] Meanwhile Chudleigh's inability to rally his exhausted horse, or to deploy his infantry effectively against the growing opposition of the enemy, forced him to withdraw his men into Okehampton.[116] A violent thunderstorm soon persuaded the royalists to retreat from the down and to retrace their steps to the security of Bridestowe, which they had left only hours before. The following morning Sourton Down was deserted (save for sixty royalist dead) and Chudleigh had by then collected almost 1,000 muskets and pikes, five barrels of powder, and other equipment left behind by the fleeing cavaliers.[117]

Such a severe blow dealt by inferior forces was a major coup for the parliamentary cause. The London pamphleteers could not find sufficient words to praise the Devonian valour and resolution, and pointed significantly to the storm as a providential gesture which had made the victory complete. Although the royalists struck back with their own satirical writings, their cause had been dealt a severe psychological setback, while the Cornish advance to the east was considerably delayed.[118]

Having retreated to Launceston, Hopton quickly reformed his army and determined to make another attempt to rendezvous with the king. This time the Cornish army headed southeast towards Tavistock, where they remained for several days before moving on toward Okehampton. Only a few miles outside of Tavistock, however, the royalists received news of the gathering of a formidable parliamentary army at Okehampton, and immediately decided to retrace their route.[119] Back in Cornwall, the royalist forces were dispersed all along the border and sat facing the gathering force of Devon volunteers and trained bands.[120] On this occasion Hopton's information about a strong enemy force was accurate as the Earl of Stamford had personally taken the field on 11 May, leaving the comfort of Exeter to join with the newly raised militia forces at Okehampton.[121] By Saturday, 13 May,[122] the main body of Stamford's forces, numbering some 5.400 infantry and 200 horse, had reached Holsworthy, and steadily advanced toward Stratton in northeastern Cornwall where they established their headquarters. The majority of their horse, however, had been sent towards Bodmin in order to disperse the sheriff's posse being assembled there, and if possible to block a royalist retreat to the west.[123]

Taking advantage of this division of the parliamentary forces, the Cornish troops regrouped and marched toward Stratton, arriving in the vicinity on the evening of 15 May. Numbering about 2,400 foot and 500 horse and dragoons, the Cornish army, supported by eight cannon, moved to the attack early the next morning, and successfully defeated and dispersed a force twice their size.[124] Altogether some 1,700 prisoners were taken, including Major-General James Chudleigh, while almost 300 Devonians were killed.[125] The courage and resolution of the Cornishmen exhibited in this encounter more than made up for their inglorious defeat at Sourton Down. Stamford's army was completely broken, and the commander fled to Barnstaple, and then to Exeter. Cornwall was thus freed from further threat of invasion for some time, while the way was now open for the Cornish to advance with greater likelihood of success through Devon and into Somerset. Two days later, having again moved back to Launceston, the Cornish leaders received information of the advance into the west of a royal army led by the Marquis of Hertford and Prince Maurice, the king's nephew. The Cornish task was now to join with Hertford's army and to establish royalist control over the entire West Country, against the threat of the imminent arrival of Sir William Waller with additional forces from London.[126]

Leaving behind a small force at Saltash and Millbrook to guard the border, the Cornishmen moved into Devon once again and struck immediately eastward. Largely unopposed, the royalists travelled by quick stages from Okehampton to Crediton and on to Exeter, spending several days in each place to rest, recruit, and replenish supplies. Sir John Acland's house at Columbjohn was strongly garrisoned against the threat of the Exeter parliamentarians just three miles away, and orders were issued to the local gentry to rally more forces from the area.[127] Moving on to Honiton by way of Tiverton, Bradninch, and Cullompton, the royalists proceeded without interruption from parliamentarian forces which fell back before the invaders. Except for a brief skirmish at Honiton, and a day's rest at Axminster, the Cornish were able to advance swiftly to Chard where they joined with Hertford's army on 4 June.[128] Together the joint force numbered about 7,000 men, Hopton having brought 3,000 foot, 500 horse and 300 dragoons, while Hertford had 1,000 new foot and 1,600 or more horse.[129]

Despite an uninterrupted passage through Devon, Sir Ralph knew full well that that county was far from being safe for the king. All major towns and ports were still in parliamentary hands, with Stamford securely settled in the county town itself and in control of much of the county's wealth and resources. Only overwhelming force could dislodge the parliament's grip in Devon and Exeter, and just then it appeared that Waller would see to it that no such thing occurred. However, many of the pro-royalist gentry had shown their willingness to commit themselves to the royalist cause and, together with the combined armies then in the West, the king could look forward to quick success.

Notes to this chapter are on page 200

6

Royalist Conquest of Devon and Exeter

june-december 1643

For months before his meeting with the army under the Marquis of Hertford, Sir Ralph Hopton had repeatedly attempted to conquer Exeter and Devon, establish royalist domination in the West Country, and march his army to join the king. Consistent failure had resulted, due more to lack of numbers than to lack of energy. With Hertford's additional forces, and the decisive victory over the enemy at Stratton, the earlier goals were now within reach, and the cavalier cause in the west could look forward to some real measure of achievement.

Rapidly collecting reinforcements from the Devon and Somerset gentry, the combined royalist army under the command of the Marquis of Hertford and Prince Maurice advanced quickly eastward. Taking advantage of the parliamentary retreat they controlled Taunton and Bridgwater by 7 June.[1] By the time Sir William Waller had reached Bath, with troops intent upon halting the royalist forces, Hertford had already arrived at Wells.[2] To protect their rear while confronting Waller's army, a royalist council of war decided to send Sir John Berkeley back into Devon with a regiment of horse to ensure the blockade of Exeter and to recruit more troops for the security of the county.[3]

While this was being effected, the main body of the cavalier army advanced to Bath, and thence the short distance to Lansdown Hill, where on 5 July they soundly defeated the parliamentary forces.[4] With no further serious opposition, the victorious Cornish moved on to Bristol, laying siege to, and finally storming, this western metropolis on 26 July. This bloody victory, however, cost the lives of Sir Nicholas Slanning and John Trevanion who,

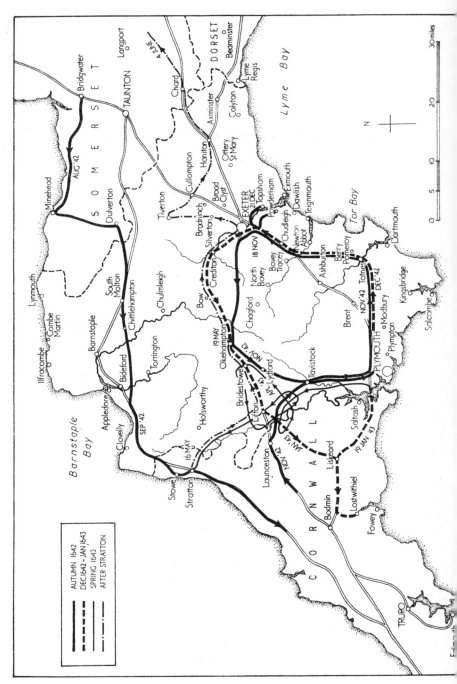

March of the Cornish Army through Devon, 1642-3

together with Sidney Godolphin and Sir Bevil Grenville, had been instrumental in raising the Cornish army and holding it together. Deprived of this leadership, and with Hopton wounded, the Cornishmen lost interest in further activity away from home, and sought to return to ensure the security of their own county against the threat of Exeter and Plymouth. Devon was by no means safely under the control of Berkeley's relatively few regular and volunteer forces, although his numbers had significantly increased since his return to the county.[5] While Colonel John Digby manoeuvred to prevent reinforcements from reaching the several beleaguered communities, all major urban centres in Devon still remained in the hands of the enemy.

Shortly after the fall of Bristol, Charles travelled west in order to settle the command of that city and to confer with his commanders as to future royalist strategy. As a result of their discussions the fateful decision was taken to divide the recently united cavalier forces and, rather than proceed directly toward London, to send the main body off to besiege Gloucester, while Maurice led the western army back into Dorset and Devon. Failing to capture the small fishing town of Lyme Regis, Maurice decided to march directly to the siege of Exeter, hoping by the capture of this important stronghold to reduce the determined opposition of the county.[6] The appearance of a royal army within the county was expected to stimulate recruitment and to bolster significantly the royalist cause, reinstating the authority which had been overawed by the parliamentary agents and militia.

Exeter had been in a state of siege since the Cornish victory at Stratton, but steps had been taken to fortify and repair the defences of the city from December 1642 onwards. From late March (1643) a great deal of work had been necessary on the castle, city walls and gates, trenches, towers, and outer fortifications.[7] On 23 May an additional company of 100 foot was raised under the command of Captain Thomas Ford, and by 19 June it was necessary for the Chamber to authorise the raising of £2,000 for the further payment of military expenses.[8] Stamford's forces in Exeter were not permitted to remain idle during the summer months. Throughout the weeks of July and August isolated skirmishes took place between members of the garrison and the besiegers.[9] The siege accounts of the Exeter Chamber record payments during this period to wounded soldiers and to widows for burials and pensions, as well as large sums distributed as rewards for 'extradordinary service'.[10] An especially severe encounter took place in the outlying parish of St Thomas on 31 July in which more than 1,100 parliamentary troops were engaged. As a result of this 'hot fight' the parliamentarians claimed to have taken almost eighty royalist prisoners.[11] But in order to maintain their defence, the corporation had been forced to expend a total of £18,479.12.0 (£18,479.60) borrowed on the bond of the city and the DLs.[12]

The cavaliers, reportedly numbering almost 3,000 horse and foot by early August, had cut off all access to Exeter from the north and west, but had left the city free to the south and east.[13] Exeter was kept in constant alarm by the attempts of Berkeley's men to cross the river Exe on their numerous raids and foraging expeditions. Stamford's cautious nature, however, would not permit his parliamentarians to take chances 'for fear of being put to retreat and disorder', and thus losing the men needed to defend the city.[14] The parliamentary strategy was to hold tight until relief came from the Earl of Warwick, from Plymouth and Dartmouth, or from the strongholds in north Devon. In any case, they hoped that reinforcements would arrive before additional enemy troops appeared following the capture of Bristol.[15]

During the third week of July the citizens could look with reasonable optimism toward early relief from Admiral Warwick, then anchored at Topsham with six vessels and 1,000 men.[16] On 18 July Warwick had succeeded in gaining control of both sides of the Exe estuary, and had sent ships and men to establish themselves further up river.[17] Three days later the parliamentarians pushed on beyond Powderham and attempted to take the port of Topsham. In anticipation of their attack Berkeley had had five vessels sunk in the river to block the enemy's passage, and at the same time constructed defences to ward off a landing party.[18] After a fierce engagement, the parliamentarians withdrew, leaving three of their ships victims of the tide.[19]

In addition to this unsuccessful attempt, forces from Plymouth under Sir Alexander Carew had been recently halted by Berkeley in their advance to the relief of Exeter. Having been notified of their plan to join with another enemy force raised in the northern part of the county, Sir John sent Colonel John Digby north in late July with a force of horse and dragoons to attempt to halt any such enterprise.[20] Digby stationed himself at Torrington where he was soon joined by newly raised troops from Cornwall, which brought his combined strength up to 300 horse and from 600 to 700 foot.[21] Greatly alarmed at this sudden and immediate threat, the people of Barnstaple and Bideford were spurred into action.[22] Barnstaple mustered some 400 horse and foot under Colonel Bennet which marched by night to Bideford where they joined with enough addtional men to double that number.[23] Aware of their advance, Digby kept his men on the alert until noon of 19 August. Not receiving any further intelligence of enemy activity, the royalist commander withdrew his foot into Torrington and dispersed his horse to their quarters. Within an hour of having accomplished this word arrived of the rapid approach of the Devonian forces. Arranging his men as best he could, Digby took advantage of the element of surprise to attack the parliamentary 'forlorn' with the 150 horse he had available. The aggressive nature of the royalist charge quickly spread fear and panic amongst the citizen army of north Devon, resulting in the rout of their entire force.[24]

Following up his victory, Digby marched his men to Bideford and laid siege to the town, sitting as it did astride the river Torridge. But despite substantial aid in money and supplies from neighbouring Barnstaple, neither Bideford nor Barnstaple were able to hold out against the royalist siege much longer than the strategically placed port town of Appledore.[25] From his headquarters in Polsloe, just outside Exeter, Prince Maurice sent a gracious message to the mayor and corporation of Barnstaple on 27 August offering free pardon and liberal conditions of surrender if the town would return immediately to its true allegiance.[26] In less than a week Maurice received an affirmative reply from the Barnstaple authorities, indicating their willingness to disband their forces and to submit to the prince's authority, which was duly performed on Saturday, 2 September. During that week Bideford and Appledore had also surrendered—circumstances which probably contributed to the decision of those at Barnstaple to end their fruitless opposition. Colonel Digby immediately took possession of the town where he remained for eleven days, supervising the destruction of the borough's fortifications before moving on toward Plymouth.[27]

The sudden surrender of the three north Devon towns, without long siege or bloody fighting, had a demoralising effect upon the

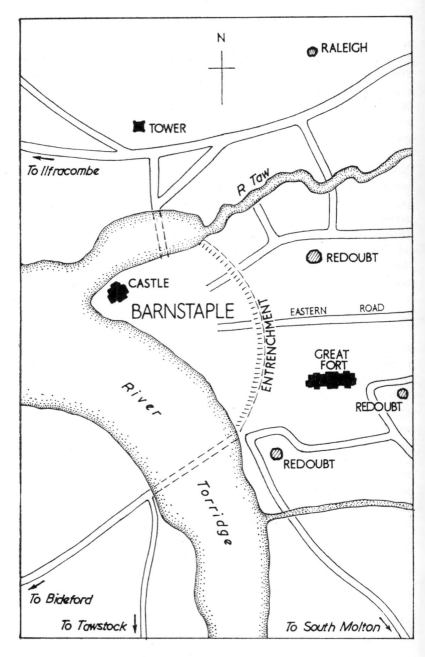

The Defences at Barnstaple

rest of Devonshire, and certainly upon long-suffering Exeter. The county town was now ever more closely besieged with the recent arrival of Maurice, and quite despondent as one hope for relief after another was destroyed by royalist forces.[28] In addition, the recent defection to the royalist cause of the Earl of Bedford, parliamentary lord lieutenant for Exeter and Devon, probably persuaded Stamford and the Exeter commissioners to decide in favour of a quick surrender, especially in the face of the large royalist minority within the city.[29] Within several days of the surrender of Barnstaple, the commissioners agreed to negotiate with the enemy, and on 7 September the garrison marched out with full honours of war.[30] Prince Maurice had been most generous in the terms granted to this obstinate enemy stronghold but, notwithstanding solemn agreement to the contrary, immediate changes were made in the municipal government to suit the new rulers.[31] Rapid steps were also necessary to prevent the spread of plague which threatened the city as a result of the insanitary conditions that followed from months of siege. At the same time, general repairs to bridges and walls were needed, while means had to be found to support the new royalist garrison under Sir John Berkeley, Governor of Exeter.[32]

Leaving Exeter to return as well as it could to normal life, Prince Maurice led his forces into the South Hams to besiege Dartmouth, while Digby proceeded with a sizeable force to the Plymouth area.[33] Mistakenly thinking that the port of Dartmouth would be an easy prize for his victorious army, Maurice fell into the fatal error of squandering a full month besieging that town, during which time he could have cracked the real nut of resistance in the West Country, ie, Plymouth. Plymouth was still recovering from the shocking discovery of Sir Alexander Carew's attempted betrayal of St Nicholas Island,[34] and at the same time desperately trying to repair defences and make preparation to stand against the victors of Bristol, Barnstaple, and Exeter. Had it been caught at this moment of despondency in early September, when Digby was pressing hard upon it, the city might well have been captured and the royalists' Achilles heel in the west would have been eliminated.[35]

Instead, by 19 September Maurice was at Totnes with more than 1,000 men and only seven miles from his Dartmouth objective.[36] Having reached his goal, the prince found the citizens stubbornly

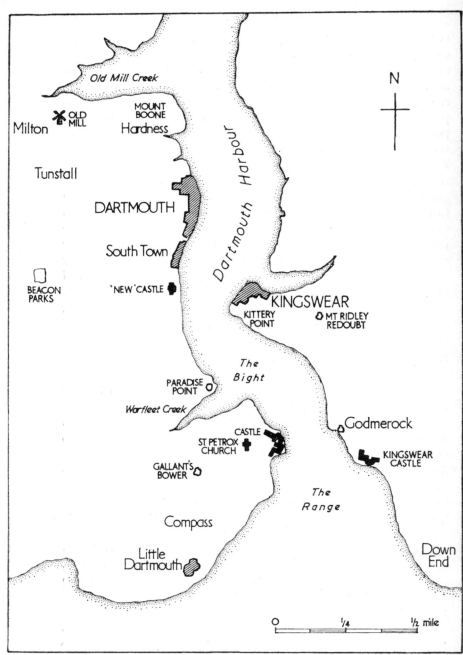

N

Old Mill Creek

Milton ✶ OLD MILL

MOUNT BOONE

Hardness

Tunstall

Dartmouth Harbour

DARTMOUTH

South Town

☐
BEACON PARKS

'NEW' CASTLE

KINGSWEAR

KITTERY POINT

⚐ MT RIDLEY REDOUBT

The Bight

PARADISE POINT ⚐

Warfleet Creek

Godmerock ⚐

CASTLE

ST PETROX CHURCH ✝

KINGSWEAR CASTLE

GALLANT'S BOWER ⚐

The Range

Compass

Down End

Little Dartmouth

O   ¼   ½ mile

Fortifications in the Dartmouth area

determined to resist royalist control as long as possible, having already refused to capitulate to Colonel Edward Seymour and Sir Edmund Fortescue the previous week.[37] As a result of this opposition, the cavaliers decided to settle down and wait for the surrender of this obstinate stronghold for as long as it might take.[38] Unfortunately for the cavalier forces, the weeks spent in the siege of Dartmouth were extremely wet and damp, and gave rise to considerable illness among the troops forced to camp out-of-doors.[39] Added to the discomfort of the elements was the generally dull and idle nature of the siege. Little could be attempted under the circumstances and it was only at the end of the month that a clash occurred at one of the outposts. Not until 4 October was Maurice able to put any definite plan into effect. Then, by dominating both sides of Warfleet Valley with his superior artillery, he was able easily to overawe the castle from Gallant's Bower and to take Paradise Tower, as well as the hastily constructed Starthay fort.[40] By separating the town from its major fortifications, the cavaliers finally managed to force Dartmouth into surrendering on 5 October. As with other Devon towns recently taken, Dartmouth received generous terms, and was allowed to retain its former charters and privileges, while being granted the right to sue for a free pardon. At the same time, those soldiers unwilling to serve in the cavalier army were permitted to pass freely to the nearest parliamentary stronghold.[41]

Notwithstanding their success in taking Dartmouth, and the subsequent benefits which it brought, the royalist victory in the South Hams had been purchased at a very dear price.[42] Plymouth was not as weak as it had been and it no longer trembled unprepared before the advancing royalist victors.[43] The townspeople had had several weeks in which to reaffirm their determination to resist, at the same time working consistently to repair their fortifications, strengthen town walls, and bring in recruits.[44] Especially important in bolstering morale were the 500 men sent by parliament under the command of Colonel James Wardlaw, who arrived in Plymouth on 30 September and made it immediately clear that no thought would be given to surrender.[45] Wardlaw replaced the mayor of Plymouth as military governor and subsequently led the determined opposition to the combined royalist forces under Maurice, Digby, and Sir William Courtenay.[46]

Colonel Digby's forces had done an effective job of blockading

Plymouth since the middle of August.[47] No attempt was made by the besieged forces to strike back until Wardlaw's arrival. On 8 October, just as news arrived of the fall of Dartmouth, the parliamentarians sent 300 men over the Cattewater to Mount Stamford at night. The following morning, taking the royalist force at Hooe completely by surprise, they dispersed the guard stationed there and captured fifty-four men and three barrels of powder. Having been so successful on this first venture, and realising that larger royalist forces would soon arrive, the men of Plymouth sent out a body of horse with 200 musketeers on 15 October to surprise the two troops of cavalier horse stationed at Knackershole (Knackersknowle), some two miles from their defences. Initially successful in their raid, the parliamentarians unfortunately over-extended themselves in their pursuit of the enemy, and had sixteen of their horse captured by royalist reinforcements.[48]

In less than a week such parliamentary sallies became extremely hazardous as Maurice arrived in the Plymouth area to take command of the blockade. He brought with him a force consisting of nine regiments of foot and five of horse which were quickly dispersed in a tight semi-circle from Plymstock to Plympton St Mary to Egg Buckland to Tamerton, and as far as Saltash and Mount Edgcumbe. Wasting little time, the royalists took the offensive immediately. Putting the garrison off their guard by hostile movements in the Cattedown, they quickly shifted the scene of operations to within a short distance of Mount Stamford, which they finally managed to capture after a two-week struggle.[49] This loss of Mount Stamford and the subsequent bombardment from royalist batteries set up on the south Cattewater caused greater harm to the morale of the town than actual damage to buildings or shipping.[50] Internal dissension was once again a serious problem for the Plymouth authorities, and their recent losses gave added confidence to those inhabitants who wished to negotiate a settlement.[51] During the early part of November, Wardlaw asserted his absolute control over the town, its fortifications, and magazine, in order to end the long-standing dispute over jurisdiction between the military and civilian authorities.[52] At the same time, steps were taken to secure the persons of a number of suspected royalist sympathisers, amongst whom were four DLs.[53] The new military authorities made it clear that they would burn the town before allowing it to pass under royalist control.

To assure themselves of general support, the parliamentary
council of war issued an order on 4 November demanding that all
military and civilian personnel within the garrison and town sub-
scribe to an oath to 'faithfully maintain and defend' the beleaguered town against enemy action.[54] On 9 November the mayor and
Colonel Wardlaw were the first to swear to this Vow and Protestation, which was soon taken by everyone within the walls.[55] With
parliamentary authority thus firmly established, and the fortifications in safe hands, the council directed its attention once again
to the external threat which still faced them. Efforts were made to
strengthen the outposts, and to bring in additional wood and hay
from the surrounding countryside.[56]

For most of November, however, there was little skirmishing
between the opposing forces. On Thursday, 16 November, the
royalists renewed their assault on the northern line of defences,
presumably to soften up the garrison for the summons which was
sent to the mayor and governor that Saturday.[57] Signed by eleven
of the leading county royalists, this offered a full pardon for past
offences, and guaranteed future security for the people within the
town.[58] No response forthcoming, the cavaliers resumed the attack
on 28 November with a bombardment on Lipson Work. This
assault continued for three days without doing much damage because of the steep valley which separated the royalists from their
target.[59] During the last week in November a plot was revealed
which was aimed at destroying Maudlyn Work, one of Plymouth's
most important outer defences. Ellis Carteret was arrested, and
Henry Pike and Moses Collins nearly apprehended, for an attempt
to bribe the chief gunner at Maudlyn into blowing up the magazine. Escaping to the royalist camp, Pike and Collins reportedly
volunteered to lead 400 enemy musketeers through the Plymouth
defences.[60] Surprising the guard at Laira Point shortly before day-
break on 3 December, the royalists were easily able to assault Lipson from behind, but were unable to take it. The alarm being
given, some 450 parliamentarian horse and musketeers rushed
from the town to drive off the enemy, only to come up against a
much larger royalist reinforcement which had been held ready at
Compton. The defenders were forced to give up considerable
ground until sufficient reinforcements could come to their aid.
Making a stand on the hill above Lipson Work, the parliamentarians put up a determined resistance for four hours before launch-

ing a successful counter-attack with the help of 200 additional men from the trained bands of the town. The royalists were forced to retreat, only to be caught by the incoming tide and the fire from a parliamentary ship near Laira Point.[61] Losses on both sides were particularly heavy as a result of the action on this Sunday morning, and the fierce encounter proved the turning point of the Plymouth siege. If Lipson had been taken the entire system of defence would have been difficult to maintain, and the town would have been placed in great jeopardy.[62]

Not successful at Lipson or Laira Point, the cavaliers turned their attention once again to Maudlyn Work, near which the defenders had set up a platform with a demi-canon to counterbalance the enemy battery. On 18 December the royalists began a bombardment of Maudlyn which went on for two days. At the same time, they constructed an entrenchment between Maudlyn and Pennycomequick in order to cut off possible relief from that quarter. Wasting no time in reacting to such a threat, the parliamentarians attacked this outpost the following day and, although twice repulsed, finally succeeded in destroying it.[63] With this final rebuff, the cavalier council of war decided that Plymouth could not now be taken. The victorious royalists had been stopped as repeated failure met their every attempt to conquer this single remaining parliamentarian stronghold in Devon. On 22 December the royalist withdrawal from the Plymouth area began, and on Christmas morning the strict siege was lifted, although a blockade was still maintained. Maurice moved the greater portion of his army into winter quarters at Tavistock and Plympton, but at the same time issued his warrant to the surrounding hundreds forbidding any one to aid the blockaded town with food or provisions, and making it clear that Plymouth had not yet escaped royal justice.[64]

Maurice's inability to take Plymouth was to have serious consequences for the future. As a result of this failure, the royalists would continue to find it necessary to squander men and material to keep the city isolated. Needless to say, the army under Digby, and later under Sir Richard Grenville, could have been put to better advantage elsewhere in England. Parliamentarian control of this important seaport permitted unimpeded sway over traffic in the channel, and guaranteed that Plymouth would remain a bastion of defiance against complete enemy domination of the

West Country. By depriving the king of their town, the men of Plymouth also hampered the outfitting of a new royal navy.

On the other hand, control over the rest of the county did permit the royalists to establish a headquarters at Exeter from which they could dominate both Devon and Cornwall, as well as overawe neighbouring Dorset and Somerset. The rich resources of the county could help recoup armies and treasure depleted during the past year and a half, and provide an essential base for future operations into eastern and southern England. At the time the fall of Devonshire, with its important ports on both coasts, revived the long-standing parliamentary fears of possible invasions from Ireland, Spain, and France, as well as the resurgence of royalist sea power.[65] In the event, the royalist cause never did receive substantial foreign aid. On the contrary, the rumours of possible assistance did them great damage. However this may be, by the end of 1643 the king was triumphant in the West and looked forward to receiving increased forces and supplies from this area with which to carry on the struggle in the rest of England.

Notes to this chapter are on page 206

7

Royalist War-Time Administration
of Devon and Exeter
1643-6

Royalist control brought with it very little change in Devon or
Exeter life. True, the military garrisons now consisted of cavalier
soldiers and commanders instead of roundheads, pro-royalist officials dominated where parliamentarians had once held sway, and
all ports (except Plymouth) were closed to the navy where they
had recently been open. But the people of the two counties, with
the inhabitants of Plymouth as the constant exception, continued
to pay a weekly assessment, or martial rates, just as they had done
before; Quarter Sessions met regularly to administer justice, and
the JPs continued to supervise local activities. The new dispensation brought with it a royalist committee which controlled the
two counties for the king in place of a similar group which the
enemy had employed,[1] but taken together Devonians knew only
that they had exchanged one set of masters for another, and one
army for another. Peace had not come to the West Country as
many wished, nor were the financial assessments abated as most
would have hoped. The war still continued and the constables
made their regular rounds to collect men, money, and supplies to
reinforce the military might of the new authorities.

Although ultimate authority within the two counties rested
with the commissioners who were appointed by the king and
resided in the Chapter House at Exeter,[2] the JPs, singly and in
Quarter Sessions, were allowed to maintain a large measure of
their former authority. Their jurisdiction, although limited by
the exigencies of war, continued to extend over such routine
matters as petty criminal offences, illegitimacy, road and bridge
repair,[3] runaway apprentices, and broken contracts.[4] The amount

of time spent and the quantity of business covered in Quarter Sessions was greatly reduced over that of previous years, however, and in 1645 little business was conducted at all.[5] And, as might be expected, an increasingly large part of the court's agenda involved military matters, while civil cases received less attention as the war progressed.

Notwithstanding the powers of military commanders and royal commissioners, the Quarter Sessions therefore continued to act as the central agency for county control, especially with regard to minor officials.[6] It was through the hundred and petty constables that all civil and military orders were to be carried out. Consequently, as civil war dragged on, the Quarter Sessions court was increasingly hard-put to insure the honesty and efficiency of these minor officials, and numerous orders and reminders were necessary to keep them at their task. This was particularly the case with regard to the collecting of money and supplies, and the impressment of men for the royal armies, for which warrants were sent out by the court, the county committee, or the appropriate military commander. At the same time, the constables were responsible not only for calling out men for the posse comitatus, but also for collecting assessments for hospitals, gaols, and wounded soldiers.[7] In some cases the constable was required to appear before the neighbouring JP to explain his tardiness in following instructions, but more often was instructed to make good the remission under threat of answering before the next Quarter Sessions for his 'neglect and contempt'.[8] The court was obviously more concerned that its county treasurers should obtain the assessed rates to pay for pensions, medical treatment, hospitals, and gaol up-keep, than it was in punishing recalcitrant individuals.[9] But as the petitions to the court show, the constables grew ever more reluctant to increase the burden of taxes on their friends and neighbours, and were continuously complaining that the sums which they themselves spent for purposes of troop impressment, messengers, and distribution of warrants were not being repaid.[10]

Repeatedly the business which could not be handled during the shortened Quarter Sessions was delegated to a select number of JPs to settle out of court. The most persistent problem requiring such attention involved quarrels between tithings and parishes concerning their assessment toward the martial rates. Such disputes would often require days of examination in order to determine what portion of the county assessment each village and parish could afford to pay without placing it under an excessive hardship. Although the justices probably did not decide initially what each section of the community should contribute toward these weekly collections, the Quarter Sessions did consider the revision of the rates demanded by the county committee.[11] In such cases the decision reached by the committee of JPs, after hearing testimony from the representative tithings and parishes, would be binding unless good reason could be shown. Individuals who had not paid their martial rates, and constables who had failed to turn in funds collected, were given short shrift by the authorities and told to pay up or face imprisonment.[12]

It is important to notice that a significant amount of overlapping existed between the membership of the Quarter Sessions bench and the county commissioners at the Chapter House. Since it was only the more prominent local magnates that would be regularly selected as JPs and as deputy lieutenants, it was similarly from this group that the king chose the men who were to govern the counties of Devon and Exeter during war-time.[13] Under these circumstances it is reasonable to expect that such men would take a greater interest in the well-being of their counties than would the military commanders and soldiers who had achieved the royalist conquest of the West Country. During the Michaelmas session (1643) a strong statement of policy was issued by Quarter Sessions in an attempt to halt the indiscriminate plundering and confiscation which apparently had accompanied the cavalier advance under Prince Maurice. By taking this position the justices recognised the absolute necessity of obedience to warrants from high military and civil officials during this period of civil strife with regard to the acquisition of supplies, equipment, and billeting. But at the same time, they were most 'unwilling that the County should be subject to the extravagant and illegal commands of inferior officers or the violence of common soldiers'.[14] Those guilty of such behaviour would be prosecuted under the law, while civilians were urged to refuse obedience to such requests. Thus, while no exception was taken to the extraordinary jurisdiction granted to the authorities as a result of the war, neither were the justices willing to forgo their responsibility for the peace, safety, and well-being of the county inhabitants.[15]

The ultimate responsibility for the royalist control of Devon and Exeter, however, rested with the royal commissioners at Exeter, in co-operation with the commanders of the several royal armies and garrisons then in occupation. As no records remain extant of the activities of the Exeter Committee, the functions and membership of that group cannot be accurately or completely described. What is certain is that the commissioners were mainly concerned with the raising of the £3,000 in weekly martial rates for the support of the cavalier forces in the two counties.[16] In addition to this regular assessment, the committee took within its jurisdiction the confiscation and sequestration of enemy property taken on land or sea, the collection of funds and equipment, the raising of troops for the reinforcement of the armies, the direction and supervision of the county trained bands and militia, as well as other aspects of military preparedness and civilian control necessary for the advancement of the royalist cause. Within this context fell the maintenance of the military garrisons at Dartmouth, Barnstaple, and Exeter, as well as the support of the forces surrounding Plymouth. Further, it was by the authority of the commissioners, often with the approval of Prince Maurice, that major policy decisions were taken for the two counties.[17] In an emergency situation, such as that precipitated by Essex's march into the West Country during the summer of 1644, it would be only by action of the committee (in conjunction with the deputy lieutenants) that the forces of the area could be rallied for purposes of defence.

The committee's major concern being the financing of the royalist armies, it was found convenient to divide Devon into three areas to facilitate the collection of money and supplies. Depending upon the needs of the time, sections of each area would be assigned to particular commanders or garrisons for their support, leaving it up to them to collect what was due. The only considerable body of information extant is the records of the Dartmouth garrison under the command of Colonel Edward Seymour.[18] From these records it appears that the garrison obtained support from Stanborough and Coleridge hundreds on a fairly regular basis. Thus, the appropriate parish and hundred constables were held responsible for collecting the sums fixed on the area within their jurisdiction and turning them in weekly to the treasurer, John Thomasius, or his agents. Thomasius, in turn, would pay the officers and men of the garrison, settle accounts with merchants,

and otherwise see to the maintenance of the forces there.[19] Together with the funds collected, lists of those who refused to pay
were returned to the treasurer. Judging from the numerous lists
of those in arrears, many people in south Devon were not paying
what was required of them. As the war continued, many became
increasingly incapable of doing so, while others withheld funds in
protest against continued royalist occupation of the region. For
those who proved backward in support of the royalist cause, recourse was taken to confiscation and distress of goods by troops of
horse sent out for the purpose.

In addition to this routine levy of the martial rates, however,
the inhabitants of Devon and Exeter were susceptible to further
demands for such supplies and men as were needed in an emergency. Numerous receipts amongst the Seymour Papers give evidence of supplies of hay, straw, wheat, oats, and other provisions,
as well as of horses and equipment, which were called in from the
surrounding parishes for use by the Dartmouth garrison from
time to time. The constables were clearly instructed as to the items
desired, and strictly ordered by their warrants to see to the collection and delivery of these goods by a specific date. Each parish
took good care, therefore, to maintain an equally strict account
of what goods and services were provided for the cavalier cause,
in expectation of eventual reimbursement. In those few accounts
which survive, it appears that great stress was placed on the expense widely incurred by the parishioners in providing free food
and billeting for soldiers quartered in their homes. Matters became
so desperate for the parish of Harberton in Coleridge hundred
that they eventually petitioned Maurice for relief from the repeated burden of free billeting.[20] This became increasingly the
case throughout Devon as irregular demands were piled upon the
regular contributions of the martial rate, to cause a severely depressing effect upon local conditions. In some areas, as with Harberton parish, the parishioners found themselves cultivating fields
for the exclusive use of the military. More remote regions, where
troops were less likely to be stationed, would be spared such visitations. Increasingly, individuals came to make their own arrangements directly with the Exeter commissioners, paying £5 or more
in lieu of the horse, arms, or other items demanded. With such a
contribution a person could free himself from disturbance for
some time, or until a further emergency occurred.[21]

The accounts of Mayor Philip Ley in the Totnes Guildhall provide a similar tale of unusual and extraordinary expense as one group of soldiers after another passed through the town, or made demands upon it for free quarter and supplies. If the town treasury could not provide the funds necessary for the immediate needs of the rival forces, the mayor had to take it from his own pocket.[22] Much of the money spent by the Totnes authorities was for the simple preservation of their town from occupation, blackmail money which went to high-ranking royalist officers (particularly Goring and Grenville) to keep their troops beyond the walls.[23]

The only account of extraordinary expenditure incurred by the people of Okehampton is found in the documents reprinted in E. H. Young's 'Okehampton during the Civil War, 1642-46'. These papers show the role played by the hundred and parish constables as the essential agents of local government in war as in peace. Warrents sent to the constables from military and civilian authorities, whether JP or general, would be executed only as quickly as the man concerned felt necessary. He might be threatened, or sometimes arrested, but such an official in a strongly pro-parliamentarian area could do little or nothing to collect arrears or supplies for the royalist cause. The enthusiastic constable got into trouble with the populace; the recalcitrant one felt the wrath of the authorities. Little wonder that the job was unpopular, and that petitions and complaints from these minor, but important functionaries were so numerous.[24]

The tithingmen of the various tithings within the parish found themselves in the same situation, but more so in eastern Devon than elsewhere. Colyton hundred, and especially the parishes near Lyme Regis, were particularly susceptible to demands, not from the royalist authorities, but from the parliamentarian garrison holding that Dorset stronghold. Documents in the Exeter City Record Office show that within the limited area of their control, the parliamentarians assessed and collected regular martial rates, at the same time sending out periodical warrants for men, money, and supplies to reinforce or maintain the garrisons at Lyme Regis and Axmouth.[25] Failure to provide what was demanded was punished by 'plundering' or legal confiscation. In this eastern section of the county, however, the people appear to have been little troubled with the extra burden of the free quartering of troops which seems to have been fairly common elsewhere.

Financial and administrative records do not exist for other sections of Devon and Exeter, but what is known of the establishment of the Royal Mint in the county town has been described by Miss Mary Coate.[26] Under the direction of Sir Richard Vyvyan, the mint accepted plate from wherever it could be obtained and, from September 1643, successfully produced money for the support of Berkeley's garrison until the spring of 1646. As the Seymour Papers show, these sums were not sufficient to meet the royalist needs, but they certainly contributed a good deal toward maintaining the control of Devon and Cornwall which was so important to the royalist success in the West Country. As with the parliamentarians, however, it proved necessary in the last resort to turn to legal confiscation to collect outstanding dues. After almost two years of such widespread royalist 'plundering', the entire county was more than ready to accept the control of the parliamentarian army under Fairfax when it eventually arrived, well-supplied with money and ready to pay for all it should need.

Notes to this chapter are on page 210

8

Consolidation of Royalist Control
january-september 1644

Early in 1644 the royalist commissioners for Devon and Cornwall agreed to an association of the two counties 'for the preservation of the Peace already obtained among us, and for a farther increase and security of it'.[1] Finding it necessary to co-operate in order to maintain royalist control in the West Country, the authorities in both counties were more than willing to combine their resources for the duration of the war. Their particular target, of course, was the reduction of Plymouth and the complete withdrawal of all parliamentarian forces from the area. To this end steps were taken to recruit additional men for Maurice's army, to regularise the assessment and collection of weekly rates, as well as to confiscate delinquent property and accumulate military supplies and provisions. At the same time, overtures were made to neighbouring Dorset and Somerset to invite them to join a union of co-operation to ensure the peace of the entire region.[2]

The articles of association required all inhabitants of the two counties to take an oath of 'Protestation' before 20 February in which they promised to support the royalist cause against the parliamentary and Scottish armies, and to work for the reduction of Plymouth.[3] Copies of the Protestation were sent to all parish constables and then to all ministers who were to administer it to their congregations on the following Sunday. Many of the parliamentarian sympathisers in the two counties, however, had not yet reconciled themselves to their new masters. Refusing this oath, they were swiftly arrested.[4]

Retaliation against the Scottish invasion was not the immediate problem confronting the associated counties. In mid-February enemy sympathisers in Barnstaple took what was thought to be a favourable opportunity to revolt against their royalist conquerors.[5] This disturbance was quickly crushed.[6] The cavaliers had greater difficulty, however, in restoring peace to portions of east Devon which were constantly disrupted by parliamentary forces from Lyme Regis who were successful in garrisoning Axmouth and the neighbouring Stedcombe House.[7]

The last week on March 1644 proved to be a significant one for the royalist cause, and especially for the people in the West Country. On 29 March Lord Hopton's army, which by now had reached Hampshire, was decisively defeated at Cheriton, near Alresford, and the enemy's path into the West was opened.[8] At the same time, Maurice was bringing up his army before Lyme Regis with the expectation of quickly capturing that trouble-spot. In order to augment his army, garrisons throughout Devon were reduced.[9] But although troops were also withdrawn from before Plymouth,[10] steps were taken to ensure the continued siege of that place under Colonel John Digby and Sir Richard Grenville.[11] Maurice arrived in the Lyme Regis area from Beaminster on 19 April and established his headquarters at Axminster while deploying his men in the surrounding countryside. The next day he proceeded with the bulk of his forces to the outskirts of the beleaguered town and tightened his blockade. Finding only slight opposition from the defenders, the prince at first anticipated an easy conquest of the small fishing village. Instead, the inhabitants of Lyme Regis, with constant access to the sea, exhibited a strong and continuous determination to resist capture as long as possible, and were ultimately successful in withstanding vastly superior forces 'with extraordinary bravery and success'.[12]

Just as her nephew was organising his siege of Lyme Regis, Queen Henrietta Maria was making her way into the West Country for what she hoped to be a quiet delivery of her forthcoming child. The recent build-up of enemy forces around Oxford during the spring campaign had greatly increased the queen's apprehension as to her personal safety, and supported her resolution to leave the university town.[13] Thus, on 17 April, much to her husband's regret, Henrietta began her journey west, parting from her family at Abingdon on the following day.[14] By slow stages the queen reached Exeter on 1 May where she intended to remain until her baby was born.[15] The royal physicians were allowed to leave London early in May to attend to the queen in her generally weakened condition.[16] Between the hours of 10 and 11 o'clock on the morning of Sunday, 16 June, she gave birth to the Princess Henrietta at Bedford House in Exeter.[17] On 21 July the baby was baptized in the cathedral 'with becoming fortitude and in great state'.[18]

Meanwhile, on 6 June Lord General Essex had informed the ruling Committee of Both Kingdoms of his determination to give up his attempt to capture the king at Oxford and to march into the West for the relief of Lyme Regis. The general claimed that this western campaign, to recapture the Devon and Cornish ports for parliament and to relieve Plymouth, was of such great importance that he considered it essential that his entire army should be employed.[19] In Essex's view, the forces with Sir William Waller would be sufficient to keep the king's army under guard. However, with the help of Warwick and the fleet, Lyme Regis had managed successfully to resist royalist control.[20] Although reinforcements were vital to its continued safety, it was not just the plight of this beleaguered village which had caused the Commons to recommend this project to the lord general. Instead, political pressure had been brought to bear by influential 'western gentlemen' in order to get additional forces into the West.[21] Coincidental with this pressure, Essex had been listening to some of his officers, most particularly Lord Robartes of Lanhydrock, who impressed upon him the ease with which he would be able to gain control of the entire West Country, especially as the parliamentary army need not live off the land.[22] This would offer the dual advantage of sealing off one of the most productive royalist supply areas, as well as halting the organisation of further armies, which the new western association threatened.[23] Thus, despite the wishes of the Committee of Both Kingdoms that Waller undertake the reconquest of the West, Essex refused to retrace his steps from Blandford (Dorset) and to take up the unpleasant task of pursuing the king. The lord general was determined that he, and not his rival Waller, would gain the plaudits for the restoration of the West to parliament's authority.[24] The House of Commons was forced to concur reluctantly with a strategy which they could not change.[25] On the last day of June Essex led his victorious army from Chard (Somerset) into Devon, stopping at Axminster to rest his men.[26] Two weeks earlier Maurice had raised his siege of Lyme and withdrawn his forces, numbering more than 4,000 horse and foot, to-

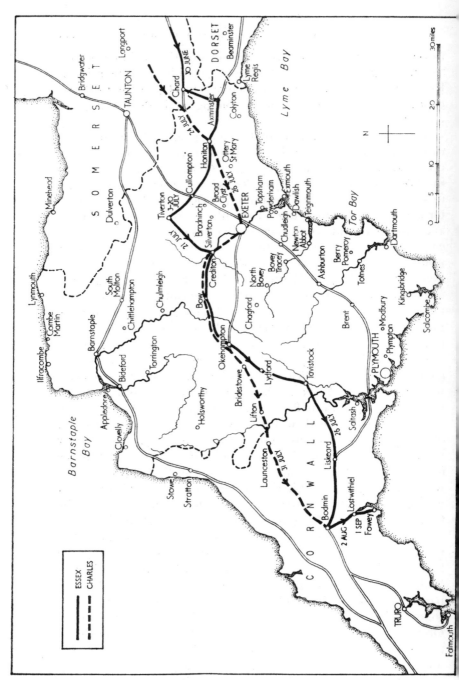

The Campaign of 1644

ward Exeter, where he intended to put up a strong resistance.[27]

The royalist commissioners at Exeter were doing everything they could to prepare for the expected invasion. Instructions were sent out to the colonels of all militia regiments to bring their forces up to full strength and to see to the equipment of their men by the 22nd of the month.[28] Efforts were also made to prepare the association forces (now including Somerset and Dorset) by drawing together all men able to serve within the four counties and placing them under Hopton's command.[29] At the same time, warnings were sent out to the royalist garrisons throughout Devon, and especially to the governor of Dartmouth and to the forces before Plymouth. On 19 June the prince wrote to Colonel Seymour to warm him that Dartmouth might well be a target for parliamentary attack, and to take care that 'watchfulness may timely prevent their wicked purposes'. The following Monday (24 June) Sir John Berkeley exhorted Seymour to reinforce his garrison as quickly as possible, and to take prisoner those known to oppose royalist control.[30]

Typically, however, money was in short supply. On 25 June by order of the Grand Committee of the Associated Counties the martial rates from the eleven hundreds of South Devon were assigned toward the support of the army besieging Plymouth, and very little cash was available for purposes of garrison support.[31] The commissioners sent Seymour £50 on the 25th but told him to expect no more from them. Instead, he was told to:

> put in execution the Commission of subscriptions, that all able men that have not had privy seals may advance considerable sums towards the maintenance of the Army, and that way, if you shall find necessity, you may be also supplied.[32]

In the meantime, with the enemy forces drawing ever closer, Henrietta Maria remained in Exeter in very poor health.[33] By 3 July Essex had advanced into Devon, and was encamped at Tiverton, where he remained until the 20th.[34] In great apprehension of being taken hostage by the parliamentary forces, as well as of the difficulties of a long and arduous siege, the queen decided to leave Exeter on 30 June and to make her way to the coast and thence to France.[35] On 1 July she arrived in Okehampton where she stayed for two nights, and by 3 July had reached Launceston (Cornwall) under the protection of her nephew Maurice.[36] By slow stages she finally came to Falmouth, from which place she set sail on 14 July for her homeland.[37]

In order to get the queen safely into Cornwall, Maurice had withdrawn a large portion of the Barnstaple garrison to act as an escort. As soon as the royalists had departed, the men of Barnstaple, long supporters of the parliamentary cause, made a second attempt to regain control of their town.[38] This time they were more confident of success, as news had reached them of the approach of Essex's army. Apparently informed of the possibility of 'disturbances', Maurice sent Major Paget northward to crush any uprising that might occur. Having been forewarned of this move, the townsmen 'shut the gates against them, and slew several of them', forcing Paget to retreat until reinforcements were sent.[39] Finally realising the magnitude of the problem, the prince ordered Colonel John Digby to march with a detachment of some 500 to 600 men with instructions to reduce Barnstaple to obedience. The royalists attacked the town on 1 July, but following severe and determined resistance, were once again forced to withdraw.[40] Two days later Essex received word of the situation at Barnstaple and quickly despatched Lord Robartes in command of a strong force to garrison the town.[41] Robartes remained in Barnstaple for ten days before turning over command to Colonel Luttrell, confident that it would be secure for the parliamentary cause.[42] Lord Robartes' confidence was justified, as this north Devon centre was to hold out against the royalists until 18 September, surrendering only after Essex had lost his entire army. Luttrell immediately set about raising additional forces with which to support his position, and was provided with much-needed arms and ammunition with the arrival of Captain Bennett on 13 July.[43] Although secure from aggression, Barnstaple continued to suffer from enemy control of the fort at Appledore, which dominated the estuary of the rivers Taw and Torridge. Attempting to remove this hindrance to trade and supply during the last week of July, Luttrell led an unsuccessful expedition against the small cavalier outpost which turned into a prolonged, and eventually ill-fated, siege.[44]

During July Essex continued his triumphal march through Devon, although with a somewhat reduced army due to the reinforcements left at Weymouth, Taunton, and Barnstaple. On 3 July he had arrived at Tiverton where he remained for more than two weeks bringing in recruits from the county and waiting for supplies from London.[45] Although the lord general was finding much local support for the parliamentary cause, he was being severely hampered by the persistent lack of arms with which to supply the new recruits. At the same time, he had difficulty with many Devonians who refused to be led by regular army officers, and demanded to follow locally prominent gentlemen. The recruits were willing to co-operate with the army, but not to become an integral part of it. Essex therefore pressed the Committee of Both Kingdoms to send back to the West as many Devon gentry as were then in London to aid in bringing in the country forces, as well as to re-establish parliamentary control over the machinery of local government. By 10 July the £20,000 being sent by sea for the pay of his army had still not arrived, and the lord general admitted 'that the country has suffered somewhat of late for want of the soldiers' pay'.[46] What was of greater concern was the constant threat from the royalist garrisons throughout the West Country, most of which he had made no attempt to reduce and which subsequently remained as so many danger spots in the rear of the army. Particularly significant was the dampening effect which these garrisons had on the response expected from the local inhabitants.[47]

One such garrison, of course, was at Dartmouth, the scene of frantic activity during the middle of July. The orders of the councils of war held there on the 15th and 24th of the month show attempts to get men and supplies into the strategic points of defence from Mount Boone to Dartmouth and Kingswear Castles as quickly as possible.[48] Two parliamentarian ships had been riding in front of the harbour since early July, making it difficult for trade and supplies to enter or leave the town, while at the same time Colonel Seymour was momentarily expecting to be confronted with Essex's entire army.[49] Seymour was only too well aware that his garrison was small, and that he might expect a revolt amongst the townspeople at any time, the more so as Essex's army drew closer.

One insurrection had already broken out in the Torbay area near Dartmouth. Seymour, in conjunction with Colonel Cary's forces, was ordered by Maurice 'to repress and reform the same' using all means necessary to keep order in the South Hams, especially at a time of such great danger to the entire royalist cause in the West. On 15 July, and again on the 25th, the Exeter commis-

sioners authorised Seymour to take what immediate steps he felt
necessary to strengthen his garrison with men and supplies from
the surrounding countryside.[50]

The royalist commissioners were also concerned with the well-
being of Exeter itself, which was called upon to surrender by Essex
during his stay at Tiverton. But instead of besieging the city, the
lord general sent a letter to the governor, Sir John Berkeley, in
which he attempted to bargain the royalists out of their stronghold. Essex maintained that the cavaliers were grossly misinformed
as to the recent outcome of the battle at Marston Moor. He proposed a bargain by which Berkeley would agree to surrender
Exeter if the parliamentarians had indeed overcome Rupert's
forces in the north, while Essex would agree to deliver up Weymouth and Melcombe Regis if the royalists had been victorious.[51]
The cavaliers were not to be taken in, however. Berkeley responded that even if his news were false, and the royalists had suffered a
severe defeat at Marston Moor, that was no reason for him to
surrender such an important post as Exeter.[52] Essex does not
appear to have made any further attempt on the city.

Although the lord general had thus far received no opposition
from Maurice's forces, he was informed on 18 July of a definite
threat to his position with the rapid march of the king's army into
Somerset.[53] Therefore, immediately upon Robartes' return from
the relief of Barnstaple, a council of war was held in Tiverton to
decide whether to continue the advance further west, or to turn
back and face the challenge of the king's forces. Expecting that
Sir William Waller would be able to handle the king, the council
decided to move immediately toward the relief of Plymouth, then
reported in very dire straits.[54] Lord Robartes' influence seems to
have been paramount in this decision, convincing Essex that their
appearance in Cornwall would result in a great uprising for parliament.[55] Therefore, on 20 July the parliamentary army moved
from Tiverton to Crediton, and subsequently to Bow, Okehampton, Tavistock, and finally to Horsebridge (5 miles west of Tavistock), where they crossed into Cornwall.[56]

Upon the certain knowledge that Essex was marching toward
Plymouth, Sir Richard Grenville quickly raised the siege of that
stronghold and retreated over the Tamar, leaving forces behind to
hold the bridges.[57] Essex having been reinforced with some 3,000
horse and foot out of Plymouth, followed the royalists further into

Cornwall.[58] Instead of keeping open his supply lines with Plymouth, the lord general led his army further west until he found himself caught between the combined forces of Charles and Maurice (by now grouping at Exeter), and the royalist forces of Cornwall under Grenville. Essex's intention was 'to clear that country [ie, Cornwall] and to settle the same in peace'.[59] It does not appear that the general actually gave much thought as to just how he would accomplish this major task. Instead, he walked into the trap of the narrow Cornish peninsula, where he found a hostile countryside, limited supplies, and meagre contributions.[60]

It was only on 31 July that Robartes appears to have given thought to the whereabouts of Waller's reinforcements, and by that time it was too late as the king had decisively defeated them at Cropredy Bridge on 29 June.[61] Charles was then free to move as he wished. Extremely concerned over the queen's safety, he decided to follow Essex into Devon 'in hopes that he should be able to fight a battle with him before Waller should be able to be in a condition to follow him'.[62] Marching swiftly and unopposed, the king's army reached the Devon border by 24 July. The following day the royalists advanced the twelve miles to Honiton, and on 26 July arrived in Exeter.[63] In order to put a halt to the activities of the Lyme Regis garrison, Charles dispatched Sir Richard Cholmondeley to occupy Axminster with 300 men.[64] At the same time, Lord Henry Percy took advantage of the royal presence to take possession of Colyton and to threaten Lyme Regis directly. The parliamentary garrison there was not readily overawed, however, and swiftly attacked Percy in his own quarters, with considerable success.[65]

Upon arrival at Exeter the king took up residence at Bedford House, the Prince of Wales was settled at the Deanery, and the rest of the court quartered on the leading citizens.[66] As an expression of their loyalty, the Exeter Chamber presented a gift of £500 to Charles, £100 to the prince, and lesser sums to various royal officials.[67] Such generosity was well-received by the king, all the more so as it came on the same day that he first beheld his newborn daughter, Princess Henrietta. To show his appreciation for their loyalty, Charles responded by knighting the mayor, Hugh Crocker.[68] Quite conscious of the apparent wealth of the city, the king let it be known that the army at Bristol was in great need of shoes, and that it would not be taken amiss if the Exeter Corpora-

H

tion would do something about it. Thus, the Chamber Act Book records that the bond of the city was given for the payment of £200 for the purchase of 3,000 pair of shoes:

> . . . which said sum of £200 together with three former sums formerly advanced to her Majesty the Queen and Prince make up the full sum of £1000, advanced to his Majesty in testimony of the loyal and dutiful respect of his Majesty's present affairs and his happy access to this City.[69]

This was not all however. A further £60 had to be paid for the royal pardon for having been in rebellion against the Crown.[70] In addition, of course, there was the actual cost of entertaining the royal party.

On 27 July the king travelled the seven miles from Exeter to Crediton in order to review the army gathered there by his nephew.[71] Returning that evening to the Exeter area, Charles spent the night in Peter Sainthill's home at Bradninch, where a council of war was held before launching an expedition of 'Essex-catching'. The king returned to Crediton on Sunday where he spent the night, and on Monday began his advance toward Cornwall through Bow to Okehampton and Lifton, averaging about ten miles each day and reaching the border on the last of the month.[72] Taking care to pull down two of the bridges over the Tamar, the king, Prince Maurice, and their aides consulted once again before crossing into Cornwall with an army of 10,000 foot, 5,000 horse, and 28 cannon. This force was soon joined by the large body of men which Grenville had managed to recruit.[73] The trap was set and ready to spring as Essex, moving away from his base of supply, was followed by no less than three armies in a country very favourably disposed toward the cavalier cause.

Once in Cornwall the parliamentary forces moved late in July to Linkinhorne, Bodmin, and then to Lostwithiel where Essex established himself by 2 August.[74] With access to the sea and to possible reinforcement,[75] the lord general refused every overture proffered by the royalist commanders and instead sent off urgent messages to the Committee of Both Kingdoms.[76] In his letter of 4 August, Essex explained once again that he had marched into Cornwall on the assurances 'of the western men' who had stressed the importance of that county to the control of the West, and had given 'their promise that we should not want victuals, and that a great part of the county stood well-affected . . .'.[77] It had now become apparent that no such local help could be expected. Quite the contrary: the Cornish were flocking to the enemy camp. What made matters worse, the royalist armies were converging around his quarters undeterred by any parliamentary force to harass them in the rear.[78] On 10 August the committee was able to respond that £20,000, and additional supplies, were being rushed to his assistance by sea.[79] At the same time Colonel Middleton had been ordered to move into the West with what troops he could collect. Meanwhile, however, the cavalier armies were closing in around the parliamentarians and August was spent in minor skirmishes as Essex attempted to maintain his position as best he could.[80]

It was not until the end of August that Middleton was able to move into Devon with the 2,000 horse and foot under his command.[81] Vastly outnumbered by the royalist forces then in the southwest, the most he could hope to do was disrupt the cavaliers' supply lines and act as a general nuisance in the rear of the royal armies.[82] By the 28th he had reached Honiton, and the next day was in the Tiverton area.[83] Middleton was not completely free to do as he wished, however, as Sir Francis Dodington had been left behind in Devon with 1,000 horse to protect the king's rear from surprise.[84] It was because of this body of men that Middleton was eventually forced to retreat into north Devon and to quarter himself on Barnstaple.[85]

Lord General Essex did indeed acknowledge with gratitude the efforts of the Committee of Both Kingdoms to send reinforcements and supplies to his rescue. But in his letter of 27 August he was at pains to add:

> ... had I known that Waller, who was to attend the King's army, had wanted either power or will to have a care of it, no persuasions of those who are interested in these counties should have engaged me so far in a country so ill-affected to the Parliament.[86]

No such bitter afterthoughts, however, could rescue his army from its present predicament. By the end of the month Essex recognised the hopelessness of his situation. Therefore, on 31 August he ordered his entire body of horse (nearly 2,000) to attempt an escape through the encircling royalist lines. Although warned in advance of the parliamentary intentions, the cavaliers were unable to prevent the escape of the enemy horse. The Earl of Cleveland's brigade, and some others, followed the fleeing cavalry as best they could, but apparently because of General

Goring's slackness, the majority made good their escape.[87] Dividing into various groups, some of the parliamentarian horse found refuge in Plymouth, while the majority appear to have made for Crediton and Barnstaple, and then to Taunton, managing to avoid the many royalist parties looking for them.[88] One body of horse that moved toward Tavistock was attacked by Goring's men. Some were captured in this skirmish, only to be quickly freed in a counter-offensive on 4 September. At the same time, Sir Francis Dodington encountered some 600 of the enemy on Hatherleigh Moor, and decisively routed them, chasing the fugitives to Little Torrington where they eventually joined Middleton's forces stationed there.[89] For more than a week Devon was thus astir with the constant movement of cavalry as the fleeing parliamentarians attempted to avoid contact with cavalier garrisons and search parties. By 5 September, however, Goring and Berkeley had to admit defeat in the essential task of destroying a body of horse which would survive to fight again.[90]

His horse safely away, Essex fell back to Fowey, still hoping for some means by which his foot might be saved. On 1 September, following only a slight skirmish on Broadoak Down, near Boconnoc,[91] the lord general informed the king of his desire to negotiate for the surrender of his army. That evening, unable himself to accept the humiliation of surrender, Essex took sail for Plymouth in the company of his chief officers, leaving Major General Skippon behind to command the army.[92] Terms were quickly agreed upon and, with the enemy's foot on the march under guard through Devon, the king returned briefly to Boconnoc.[93] There it was determined to return immediately eastward, and to stop at Plymouth to see if that place would finally capitulate to the victorious royal army.[94]

Charles led his armies to Liskeard on 4 September, and the following day crossed into Devon, establishing himself at Tavistock. Immediately upon arrival the king authorised Sir Richard Grenville to send a messenger to Plymouth demanding that the garrison 'render the town'. On 6 September the trumpeter, who had suffered some physical abuse on his mission, returned to say that a reply would soon be forthcoming.[95] This eventually proved to be a flat refusal. Determined on a show of force,[96] the king sent out warrants to his officials in Devon and Cornwall to bring in deserters, recruits, and supplies for an assault.[97] On 9 September the royalist armies were paraded on Roborough Down, just four miles from Plymouth, presumably to frighten the garrison, for only one regiment was actually 'sent to face the town'. The next day, however, the siege began in earnest as the cavaliers took up positions close to its outer defences. While laying siege to the place, Charles tried on two occasions to summon the garrison on reasonable terms, both offers being rejected.[98]

News reached the forces before Plymouth on 13 September that the rebellious town of Barnstaple had once again submitted to royal control. The Barnstaple garrison had been greatly shaken by Essex's defeat in Cornwall and the subsequent chase of the parliamentary cavalry. Somewhat fortified by Middleton's call for resistance, the townsmen however thought better of it when he withdrew his forces on 5 September and when their walls were besieged by Goring's troops.[99] The town was summoned on the 12th and surrendered on 17 September, 'upon such fair and reasonable conditions as no town ever had the like'.[100] Goring then withdrew to Sir John Chichester's house at Raleigh, one mile north of Barnstaple, where he set up headquarters, having agreed not to quarter a garrison in the town itself. Not until December were troops actually stationed in Barnstaple, and then under the command of Sir Allen Apsley.[101]

Throughout that week the royalist forces continued their siege of Plymouth, giving the garrison 'strong alarms' and continuously pressuring the outworks. Early on Saturday morning, however, the the main body of cavaliers broke off their activities and marched away from Plymouth, leaving Grenville to continue the blockade with fewer than 1,000 men. An easy success not possible, the king was unwilling to waste further time around Plymouth. Marching through Lydford to Okehampton, Charles finally arrived at Exeter on the evening of 17 September.[102] As before, the citizens contributed generously for the honour of the royal presence, and the corporation succeeded in raising £500 as a gift.[103]

During the five days spent in the city, Charles was constantly occupied with matters of supply and recruitment. Shoes, stockings, and other clothing were ordered to be brought out of Cornwall, deserters were to be apprehended and returned to their colours, arms had to be repaired, and arrangements made for the provisioning of the two armies. Further, steps were taken to restrain the parliamentary forces still active in the region of Lyme Regis and Taunton.[104] At the same time, because of constant complaints from Cornwall and Devon, it was necessary to appoint commissioners to audit the accounts of all funds collected for the royalist cause in the Southwest.[105]

Leaving Exeter on 23 September, the king moved on to Chard, via Honiton, where he remained until 1 October.[106] From Chard he was pleased to grant the petition of the Corporation of Totnes for a full pardon for their previous acts of rebellion and for a confirmation of their ancient liberties and privileges.[107] There he issued his 'Propositions' to the people of Somerset, requesting that they follow the example of their neighbours in providing such necessary clothing, money, and carriages as had been so freely contributed by the Devonians.[108]

Although he had failed to take Plymouth, and he was never again to have such an opportunity to do so, Charles' campaign, and especially his efforts in Cornwall and Devon, had been extremely successful. He left Devon at the head of a well-supplied army which had completely freed the peninsula (with the continued exception of Plymouth) of parliamentary control, had restored Barnstaple to its allegiance, and had crushed a large and dangerous enemy force. Most of Devon could now return to a peaceful routine under an established royalist regime.[109]

Notes to this chapter are on page 211

9

The Siege of Plymouth
january 1644-january 1646

Plymouth was in a class by itself. In all of Devonshire it was the
only community which did not change hands during the entire
civil war, but remained staunchly parliamentarian throughout. At
no time during this period was Plymouth as seriously threatened
as during Christmas week, 1643, although it had been continuously besieged or blockaded from the previous summer. With the
new year, and the institution of a mild blockade by forces under
Colonel John Digby, the garrison had several weeks of respite
from assault which were spent on repairs and expansion of fortifications, and the destruction of enemy trenches and outworks.[1]

Internally, however, Plymouth was in poor condition. Although
provisions were limited, quarrels and suspicions were abundant
and widespread. In the last week of January 1644, Colonel James
Wardlaw, parliamentary general for Devon and Cornwall, was
replaced as commander of the Plymouth garrison and as governor
of St Nicholas Island by Colonel Gould.[2] Recriminations and
accusations amongst officials resulted until recourse was taken to
the parliamentary authorities at Westminster. Gould was able to
retain his new command until it was abruptly ended by his death
on 27 March.[3]

In the meantime, Sir Richard Grenville had replaced Digby as
royalist commander before Plymouth and was actively bringing in
recruits for his blockade, as well as increasing his own private fortune. According to Clarendon: '. . . for though he suffered not
his soldiers to plunder, yet he was in truth himself the greatest
plunderer of this war; . . .'[4] As a means of introducing himself
to the parliamentarians, Grenville wrote a letter to the Plymouth
authorities on 18 March in which he explained his past behaviour

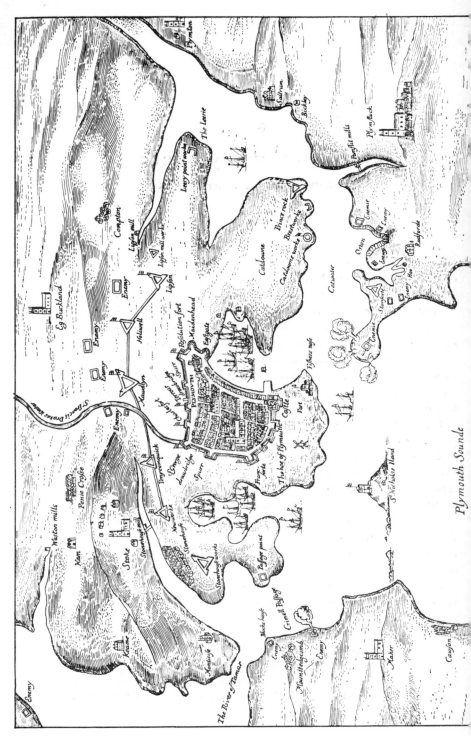

Plymouth Defences

in going over to the king, and at the same time attempted to convince them that they should follow his example.[5] That same day the parliamentarians returned a scornful reply to their notorious enemy, rejecting his arguments and refusing to treat for peace.[6]

During this period the garrison was quite active in sending out raiding parties and sorties to harrass the cavalier outposts and to reciprocate for the attacks 'on some of our men, that were abroad in the Country, . . .'. On 24 February, and again on 15 and 20 March, parties advanced as far as Trinaman's Jump where they attacked the cavaliers stationed there and did what damage they could. But in large measure these raids were punitive in nature, and it was not until Colonel Robert Martin took command in mid-April that the garrison took the initiative.[7] Thus, on 16 April a force of 600 musketeers was despatched to St Budeaux to surprise the royalist soldiers recently quartered there and at the same time forces were sent to alarm the main enemy headquarters at Plympton. Having great success at St Budeaux, Martin sent out 200 musketeers toward Newbridge on the 19th. Parliamentarian enthusiasm over-extended itself, however, and the party was forced to retire in the face of overwhelming odds.[8] Colonel Martin was not content with this. The successes at St Budeaux were followed by minor skirmishes with the growing enemy forces. On 13 May Martin personally led a force of 1,000 foot and almost 100 horse toward Trinaman's Jump and, while 400 musketeers and 25 horse protected their flank around Compton, he directed the attack on Hopton's Work. With no great difficulty that outpost was taken and a safe retreat made to Plymouth. Keeping the initiative, Martin then sent out 300 musketeers by boat to Mount Edgcumbe where, although unable to take that stronghold, they succeeded in capturing several of the royalist outposts in the vicinity and carrying off valuable equipment, livestock, and prisoners.[9]

Barely two months after having obtained sole command, Martin was replaced by Colonel James Kerr, who arrived from London on Friday, 14 June.[10] Notwithstanding the petitions of various influential western gentlemen, Kerr had been named in preference to Lord Robartes for this essential post, while Sir John Bampfield was placed in charge of St Nicholas Island.[11] Under Kerr's command Plymouth's problems were at first greatly eased, as Essex was then moving into the west and his presence caused the lifting of the blockade of the town. This relief of tension was short-lived, for the lord general's defeat put Plymouth in a generally weaker position, so many of her best men having accompanied Essex into Cornwall. Warwick's report reflects this: 'I find the town unsettled, the soldiers complaining for want of victuals and pay, and the townsmen not very forward to content them.' The garrison was then down to 800 men who were expected to defend a four-mile long line of fortifications. Just as bad: 'There are daily controversies between the Mayor and Governor, . . .'.[12] During the first week of September the garrison was hourly in expectation of attack and feverish steps were taken to prepare against assault. Kerr wrote on 3 September to urge the Lords to 'hearken to the Earl of Warwick in all his solicitations for assistance'.[13] Men and supplies were desperately needed if Plymouth were to survive another siege.

As the royal armies once again drew up around Plymouth in early September, parliament moved quickly to reinforce this western bastion. Orders were sent to Waller and Essex to provide the garrison with 1,000 and 500 men respectively, from whatever forces were then available.[14] All provisions en route to Cornwall for Essex's use were to be diverted to Plymouth for the use of that town and garrison.[15] Essex's defeat thus brought some good to Plymouth in the form of supplies which she would not otherwise have obtained. His most enthusiastic supporter, Lord Robartes, was swiftly appointed governor, relieving Colonel Kerr. Robartes was notified of his new authority in a letter from the Committee of Both Kingdoms on 8 September, and told at the same time that men, arms, and supplies were being rushed to his aid.[16] The following day the committee also wrote to the Earl of Pembroke to order the transfer of an additional 400 men from the Isle of Wight to Plymouth, and to give what encouragement he could to the raising of £1,000 worth of provisions for the same cause.[17] In Plymouth Robartes and Vice-Admiral Batten were, in their turn, urgently requesting assistance as the royalist pressure on their defences became almost irresistible.[18]

These preparations were made just in time. As mentioned above, the royalists waited almost a week after returning to Devon before making their fierce, but unsuccessful, attempt to gain Plymouth, by fair means and foul, through strength and persuasion. Finding the townsmen and garrison as determined as ever to resist royal control, the king moved his armies further eastward, leaving Grenville in charge of the reduced blockade.[19] Once the immediate crisis had passed, Plymouth again found itself neglected by the Committee of Both Kingdoms whose members turned their attention to more pressing problems, halting whatever supplies were destined for the western outpost.[20] Although not threatened by the enemy, the authorities were faced with the discontent of the soldiers who lacked pay and supplies, and the unrest of the civilians who saw trade and commerce decline.[21]

Following the king's departure with the majority of the royalist troops, Grenville set to work recruiting his forces so as to prosecute the siege and make good his boast of an early victory. In large measure, his men came from his native Cornwall where the Grenville name and Sir Richard's military reputation brought numerous recruits.[22] To pay and maintain these men, and to provide the necessary arms and ammunition for a besieging force, the Devon commissioners granted him one-half of their weekly contribution (£1,100), in addition to the right to collect some £6,000 in arrears from the western portion of the county. This sum was combined with £700 from Cornwall which constituted that county's entire weekly martial rates.[23] Clarendon makes clear that Grenville in no way raised the full number of men for which he was being paid, but rather looked to his own interests.[24] These huge sums do not appear to have satisfied him, for as early as October 1644 he was accusing Colonel Edward Seymour of encroaching on his area of contribution, and beginning the long struggle over jurisdiction and privileges which was to hamper so seriously the royalist cause in the west.[25]

Taking advantage of this lull in the enemy's activities, the Plymouth forces once again took the initiative. On 4 October a party of men was sent into Cornwall and successfully captured Saltash.[26] The next day another group crossed the Tamar by boat and easily took Millbrook and the nearby fort at Insworke. Reacting swiftly to these attacks, the Cornish forces recaptured Millbrook in short order, inflicting severe damage upon the enemy in doing so.[27] It took three days, however, before Grenville was able to regain Saltash, and then only after a fierce two-hour battle.[28]

The last two months of 1644 found the defenders of Plymouth continuously on the alert as the royalists tried first one thing and then another in hope of success. An attempt to fire the town was thwarted and the royalists suffered a severe setback in their simultaneous efforts to storm the defences.[29] Further efforts were made to bribe malcontents within the garrison to blow up the magazine, but this also was discovered.[30] At the same time that force and subterfuge were being employed, the royalist commissioners at Exeter sent a plea to the Plymouth authorities in the hope of bringing about a 'reunion' of that town with the rest of Devon in order to thereby restore 'the exceeding great commerce and profit' which they had previously enjoyed.[31] Certainly the parliamentarians could have wished for nothing better than a restoration of peace and a resolution of 'this unnatural difference', as life had been extremely difficult for them during almost two years of continuous siege. As the 1644-5 winter approached the inhabitants of town and garrison had difficulty in obtaining the necessary provisions for themselves, as well as for their livestock and horses.[32] Luckily for the besieged, in November the navy captured two royalist ships bound for Topsham and Exeter, whose confiscated cargoes provided useful means of supplying the town with money and provisions.[33] In his letter of 16 November to the Speaker of the Commons, however, Lord Robartes stressed the need for additional ammunition and money with which to maintain this essential outpost.[34] Robartes further hoped that more vessels could be sent into the western waters in order to intercept the supply ships bringing aid to the royalist forces in the county.[35]

The onset of winter did not halt Grenville's activities. A correspondent from Plymouth, writing on 22 December, stated: 'We are here upon very hard duties, and have many alarms, but our Governor (the Lord Robartes) is very vigilant and active'. Although nothing could be done to prevent the royalist horse from raiding 'within a mile or two of us', Robartes took every opportunity to strike out at the cavalier forces which approached the town, and did what he could to harrass the enemy.[36] It was not until just after Christmas, however, that Commons decided to send down 200 barrels of powder to aid in the defence of the town.[37] Notwithstanding irregular supply and limited provisions, the garrison worked continuously to repair weak fortifications, construct new outworks, and significantly strengthen the line of defence in anticipation of renewed royalist attacks.[38]

Sir Richard was not long in providing the test of strength for which the men of Plymouth had prepared. On Wednesday, 8 January, he drew up a force of 5,000 men to attack the town and outworks but, due to extremely wet weather, was unable to begin an assault until the Friday.[39] Then, dividing his men into several groups, Grenville attacked four outworks and 'after a very hot dispute', gained control of Pennycomequick, while being repulsed at the other defences.[40] William Thomas aboard the *Warwick* wrote to Westminster shortly thereafter reporting on the role played by the seamen in the defence of Plymouth, and added: 'As at the expiration of my victualling I have to come in, some shipping should be sent down, for the place needs support, and the State might as well lose London as this town'.[41] Mayor Justinian Peard and the other Plymouth authorities also wrote to request further aid from parliament, which the MPs were more than ready to provide following the recent successful repulses of the enemy.[42] Although decisively repulsed and suffering severe losses, however, Grenville was not discouraged. He immediately sent out instructions to the commanders of local garrisons to bring in their regiments to Plympton as quickly as possible so that he might make another attempt.[43] By the middle of the month he was once again prepared. During the night of 17 February Grenville sent a large force to reoccupy and reconstruct a work on the site of Mount Stamford, across the Cattewater from Plymouth. The following day, realising what danger such an outpost would constitute to the town's shipping, the Plymouth authorities acted quickly. At noon a group of horse and foot were rushed into the nearby Fort Batten to reinforce that garrison against possible attack.[44] From Batten and the ships in the Cattewater, parliamentarian artillery pounded the new royalist position all day. Then, while a diversionary assault was made out of Pennycomequick, Lord Robartes led a substantial force across the water to attack Mount Stamford.[45] Fighting broke out about 2 pm and within a half hour, following a short but fierce engagement, the royalist forces fled their new outpost, leaving behind large quantities of supplies and equipment.[46]

Much of the organisational leadership which went into the continued parliamentarian opposition came from the recently established Plymouth Committee of Defence.[47] Among the prominent citizens who made up this committee in February 1645 were Mayor Peard, former mayors Thomas Ceely and John Cawse,[48] as

well as Colonel Christopher Savery, Francis Godolphin of Tre-
veneague (Cornwall), Harcourt Leyton, and Timothy Alsop as
treasurer.[49] These men, led by Lord Robartes, organised the resistance against the fierce royalist assaults of January and February.
It was their task, and one which was carried out with notable
success, to assess and collect money and plate from whatever
source possible in order to maintain the garrison, as well as the
town's fortifications. Alsop was the agent to whom orders were
given to collect the funds and pay out all sums to merchants and
workmen for services rendered. At the same time, commissaries
Slade and Clap concerned themselves with the payment of the
troops on the mainland, and Sir John Bampfield with those on St
Nicholas Island.[50]

The Plymouth records indicate that parliament was much more
willing and able in 1645 to provide this bastion with funds than
they had been at any other time during the war. In only isolated
instances, however, was income ever above the amount spent on
supplies, pay, repairs, and other necessities. Month after month
the committee was forced to borrow from loyal supporters within
the town, and to accept services and goods for which payment had
to be deferred.[51] But as was generally the case throughout this
period, labourers and soldiers expected prompt payment for services rendered, and were greatly dissatisfied when put off. Usually
they had to wait only until the next parliamentary supply ship
arrived with money from London, and then all creditors were
promptly reimbursed, with the expectation that they would continue their support of the puritan cause. The largest portion of
this money obviously went toward the weekly payment of the
garrison, and those on duty at the outposts. But increasingly the
repairs to the town's defences became more costly, requiring attention following each attack and as the natural result of age[52] While
the outworks continued to be extended and reinforced, shipments
of arms and ammunition arrived at regular intervals after October 1644.[53] But provisions for an increasingly deprived, although
constantly enlarged, garrison still had to be found and paid for,
sick men required care, and dead men had to be buried. Thus,
from February to May of 1645 the monthly expenditure of the
Plymouth Committee was about £3,000, and as the year progressed, that figure rose until December when almost £5,000 was
spent for defence.[54]

Notwithstanding their continuous preparations, the parliamentarians had little cause for concern following the mid-Februrary assault. In March 1645 Grenville received orders to leave Plymouth fully secured and to advance eastward into Somerset with the bulk of his forces.[55] His remaining 2,400 horse and foot were quartered at Plympton, Hopton Fort, and Arundel Fort where they could easily maintain the blockade of the town and cut it off from the countryside. A letter from Plymouth on 16 March, however, claimed that the parliamentarians there were 'in a good condition', though still awaiting the expected supplies from the capital.[56] In the meantime, the besieged took advantage of the reduced enemy strength to sally out on occasion to alarm their opponents and to bring in what provisions they could.[57] Following the successful raid on 2 May these excursions became increasingly popular as a convenient means of obtaining food and livestock from the country.[58]

The only major disturbance to disrupt the calm of Plymouth life during late spring 1645 was the news of the recall of their zealous governor, John Lord Robartes, along with Sir John Bampfield, governor of St Nicholas Island.[59] Petitions were immediately sent up to parliament describing Robartes' 'indefatigable pains and vigilance' by which means alone Plymouth had been saved from enemy conquest.[60] But notwithstanding popular pressure, parliament remained determined that the Self-Denying Ordinance be enforced, and that all members should return to the service of their respective House. To replace Robartes, a committee of five was named to govern the town, including Justinian Peard, Colonel Kerr, Thomas Ceely, Colonel John Crocker, and John Beare. Kerr alone, however, was to exercise complete military control.[61]

At the end of May parliament took care to strengthen the garrison at Plymouth by approving the agreement which secured the services of Colonel Birch's Kentish regiment for an additional four months, and arranged for funds with which to pay these men. At the same time, an ordinance was passed by both Houses granting the Plymouth committee authority to institute martial law if necessary to maintain their position.[62] Concern was growing in London over the cessation of hostilities between the Irish rebels and the royal forces, a situation which greatly enhanced the possibility of the enlistment of Irishmen in the royalist armies in England. If possible, therefore, the men of Plymouth were asked to contribute 500 men toward the security of Milford Haven, the most obvious port of entry for any foreign troops.[63]

In June Sir John Berkeley was placed in charge of the royalist forces before Plymouth, but he did not consider it advisable to do more than maintain a tight blockade around the place.[64] The only skirmish recorded that summer occurred in mid-August when a party of 200 royalist horse penetrated close to the town's defences and carried off 180 sheep, along with fifteen soldiers out collecting wood.[65] Other such events probably took place as each side tried to relieve the boredom of the siege, and as the townsmen searched further afield for additional supplies.

By early September the Plymouth authorities were once again concerned over the prospect of another winter's siege. They addressed a petition to the City of London asking for support in pressing parliament for supplies and reinforcements to last until General Thomas Fairfax, then preoccupied with the siege of Bristol, could move into Devon. London gave ready support to the cause for which parliament needed little urging at that point, and the Committee of Both Kingdoms immediately recommended Plymouth's plight to the lord general.[66] At the same time, the House of Commons took steps to renew the one per cent customs duty being collected to finance Plymouth's defence, and named Colonel Ralph Welden to replace Colonel Kerr as governor of the town.[67]

That summer the command of the royalist forces around Plymouth had once again changed hands, and Berkeley was replaced by Sir John Digby. The new commander, reinforced by troops falling back into the West before Fairfax's advancing army, put additional pressure on the Plymouth garrison during October and November. Besides the continuous lack of supplies which treacherous winds made difficult to obtain by sea, the new mayor, Bartholomew Nicoll, reported a serious shortage of money by mid-November.[68] Further, there were serious intimations that unrest was growing within the town.[69] The petition sent to parliament in early November particularly emphasised the distress felt in Plymouth at seeing Fairfax go into winter quarters only fifty miles away (near Exeter), while 'the enemy between them and us most barbarously spoil and oppress the country, and streighten us, who are destitute of all things for a winter's siege'.[70] Reminding parliament again of their long-suffering devotion to the cause, as

well of the town's vital position in the West, the Plymouth authorities requested immediate action be taken to provide for their
security.

Both Houses took up the Plymouth matter immediately, with
the Lords pressing (under Robartes' leadership) for speedy action
to relieve so important an outpost. The former governor stressed
the responsibility of parliament to make good the relief of that
place which had been too often frustrated in the past by the depressing continuation of the siege. In consideration of Plymouth's
commercial and military importance, the lords advocated that
immediate steps be taken to send money, provisions, and equipment needed for the winter, that the internal affairs there be
straightened out, and that Fairfax be encouraged to continue his
western march 'with convenient speed'.[71] In ready agreement, the
Commons voted a grant of £10,000 for the immediate relief of
Plymouth, and asked the Committee of the West to settle the
internal affairs of the town and to see to the support of the
numerous refugees there. The lower House would not, however,
agree to sending Fairfax further west under winter conditions,
but desired that he continue where he was in order to recruit and
consolidate his army.[72]

No record remains of any serious skirmish between Digby's
forces and the garrison during November or early December 1645.
Instead, Colonel Digby attempted a different approach in the
hope of bringing the town over to the royalist side. Addressing
himself to Colonel Kerr on 3 December, the royalist commander
urged the parliamentarian leader to reconsider his true allegiance
now that parliament planned to replace him with Colonel
Welden, and to hand over his charge to the king's forces. Immediately upon receipt of Digby's offer, Kerr called together his
colleagues on the Plymouth Committee and informed them of the
enemy's latest manoeuvre. At first hoping to turn the situation
to their own advantage, the committee finally recommended that
Digby be sent a flat refusal. On 10 December Kerr rejected Digby's
proposal, and in the most contemptuous terms let that gentleman
know how much he scorned such an offer. Kerr went on, in his
turn, to attempt to pursuade the royalist commander to throw
over his old cause and embrace the parliamentary side.[73]

Such a strong rejection did not spur Digby into any more force-
ful action. On the contrary, December passed peacefully enough

until just after Christmas. Then, for the next week and a half, the Plymouth garrison was active in raids out into the countryside to harass the royalist quarters, take prisoners, and bring in supplies. On 27 December 600 horse and foot easily captured the cavalier outpost at Kinterbury, and then moved on to St Budeaux. Storming the church there, the parliamentarians found themselves strongly opposed in a determined engagement which lasted for almost two hours before the royalists would surrender.[74] In the course of the next few days Buckland Abbey and Fort Arundell were also attacked, but by this time the royalists were not willing to put up much of a resistance.[75] On 12 January Fairfax reached Totnes, and soon caused the rapid withdrawal of the cavaliers to the other side of the Tamar.[76]

Once again the royalists found themselves at the end of a long, fruitless siege which had occupied precious forces, supplies, and money that could more profitably have been used elsewhere. Unable to surround Plymouth completely or to cut off supplies as long as the parliamentarians controlled the sea, cavalier attempts to take this essential outpost were doomed to failure: a failure which the king's party could not sustain and still hope to remain dominant in Devon, and in the West Country. At the same time, while the outstanding endurance of the men of Plymouth had far-reaching consequences, their success had been obtained at a dear price. In order to maintain their independence the townsmen and garrison had suffered through three years of depravation, siege, and alarms, gathering courage from a determination that they were right notwithstanding what force was sent against them. Some 8,000 estimated dead during these siege years, added to the loss in trade and commerce, destruction of property, and disruption of occupations, amounted to a terrific sacrifice for the parliamentarian cause. Certainly as Worth wrote: 'The whole history of the Civil War fails to supply a parallel to this'.[77]

Notes to this chapter are on page 216

The Prince of Wales in the West
january 1645-april 1646

The siege of Plymouth did not constitute the only major problem confronting the royalist forces in Devon during 1645. For the Prince of Wales, and the council which assisted him, the entire year proved to be one of constant dissension within the royalist camp and continuous effort to reorganise and revive the cavalier cause in the West. It was originally intended that the prince should take up residence in the West in May 1644, but the king had been persuaded to postpone this course of action.[1] By 1645, however, Charles was unwilling to risk further the capture of himself and his son if the New Model Army should apply itself directly to the siege of Oxford. Placing an undue amount of trust in the idea of a Western Association then being promoted by zealous royalists in Somerset, Dorset, Cornwall, and Devon,[2] the king took this opportunity to launch his fifteen year old heir onto the stage of national politics. The prince was granted a dual commission as General of the Western Association, and 'First Captain General of all our Forces',[3] but it was never intended that he should exercise direct authority without the consent of his council.

The king's purposes in sending his son into the West were manifold. In addition to his desire that his heir come early to an appreciation of the responsibilities of authority and rank, Charles was worried about the possibility that both he and the prince should be taken at one sudden reverse in the fortunes of war. But with the prince in the West Country, exceptional vigour might readily transform the new association into a potent force for the royalist cause in this section of the country, and further spread its influence to wherever it might be needed. As important as any of these considerations was the hope that a royal presence in Bristol, the seat of the prince's court, would facilitate the reorganisation of the royalist resources, while at the same time bring about a reconciliation of the quarrelling factions amongst the king's supporters. In order to obtain the indispensable support which he needed from his western counties, the king had to re-establish a single authority from which all commanders would take their orders. The Prince of Wales could well constitute this authority.[4]

The prince and his council found their work cut out for them upon their arrival in Somerset in early March 1645. The men, money, and supplies which were to have been provided by the Western Association did not exist in fact, and even the prince's Life-Guard had not been raised.[5] General George Goring's army, some 1,500 foot and 3,000 horse, had retreated to the borders of Dorset, Devon, and Somerset where they indulged in 'unheard-of rapine, without applying themselves to any enterprise upon the rebels'.[6] Having finally made up his mind to take up the siege of Taunton once again in order to clear the West of a particularly obnoxious enemy stronghold, Lord Goring proceeded to antagonise both Berkeley and Grenville. Ordering reinforcements from each commander where he had no authority to do so, Goring found the governor of Exeter most indignant at this treatment, and the commander at Plymouth most reluctant to comply.[7] Recognising the necessity of reducing Taunton, however, the prince's council gave Goring their full support and repeatedly ordered Grenville to bring up the bulk of his troops while leaving Plymouth securely blockaded.[8] Grenville immediately blamed Berkeley for this removal eastward, claiming that Berkeley was jealous of his 'prosperity' in besieging Plymouth,[9] whereas in actual fact he had been no more successful in reducing that stronghold than had any of his predecessors. But Grenville probably judged accurately the refusal of his troops, both Cornish and Devonian, to march eastward while Plymouth remained in enemy hands, and while their counties were exposed to parliamentarian raids. With Taunton taken, the council hoped to be able to raise the force originally expected from the association, and at the same time better utilise the resources of a completely royalist West. This objective carried priority over the local interests of the western farmer and yeoman, and Grenville slowly moved east in late March with some 3,000 horse and foot. By the time he had reached Somerset, however, Goring was already moving his forces back into Dorset, and Taunton was being forgotten in an effort to halt the advancing rebel forces.[10]

Dissension, jealousy, and quarrelling, already noticeable in the royalist ranks in February and March 1645, became a constant and pressing concern throughout the remainder of the year.[11] Grenville, who had earlier refused to serve under Goring, was immediately relieved of any disagreeable service in Somerset for within days of his arrival he was severely wounded while attempting to take Wellington House, near Taunton.[12] Before retiring to Exeter for treatment, Sir Richard agreed to the temporary appointment of Sir John Berkeley as commander of his forces.[13] At the same time, Goring, probably piqued at having been passed over as commanding officer before Taunton, indicated his intention of retiring to Bath for health reasons.[14]

With the command of the royalist forces around Taunton thus momentarily settled, the prince's council turned its attention to the universally depressing situation which had grown out of the many fair promises of those promoting the Western Association. To escape from the frustrating quagmire which resulted from internal accusations and counter-attacks, the council called together commissioners from the four counties in the hope of hastening the achievement of their primary objectives—to reduce Taunton and to establish a strong western army. Representatives from Devon, Cornwall, Dorset, and Somerset subsequently met at the Town Hall in Bridgwater on 24 April. Urging them not to be hampered by previous association decisions, the prince convinced the commissioners of the necessity of raising an army of 8,000 men with which to reduce Taunton, and to include therein the forces already recruited by Berkeley and Grenville.[15] Once again the quota system was to be employed whereby each county would be responsible for supplying a requisite number of men.[16] At a time when the parliamentarians were organising a national army which would serve in any part of the realm, this new western venture, which was to constitute an essential pillar of the floundering royalist cause, was falling back on the outmoded system of impressing local levies to serve under local commanders for primarily local ends. A standing army, well-paid, and under a strong central command was what was needed if the king could ever expect to regain his kingdom.

Considering their efforts thus far successful, the prince's councillors then ran into trouble in deciding who amongst the contentious officers would command this army. It became readily apparent to Sir Edward Hyde at least that Lord Goring was anxious to assume in title an authority which he had already attempted to exercise in practice. Berkeley, as colonel-general of all forces in Devon and Cornwall, had a strong claim to the new post, as did Lord Hopton, now governor of Bristol. Notwithstanding his enforced retirement at Exeter, Grenville also made it clear that he was unwilling to serve in an inferior capacity.[17] He would either become lieutenant-general to the prince or serve the king in a voluntary capacity.

The problem of delegating authority which now faced the council was a serious one and tended only to cripple the entire royalist effort in the western counties. The situation became more complex when the Devon commissioners took advantage of the Bridgwater conference to present a petition of complaint to the Prince of Wales concerning Grenville's past activities. In a statement which was devastating in its condemnation of Grenville's behaviour before Plymouth, the commissioners pointed out their heavy sacrifices in terms of money and supplies to equip an army of 6,000 foot and 1,200 horse which Sir Richard had avoided raising until he was called upon to move into Somerset in March. In the meantime, the entire weekly contribution of Cornwall, in addition to half that of Devon, plus arrears and funds from other sources, had all been collected by Grenville but expended on non-military purposes. He had not in fact conquered Plymouth, and had moved off leaving a blockade of only 2,400 horse and foot before the town. In sum, these gentlemen maintained that it would be extremely difficult for them to contribute toward the prince's new army unless Sir Richard's authority were limited, his quarrel with Berkeley ended, and his arbitrary control of large sections of the county brought to a halt.[18] So serious was this indictment and so strongly was it pressed by the petitioners, that the prince's council determined to send three of their number to Exeter to straighten out once and for all time the question of authority within the counties of Exeter and Devon, to settle the matter of martial rates, and to arrive at some recommendation for the supreme command of the association's army. After an examination of the arguments presented by both Grenville and Berkeley (still at Taunton) it became obvious that definite overlapping in authority had grown out of conflicting commissions. Thus, in an effort to content both commanders. it was agreed that Grenville would resign his command before Plymouth in favour of Berkeley, and would be given in exchange an appointment as lieutenant-general of the prince's army.[19]

Lords Capel and Colepeper then returned to Taunton to obtain Sir John's consent to this arrangement, leaving the Chancellor of the Exchequer (Hyde) behind to organise the matter of contributions which had so strongly stirred the Devon commissioners. Once again the total weekly martial rate was redistributed in an effort to meet the complete responsibilities for defence which existed within the two counties of Exeter and Devon. The huge sums originally allotted to the Plymouth forces were greatly reduced, and the hundreds were reassigned to support the other garrisons of Dartmouth, Exeter, Tiverton, and Barnstaple. Even on the assumption that every penny of this contribution would indeed be collected, the commissioners still found themselves seeking 'other extraordinary ways' in order to obtain the funds necessary to supply garrisons, reinforce fortifications, pressure the outpost at Lyme Regis, and otherwise maintain an increasingly exhausted royalist cause.[20]

Nevertheless hopes were high once again that the cavalier cause in the West, strengthened by a fresh army, reorganised finances, and a unified central command, might yet regain for the king the advantages lost that year in other parts of the realm. But, having resigned his command before Plymouth, Grenville was never to be granted his new commission—a factor which, according to him, 'was none the weakest reasons why that associated army was not raised'.[21] An unforeseen obstacle had presented itself to the plans so carefully worked out by the prince's council. While the councillors had been struggling to reason with Grenville and Berkeley, Lord Goring had gone off to court and obtained from the king specific authorisation to command whatever forces were brought together in the West. The prince was further instructed to stay out of military matters, and to remain safely distant from any trouble spot. Letters which Goring carried with him, as well as others from the court, made perfectly clear the royal desire that Goring's voice was to be decisive in the military counsels in the West, while Grenville was given a position below him.[22] As these commands were so contradictory to existing commissions and instructions, Colepeper wrote immediately to the king to explain the necessity for the compromise which he and his colleagues had arranged in order for them to retain the services of their two most valuable commanders.[23] The response from Lord Digby and Prince Rupert was to order Goring to march eastward as quickly as possible, with whatever men he could find at hand, to relieve the pressure on Oxford from Sir Thomas Fairfax and his New Model Army.[24] Instead, Goring appears to have wasted additional time in the Taunton area, neither establishing royalist control over that obstinate town, nor securing recognition of his position from the prince's council.[25]

Having recovered from his wounds, Grenville soon occupied himself in attempting to reorganise the forces which he had once commanded, notwithstanding the fact that he was now without authority to act.[26] As early as 11 May he was in touch with Colonel Seymour at Dartmouth who had expressed a willingness to add his regiment to the army which Sir Richard was working to establish.[27] Sending his warrants throughout the counties of Devon and Cornwall, Grenville soon found his orders countermanded by Berkeley who informed the commissioners of both counties on 26 May that they should make no move without his specific command as colonel-general of the area.[28] Two days later, Grenville wrote from Exeter to Lord Colepeper to complain of Berkeley's interference, and to petition that the prince's council confirm his authority in Devon and Cornwall.[29]

In early June the prince and his advisers made a rapid shift in headquarters in order to avoid the growing threat of plague in Bristol. Their choice of residence was the now well-fortified town of Barnstaple in north Devon.[30] It was to this Barnstaple court that Grenville presented himself in June in order to petition personally that 'he might be re-established in the command of those men he had formerly levied'.[31] The prince's council decided otherwise. Berkeley was reaffirmed in his command of the forces before Plymouth, while Grenville was supposed to move into Somerset to join Goring's army as field marshal.[32] This decision was presently revised.[33] Grenville was then told that he would be given an independent command in east Devon in order to confine the Lyme Regis garrison and to establish royalist control in the region of Ottery St Mary. Sir Richard's efforts to raise additional county forces and to collect his scattered troops were soon interrupted again by Berkeley's interference on the one hand, and by 'some ill-affected persons' in Cornwall on the other.[34]

On 18 June Sir Hugh Pollard, then at Exeter, had written to Colonel Seymour warning him not to reduce the strength of his Dartmouth garrison, as Grenville had requested, until the security of the town could be assured.[35] And whatever the intention had been to collect troops from Exeter, Dartmouth, Barnstaple, and Tiverton for Grenville's use in east Devon, threats of a parliamentary advance forced the return of these men to reinforce their respective garrisons.[36] Sir Richard appears to have taken this setback as a personal affront, and immediately threw up his new commission after informing the council that he desired a court-martial to clear his name, 'or else for leave to retire out of England'.[37] As it turned out, neither alternative was required.

Without any military authority beyond that of sheriff, Grenville moved to Ottery St Mary where he began to collect men and send out warrants for new recruits, using the posse comitatus as the core of a new army. Berkeley and the other commissioners took exception to this high-handed practice, and countermanded Grenville's orders, letting it be known that Sir Richard was to be obeyed only in his capacity as a county official.[38] Such being the case, the sheriff then sent out fresh warrants to those parishes within the vicinity of his quarters asking all those who had been 'plundered' by Berkeley to bring in statements of their grievances so that appropriate action could be taken. Such outrageous behaviour resulted in the Prince of Wales, who was now in Cornwall, calling Grenville for an interview in which the sheriff was told to stop interfering in military matters unless he was willing to accept orders from those placed above him. Grenville's behaviour in July improved remarkably, and he eventually began to work with Lord Goring to construct a consolidated army. But this co-operation lasted only a short time, as Goring's friendship with Berkeley soon turned Sir Richard against him.[39]

Dissension, quarrels, disputes were all working to destroy the royalist cause in the West faster than could any enemy force. Mutual recriminations prohibited active co-operation between officers whose major concerns were personal aggrandizement, profit, and glory, with little regard for the cause they served. General Goring was guilty of the especially serious error of antagonising not only his peers,[40] but also the very people whose support was essential to success—the entire body of Somerset and Devon royalists whose men and money were badly needed to carry on the struggle. Conditions became so bad in Somerset that on 15 June the prince was forced to write Goring a strong note recommending that determined steps be taken to curb the excesses of his men who plundered, took free billeting, and coerced the civilian population; and at the same time to take steps to encourage those who were favourably disposed to the royalist cause.[41] Grenville's forces were less often blamed for such outrages, but Sir Richard was not personally blameless. His reputation in both Devon and Cornwall was that of a strict disciplinarian and ruthless tyrant, who kept his men under control but looked to his own profit.[42] From whichever level of the army they came, the outrages perpetrated upon the people of the West Country were more than years of suffering could endure, and gradually produced the hostility which helped to destroy the well-laid plans of the prince's council and bring on the defeat of the entire party.

Speaking out in a letter addressed to Secretary Nicholas, Hyde expressed the regret sincerely felt by the council over the royalist defeat at Naseby earlier that month, but went on to indicate that help might yet come from the West.[43] Hyde would very much like to see Charles come there in person 'to prevent any mischief by Lord Goring', for that gentleman did nothing but drink and amuse himself. Goring appeared, in fact, to be devoting more time and effort intriguing against the prince's council than in active efforts against Plymouth.[44]

The western counties, long since weary of the exertion of sustaining one army after another and the expenses involved in weekly martial rates, were slow to bring in additional men and supplies for the new association army. The prince's council had to work against overwhelming odds to do what they could to keep alive a rapidly dying cause. But their efforts were vital as the king now had no other region to depend on, nor any other force that could provide certain support.

In early July the cavalier cause suffered another severe blow. Goring's forces had encountered the parliamentary army under Fairfax near Langport in Somerset where, on 10 July, they had been decisively defeated. Still in command of a force numbering more than 6,000 horse and foot, Goring retreated toward Bridgwater, and then into north Devon.[45] On 12 July he advised the

king's secretary, Lord Digby, that the only way to save Devon and
Cornwall was to collect into a single army all those royalist forces
then before Plymouth, in garrisons, or in trained-bands, throughout both counties and to confront the strong parliamentary army
then marching westward. If this could not be accomplished, Goring felt that the entire West would be lost. The royal council
quickly agreed to this plan, and immediately sent instructions
that it should be followed.[46]

But the threat to the West was not that imminent. Fairfax con-
tented himself with the capture of Bridgwater on 23 July which,
together with the other towns held in that region, effectively isolated royalist control to Devon and Cornwall.[47] Returning eastward, the parliamentary commander left the cavaliers to do what
they could to regroup their men and to fortify their position for
the inevitable struggle that lay ahead.

An increasingly desperate cause drove the royalist leaders to renewed efforts in the hope of raising a sufficient force with which to
confront the New Model Army when it advanced into Devon.
Berkeley sent out warrants to press men throughout the county,
while Hopton concentrated his efforts in the Exeter area and
Grenville worked directly in the South Hams and in Cornwall,
where the prince and his council were also active. Goring, meanwhile, had established his infantry at Torrington after having
called in additional forces from the surrounding hundreds.[48] At
the same time, the major body of Goring's horse was allowed to
take free quarter, and make themselves generally obnoxious, in
the region between Barnstaple, South Molton, and Torrington.[49]
The lack of discipline, and the inactivity of his men, together
with the declining confidence in the royalist cause, brought about
a rapid reduction in Goring's forces during the summer months.
He wrote repeatedly to the prince's council requesting funds with
which to pay his men in the hope of keeping them loyal to the
king.[50]

The need for drastic reform was obvious to all concerned,[51] and
for a change Goring took the lead. Temporarily enjoying good
relations with Grenville, he sent a series of recommendations to
the prince's council on 1 August which gave promise of raising an
army of 10,000 men from the Cornish deserters and Devonian
posse. The council immediately approved the idea and authorised
the two commanders to put their plan into action, giving Gren-

ville the responsibility for rounding up the forces.[52] But reports soon testified to the limited success of this latest royalist project. The Cornish were reluctant to rally to a cause which was obviously losing ground, or to leave their homes open to attack from parliamentarians and renegade royalists alike.[53] Goring, still quartered around Torrington during most of August, was reported to have a force of 5,000 foot and horse, but had to rely on the troops before Plymouth as well as in garrisons if he ever hoped to raise a major army.[54] Neither the trained bands nor the Devon posse appear to have added substantial numbers to Goring's infantry, regardless of the threats or fines imposed.[55]

The success of the parliamentary army under Sir Thomas Fairfax remained unchecked, and in August it was decided to postpone a campaign in Devon until the city of Bristol was taken. While the bulk of the force then took up the siege of that city, Major-General Edward Massey was sent to the Devon border to resist any efforts by Goring's army to bring relief.[56] With this enemy advance, the Exeter commissioners wrote to the prince's council asking for a conference to plan for an inevitable attack further west. On 25 August Lord Goring was informed that the prince would shortly arrive at Exeter in person to help provide for the supply of his forces, but that in the meantime all available troops in the county were to be called up for the relief of Bristol.[57] The attendance of the Prince of Wales was thought essential if ever the western army was to achieve some degree of unity and realise any success in recruitment and obtaining supplies.[58] But although Goring appears to have actually begun the march eastward for the relief of Bristol, he suddenly returned to Exeter during the last few days of August, and left the besieged city to its fate.[59]

The prince returned to Exeter on 28 August.[60] In addition to organising the defence of the region, his councillors were concerned to end the persistent rumour that the prince was planning to leave the country now that the royalist cause was in danger of collapse. A number of leading Devon gentry took this opportunity to petition the prince to intercede with parliament in the hope of arranging a peace on his own authority. Such a procedure, as Hyde and his colleagues well knew, would offend the king, and their efforts while in Exeter were directed toward quieting this faction.[61] To remove the prince from this ticklish situation, the council suggested that a petition be sent to Sir Thomas Fairfax for a safe-conduct so that Hopton and Colepeper might go to the king with 'such overtures for peace' as the prince thought desirable.[62]

When the shocking news of the fall of Bristol reached Exeter in mid-September, the prince's council was stung into renewed activity. A plan was hurriedly devised whereby Goring would push his horse through enemy lines to join the king who, together with Montrose's forces in Scotland, would then be in a better position to strike a last blow at London. On 19 September the Earl of Berkshire notified Goring that he was expected to march at once to the support of the king, as the prince's council fully expected to have sufficient forces raised in the near future to defend the West.[63] Goring, however, had no intention of leaving Devon, and his army remained in the same state of 'negligence and disorder' as before, while he, 'with the same license and unconcernedness remained at Exeter'.[64]

Presumably to excuse his disobedience, Goring asked for a meeting with Lord Colepeper and Sir John Berkeley in order to air the grievances and burdens under which he laboured in his attempts to build a strong army. Chief amongst his complaints was the insubordination of Sir James Smith, who had not only refused to obey orders, but actually disputed Goring's right to command.[65] The general also expressed his concern that he should not leave Devon until Grenville's Cornish forces had arrived, and the local garrisons had been reinforced. Not the least of his problems was the persistent lack of supplies and money with which to maintain the 1,850 foot which he had been able to muster.[66]

Privately Goring was still hoping to obtain full command, under the Prince of Wales, of all royalist forces in the West, with Grenville serving under him as commander of infantry. In late August he had sent Lord Wentworth to Launceston with a strong set of demands, but it was not until 29 September that Colepeper was asked to petition the prince for a direct answer regarding Goring's ambitions. The prince's council once again decided to follow Goring's advice with regard to military preparedness, granting Grenville additional command of the new levies, and taking care to collect provisions and equipment for the confrontation with Fairfax that was becoming inevitable.[67] Warrants were sent out to obtain loans from the king's loyal supporters in the two counties.[68] Early in October Goring again took the initiative and promised to curb the notorious excesses of his men in return for which the commissioners were to collect twice the weekly assessment of the counties for six weeks, and to give over half this sum for Goring's men.[69] But the plundering and free quarter of his troops did not cease, nor did Goring march eastward with his horse as the king had demanded. Instead, remaining in Exeter throughout October, the general repeatedly urged that Grenville and the Cornish foot be sent to him as soon as was convenient for a combined attack on the advancing parliamentary army, while on the 17th he finally notified the council that he was sending all but 1,000 horse further west in order to rendezvous with the Cornish foot.[70] Within the week, however, Goring decided to leave Exeter himself, and to regroup his cavalry before taking any action against the approaching enemy forces.[71] The prince's council, having nowhere else to turn, accepted with good grace the erratic behaviour of their leading commander, and ordered Grenville, then advancing toward Okehampton, to take his orders from Goring.[72]

The threat of imminent attack had once more spurred the royalist garrisons into active preparation for their defence. Berkeley petitioned the prince to be allowed to continue in his command at Exeter and thus promote the efforts for the protection of the city.[73] At the same time, the new governor of Dartmouth, Sir Hugh Pollard, requested 300 additional men from Edward Seymour's regiment, no doubt because of the trouble he had been having with the clubmen of the South Hams.[74] Grenville, although having lost the Cornish levies at the termination of their month's service, fortified his position at Okehampton where he remained as a significant barrier to Fairfax's weary army which had by then reached the river Exe.[75]

The month of November proved disastrous for the royalist cause. Although still in control of a formidable cavalry and ample infantry, in addition to having plenty of time to consolidate his position, Goring suddenly petitioned the prince for permission to leave his command for a two-month period so that he might withdraw into France to recover his health.[76] Sir Edward Hyde, for one, was delighted to see him go, attributing to Goring much of the confusion, disorder, and inertia in an army which could have become an effective fighting instrument if properly handled. For five months Goring had maintained a sizeable force in Devon,

much to the grief of that county, and yet done nothing construc-
tive for the advancement of his party or cause.[77] During the last
week of November, following Goring's departure, Sir Richard
Grenville suddenly abandoned his quarters at Okehampton and
retreated into Cornwall without any authorisation from the
prince's council. To make matters worse, he then set about preparing to defend that county against any incursion by soldiers
from Goring's forces, now under the command of Lord Wentworth
—'and so alienated all men's spirits towards the resistance of the
enemy'.[78] Such extraordinary and divisive behaviour brought a
demand from the prince, then at Truro, that Grenville explain
himself and recommend what was now to be done to hold the
West and preserve their cause.[79] In a letter in which Grenville
admitted to 'have occasioned a strange rumour in the world', he
suggested a plan which would in effect establish the Duchy of
Cornwall as a neutral region. According to Grenville's suggestion,
the prince should enter into a treaty with parliament to establish
their separate spheres of influence, each side promising not to
invade the other's territory.[80] Neither the prince nor his advisers
were attracted by this scheme and it appears to have received but
slight consideration.[81]

The council finally decided to collect what troops they could in
Cornwall and Devon, place them under the personal command of
the Prince of Wales, and then march east in order to relieve Exeter
and drive the parliamentarians out of Devon.[82] On 27 December
Prince Charles again crossed the Tamar and took up residence in
Devon, settling his court at Tavistock, and paying visits to Dartmouth and Totnes. From Tavistock a proclamation was issued to
the county on 29 December calling upon all able-bodied men to
attend the prince 'now advancing in person to meet the rebels'.[83]
While his troops were being recruited and brought together, provisions were collected at Totnes for the support of the entire
army.[84] Preparations proceeded satisfactorily into the new year,
when news reached the prince's court of the general advance of
Fairfax's army.[85] This intelligence dashed the cavalier plans, since
immediate opposition was impossible, and necessitated a rapid
retreat into Cornwall, with Wentworth's horse left to protect the
border.[86]

On 16 January Grenville bluntly told the council that the
decayed condition of the army and its desperate danger from

approaching parliamentary forces required the immediate appointment of a lieutenant-general who, under the prince, would command the entire army. Grenville recognised his own unpopularity, and suggested that Lord Hopton or Lord Brentford might be suitable for the responsibility of reconstructing an army to face the New Model.[87] That very day the prince notified Grenville of his acceptance of this suggestion, and that Hopton was to command as lieutenant-general, while Grenville took charge of the foot and Wentworth the horse.[88] Quite unexpectedly, however, Sir Richard informed the prince on 18 January that he was unable to accept such a position, 'believing he should be more serviceable to the Prince's affairs, if he were employed in recruiting the army, and guarding the passes of Cornwall'.[89] As Grenville would not reconsider his decision, the prince ordered his arrest rather than leave such a troublemaker free to do as he wished.[90] Equally surprising to the council was the easy acceptance by Lord Wentworth of the reorganisation of command.[91] Under a single commander-in-chief, the decision was then taken that the royalist army proceed immediately eastward toward the relief of Exeter and a confrontation with the parliamentarians.[92] After some delay this plan was carried out, but with unfortunate consequences.

On two separate occasions the king had given positive orders regarding the removal of his son if the prince were in any danger whatsoever, and on 7 December had sent definite instructions that Prince Charles was to leave immediately for the continent. In both instances, the council had considered such a move totally destructive to their plans. By early March, however, there was no longer any doubt that the royalist cause in the West was doomed. Therefore, on Tuesday, 3 March, the prince took ship to the Scilly Islands, where he arrived safely on the following day.[93]

Notwithstanding Hopton's final attempts to rally an ill-disciplined and disordered army, the king's cause in the West had been in a ruinous state for months. Quarrelling and bickering amongst leading officers had made a united effort impossible from the outset, and precious months were wasted when a sizeable body of horse and foot could have taken a severe toll of the enemy. The inability of Goring to take the initiative, or to follow orders, kept the horse uselessly trapped in Devon, coercing and plundering to the ruin of the countryside and the disgust of all those whom it was necessary for the cavaliers to cultivate if they expected con-

Ralph Lord Hopton

*George Lord Goring
and the
Earl of Newport*

tinued support. At the same time, this outrageous behaviour created the occasion for the rise of the clubmen who were to join with the parliamentarians in an effort to bring law and order out of chaos.[48]

Thus, from the beginning the hopes and expectations of the Prince of Wales and his council in the western counties had come to nothing. This was so not because of any fault on their part, but because of the inherent weakness of a cause upheld by individual commanders, independent of central command and supplied with conflicting commissions, with followers devoted to them and not to the cause for which they fought. Lack of unity within the army (and the inability to place merit in command above social position) combined with the fundamental weakness of a force based on the 'militia mentality' (dependent upon local committees and men unwilling to march far from home) to bring about almost certain royalist defeat.

Notes to this chapter are on page 219

K

Royalist Defeat in the West
october 1645-april 1646

On the brink of disaster the royalist force under the command of Lord Hopton was called upon to face the most effective military instrument of the entire war, the New Model Army. Originally proposed in November 1644, this army had actually come into existence in the spring of 1645 as a national body, well-disciplined, and regularly paid, to do parliament's bidding.[1] Under the command of Sir Thomas Fairfax, with Philip Skippon as major-general and Oliver Cromwell as lieutenant-general of horse, it was remarkably successful in its first campaign. By early October it was once again in the West Country, and actually crossed the borders of Devon on 14 October after having won a major victory at Naseby and taken the city of Bristol.[2] With most of England under parliament's control, Fairfax had been instructed on 22 September to take into consideration the state of the West, and particularly the safety of Plymouth, for which place the Committee of Both Kingdoms was greatly concerned.[3]

The task facing Fairfax was no mean one. His army must now contend with a large force of experienced horse and a considerable body of Cornish foot, many of whom had been put into strongly fortified garrisons throughout Devon. Exeter, Barnstaple, Dartmouth, and Torrington had been heavily reinforced, and care taken to strengthen forts at Tiverton, Salcombe, Exmouth, and Ilfracombe, as well as establish forces at a number of country houses.[4] In addition, the destruction of royalist forces elsewhere in England made it essential that the prince's council promote the royalist cause with all the resources at its disposal. Although the strongly parliamentarian element in Devon might aid in bringing about the capture of that county, the fiercely royalist Cornish

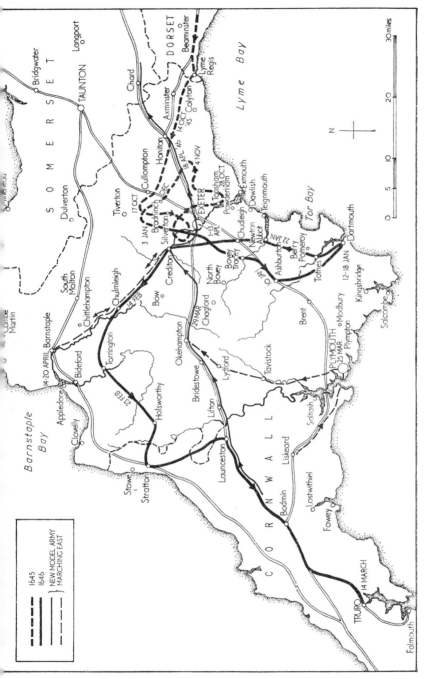

New Model Army in Devon, 1645-6

must also be tackled and could prove even more difficult when fighting on their own land.

On the other hand, Fairfax was well-informed about the disunity and dissension which was rampant within the royalist ranks, while also aware of the weakness which came from purely local forces, poorly disciplined and rarely paid.[5] It was no secret that the cavaliers were hard put to raise money and supplies, as the excessive plundering of the countryside gave testimony. The royalists paid nothing for what they took, and took whatever they wished from free quarter to farm produce and horses.[6] Such obnoxious habits, together with the looting of the troopers, had long since raised opposition from those who refused aid if they could, and joined bands of clubmen if they dared—doing anything to rid the county of Goring's horse.[7] By the autumn of 1645 the advance of the New Model was welcomed with relief by the majority of Devonians who were sick of war, desired a return to law, order, and protection of property, and did not care which side dominated as long as peace prevailed. Certainly, the fact that theirs was a losing cause did not help the royalist leaders in gathering recruits and in keeping their soldiers from deserting.[8]

Except for a damaging cavalry raid led by Goring and Wentworth at Blackdown on the night of 13 October, the parliamentary army was unopposed in their early advance into eastern Devon.[9] With the royalist cavalry retreating before them, Fairfax's forces moved to Honiton (via Axminster) on Tuesday, 14 October, and to Cullompton on Wednesday. At a council of war it was decided that Major-General Massey, together with Colonel Welden's brigade, should immediately advance to Tiverton in order to reduce that stronghold and block any effort on the part of the royalist horse to escape eastward to join the king.[10] On receiving word from Massey that the enemy forces at Tiverton refused to surrender, Fairfax called a council of war to determine whether to continue the march toward the relief of Plymouth, or to attack Tiverton immediately. It was decided that such a strategic fortification could not be permitted behind parliamentary lines, and that a sizeable force should go with the general to reduce it. The remainder of the army was posted at Bradninch, Silverton, and the mansion of Columbjohn in order to blockade the enemy forces in Exeter, and keep control of the passages over the river Exe.[11] With the region east of the Exe securely in parliamentary hands, the chances were greatly reduced that the enemy horse would be able to force their way eastward.

Reaching Tiverton on the 17th, Fairfax found batteries already in place against the 225 royalists in the castle and church. The enemy having refused a further summons to surrender, the lord general ordered an artillery attack begun in earnest on Sunday afternoon in preparation for an assault on the castle. During this barrage an accidental shot broke the chain holding up the draw-bridge into the castle and the parliamentarians poured across the bridge and into the compound. Taken completely by surprise, the royalists were easily brought to surrender without much further show of opposition. The governor, Sir Gilbert Talbot, wasted little time in turning over his command to Fairfax, along with the large quantity of arms and ammunition which had been stored there.[12]

Having easily secured this stronghold, the New Model continued its march on 20 October. Moving south toward Exeter, the entire army quartered for two nights in the Silverton area, just a few miles from the county town. At Silverton it was decided that the weather, and condition of the troops, would not permit the immediate advance toward Plymouth. Instead, Fairfax and his council determined to besiege Exeter in the hope of removing the threat of this well-fortified garrison. Following a personal examination of the enemy's defences, the lord general held another council of war on 21 October in which it was decided that the army should be split, some troops moving west of the Exe to Thorverton, and the rest to Stoke Canon.[13] That very night Goring took the opportunity still open to him and escaped from Exeter with most of his 1,000 horse, retreating toward Okehampton, and on to Tavistock, with the intention of joining the Cornish foot that Grenville was then recruiting.[14] Such a move was extremely wise as the parliamentarian intention was obviously to encircle Exeter, and establish a blockade to the west of the Exe as they had to the east. Unfortunately for this plan, heavy rains made it impossible for Fairfax to get his men from Newton St Cyres, where he arrived on 22 October, to Alphington (south of Exeter). Instead, a sudden change in plans brought his men to Crediton where they could rest, making it possible for Cromwell to bring up his cavalry to join the main body of the army.[15]

Attempts to decide on a plan of action for the parliamentary army took several days. For two days the council of war held continuous sessions to determine which of several possible courses would be most effective. It was finally agreed that, instead of marching further west to Plymouth, the army should return east of the Exe and there secure the blockade of Exeter, while taking in Topsham. Various reports had already assured the general that Plymouth was in no immediate need, nor was there any value in relieving that place only to be forced back into east Devon for winter quarters. It was also readily obvious that such a large enemy stronghold as Exeter would present a great danger in the rear of the army in any westward movement.[16] Besides, no one could doubt that the miserable weather conditions made this a most unsatisfactory time of year for further campaigning, especially in a notoriously rugged county, and with an army seriously weakened by illness. On balance, therefore, to confront an enemy reportedly equal in numbers, in a hostile territory, did not suggest itself as a wise plan.[17]

On Sunday afternoon (26 October) the parliamentarians returned to Silverton, and the next day marched on to Topsham. There it was decided that in order to block Exeter securely from all relief and supply from the east, garrisons should be established at Stoke Canon, Poltimore, along the river Clyst, at Bishop's Clyst and at Exmouth Castle at the mouth of the Exe.[18] Except for troops on garrison duty, the remainder of the army was withdrawn to Ottery St Mary to take up winter quarters.[19] In this fashion Exeter was completely cut off on the north and east, it being Fairfax's intention to secure this position, to relax his men, and to recruit the army before making any further westward advances.

Parliamentary headquarters were established at Ottery by 4 November, and there they remained for just over a month.[20] During this period Fairfax occupied his troops in securing their fortifications east of the Exe, making sure that no help reached Exeter from that side of the river, and that no enemy forces escaped eastward.[21] The lord general's primary concern was the well-being of his men, many of whom were dying from exposure as a result of the wet winter weather, as well as from lack of good clothing, adequate supplies, and sufficient quarters.[22] Meanwhile, encouraged by reports of growing parliamentarian weakness, the royalist forces were again regrouping at Tavistock and Okehampton for an attack which many hoped would again secure the county for the king.[23] But nothing came of this upsurge in energy and by the end of the month the leading royalists were in winter quarters at Truro.[24]

The weak condition of his forces was, of course, the chief motive for Fairfax's inactivity during November. But there were other factors to consider. An advance westward would bring on an encounter with a sizeable body of royalist horse still taking free quarter from the heart of Devon. This force, especially at this juncture in the war, must be confined to the Cornish peninsula, particularly now that the king had regained his headquarters at Oxford, and once again threatened the Midlands. Although too weak to fight the western royalists because of illness and lack of supplies, the parliamentarian commanders had also to consider what was to be done to safeguard the south east from enemy attack. A council of war held on 29 November determined to retain the newly secured Devon line of fortifications, while sending east as large a force as could be spared.[25]

His line of defence secure to the east of the Exe, Fairfax nonetheless decided to move westward in response to renewed enemy activity, and in the hope of finding improved surroundings for his sick men. On 7 December advance units were sent across the river to take possession of Crediton, and shortly afterwards the remainder of the forces left Ottery for Tiverton where Fairfax established his headquarters for the following month. One of the primary objectives of such a move was to do everything possible to shut Exeter off from further western aid. As a consequence, immediate efforts were made to fortify Crediton, and also to capture Powderham Castle, then being garrisoned by 150 royalists. Unable to take the castle, the parliamentarians threw themselves into the parish church which they proceeded to fortify, only to find themselves under fierce attack from royalist reinforcements. After three days of resistance, Sir Hardress Waller ordered his roundheads to withdraw (17 December), leaving this vital river fortification in enemy hands for the time being.[26]

During the next two weeks Fairfax tightened his grip around Exeter, extending his line of defences further to the south west of the city. As it was essential that Exeter be cut off from the provisions of the South Hams, parliamentarian forces took one after another of the great houses which could block these supply lines. Fulford House (six miles south west of Crediton) was easily cap-

tured and subsequently used as a base of operations against Canonteign (three miles north of Bovey Tracey) which was the scene
of sharp fighting early in the morning of 22 December.[27] Successfully driving off a sudden royalist attack, the parliamentary troops
at Canonteign were reinforced by men hurriedly sent up by Waller, and were soon able to establish their control over the area.
Several days later, Sir George Chudleigh's home of Ashton, across
the valley from Canonteign, was also occupied, reinforcing a line
of defence which ran from Tiverton in the north to Ashton in the
south west, and included Crediton, Great Fulford, and Canonteign.[28] With outposts thus established, the parliamentarians consistently harrassed the royalist garrison, going up to the very walls
of Exeter as they pleased.[29]

Just before Christmas definite word reached Fairfax's headquarters that the royalist army was in the process of massing at
Okehampton for a concerted attempt to relieve Exeter with great
stores of provisions.[30] Rather than wait for such an advance to
threaten their position, the parliamentarians decided in favour of
an immediate rendezvous, and an advance of their own with the
obvious intention of pushing further into the South Hams should
the opportunity present itself.[31] The mere show of force, however,
was sufficient to deter the make-shift and ill-prepared army which
the prince had intended to lead. With reports of the gathering of
parliamentary troops at Cadbury Hill, near Crediton, together
with the cold and snowy conditions which generally prevailed, the
royalist forces kept to their quarters and the New Model returned
to their camps.[32]

The early days of the new year were spent in continuous royalist
preparation, recruiting men and collecting supplies as best they
could. During this period the main body of horse occupied the
district around Ashburton, between the rivers Dart and Teign.
The main body of foot, mainly Cornishmen, was still in western
Devon, while others were being drawn up from Cornwall.[33] By
5 January the prince and his advisers were reportedly at Totnes
urging forward preparations for their army and for the relief of
Exeter. But apparently their great activity was not producing the
desired results as many men refused to come in to the army, and
a number of the Cornish actually deserted.[34] The startling energy
of those attempting to support a ruined cause brought the parliamentarian council of war once more into session. This time it was

decided to push west as quickly as possible in order to engage the enemy, so as to disperse their forces or to drive them further down the peninsula and thus free Plymouth from continued harassment.[35] Once in control of the South Hams, and especially Dartmouth, the parliamentarians could cut off the vital supplies which supported the faltering royalist party, and at the same time remove from enemy hands a port which might act as a base for future invasion. On 8 January the New Model, fully outfitted with shoes and stockings, began its advance after more than a month of inactivity. To mislead the enemy, Sir Hardress Waller moved toward Okehampton, and actually engaged some royalists at Bow.[36] The bulk of the army, however, while leaving a sufficient rearguard, moved off towards the South Hams.[37] On Friday evening, 9 January, Cromwell led a body of horse and foot in the direction of Bovey Tracey, where three regiments of Lord Wentworth's horse were quartered. Entering the village after dark, the parliamentarians took the enemy completely by surprise, catching a number of officers playing cards. Although many of the royalists were able to escape into the night, some 400 horse were captured.[38]

On Saturday the army continued on to Ashburton, only to find the royalists had abandoned that town shortly before. The same was true for Totnes and other south Devon villages which the royalists evacuated in their flight.[39] From throughout the county reports were received of the complete collapse of enemy opposition, the panic and defeat which had been experienced at Bovey Tracey being enhanced as fleeing troopers carried exaggerated stories of enemy strength. To keep them pressed, Fairfax sent out parties of horse to harrass their quarters and to hurry them on their way westward, as he moved the bulk of his forces to the siege of Dartmouth.[40] The flight of the royalist horse was quickly followed by the retreat of their foot.[41] By 13 January the forces still besieging Plymouth drew off for the last time and joined their comrades across the Tamar.[42] After three years of continuous siege, Plymouth was at last freed.

Dartmouth having rejected their summons, Fairfax's army spent the week of 12 to 18 January preparing to storm the town.[43] By the end of the week, with additional help arriving from Plymouth and from the fleet blockading the harbour, all was ready for the final assault. About 11 o'clock on the night of 18 January, the weather having greatly improved, Fairfax launched his attack and,

within hours, had successfully captured the entire town, its fortifications, and the old castle.[44] Taking refuge in the fort called
Gallant's Bower at the mouth of the harbour, Governor Sir Hugh
Pollard hoped to hold out against the enemy, while Sir Henry
Cary made Kingswear Fort secure across the river. Cary was persuaded to give up a hopeless struggle, notwithstanding his strongly
entrenched position. With all support lost to him, Pollard agreed
to surrender on the following day. In addition to the many prisoners and large quantities of arms and supplies captured, Fairfax
had within a short time eliminated this essential royalist storehouse and port.[45] With Dartmouth gone, the cherished cavalier
hopes of aid from France could no longer be sustained.[46] At the
same time, the relief of Exeter was once again thwarted, as the
advance of the New Model into the South Hams forced the enemy
to retreat into Cornwall. The moderation of the parliamentarians
in their treatment of the captured town, and in the freedom
granted the Cornish prisoners, created a favourable impression on
those already disillusioned with the continuing struggle.[47]

Events soon showed that the disenchanted were becoming ever
more numerous. Clubmen were already growing in strength
throughout the county, no longer taking a neutral position, but
actively supporting the parliamentarian cause.[48] More expressive
of the growing sentiment toward peace and parliament was the
overwhelming number of recruits who presented themselves at
Totnes on 24 January in response to warrants sent out by the lord
general to the four neighbouring hundreds. From the 3,000 men
who appeared, Fairfax selected 1,000 to form a new regiment
under Colonel Fowell, whose task was to remain at Totnes and
guard the South Hams from further royalist interference.[49] In this
way, the bulk of the New Model was free to continue the siege of
Exeter, and proceed against the Barnstaple stronghold as well as
the royalist cavalry still in the county.

Fairfax's men continued to encircle Exeter and to increase the
pressure of their blockade. On the 25th Powderham Castle was
captured, and additional guards were also set up at Alphington,
Barley House, and other nearby quarters.[50] Completely surround-
ed, the people of Exeter were experiencing great difficulty in keeping up the courage necessary to withstand the siege, at the same
time suffering a shortage in food and supplies which caused prices
to increase three-fold.[51] Trade had come to a halt, and the inhabit-

ants had to make do with the livestock they already had, while trying to smuggle in whatever additional food they could through loopholes in the enemy lines. Further, concern for the safety of the infant Princess Henrietta was increasing, although no effort appears to have been made to take her out of the country.[52]

Hoping to take Exeter quickly, Fairfax did not wait long after the conquest of Dartmouth to summon the county town. On 27 January he sent a message to Sir John Berkeley attempting to persuade him of the hopelessness of his situation and the futility of expecting aid either from the king at Oxford or the prince in Cornwall. Instead, the lord general was willing, in exchange for Exeter's surrender, to allow each man his freedom to return to his home, or to leave the country if he would swear never again to fight against parliament.[53] The following day Berkeley replied to this offer, in a polite but negative fashion, stressing the obligation which he had to the king to hold the city, and pointing out how probable was some relief from the large forces still under the prince in both Devon and Cornwall.[54] Seizing upon this 'modest denial', Fairfax responded immediately, suggesting to Berkeley that he take a greater concern for the well-being of the citizens of Exeter who had suffered enough during the war, and accept the conditions so generously offered. The lord general was confident that his recommendations to parliament would serve to mitigate the punishment which the defenders of Exeter might suffer.[55]

At his headquarters at Chudleigh, Fairfax received word on 29 January of the westward penetration of a portion of the king's horse from Oxford. At the same time, he obtained information that the royalist horse in north Devon were again attempting to push eastward and join with those from Oxford. Realising through intercepted correspondence that the enemy could expect no immediate aid from France while their western army was wracked with internal dissension, the lord general and his council decided once again to postpone their attack on Exeter, and leave it securely blocked up while the army marched westward.[56]

It was only on 8 February that the parliamentarians learned the extent of the danger confronting them, and realised that a general massing of royalist forces under Lord Hopton was taking place.[57] The obvious intention of this effort was to relieve Exeter and join with the Oxford horse in an attempt to recapture the West. In this strategy, Barnstaple was to be used as the base of operations

and Hopton moved in that direction, rather than by way of Okehampton as had been previously attempted. With north Devon
securely in royalist hands, there would be some hope of bringing
in additional aid from Wales or Ireland.[58] The lord general therefore decided to advance in person into the northwestern part of
Devon with a force of some 9,500 horse and foot, hoping this time
to completely destroy the royalist armies.[59]

On 14 February the New Model Army, having left their baggage
and heavy equipment at Crediton, reached Chulmleigh, on the
road to Great Torrington which Hopton had fortified four days
before. Hindered by wet weather, the parliamentarians were unable to make much progress until the 16th when they moved into
the vicinity of Ashreigney where a general rendezvous was held.
In the meantime, Colonel Cook had been sent toward Barnstaple
with a sufficient party to blockade that town and prevent reinforcements from moving to Hopton's aid.[60]

Although hearing of the parliamentarian advance quite by ac-
cident, Hopton was unwilling to retreat before the superior force.
He knew quite well of Cornwall's inability to support his army,
and particularly of the Cornish desire to be rid of Goring's horse.
Besides, Hopton had been ordered to engage the enemy if at all
possible, and this would probably be the last favourable opportunity.[61]

Driving the royalists from the Rolle mansion of Stevenstone (16
February), the parliamentary vanguard pressed the enemy back
into Torrington where the bulk of the royalists were quartered.
Toward evening both sides lined the hedges and lanes between
Stevenstone and Torrington with their 'forlorn hope of foot', supported by horse and dragoons, so as to be prepared for any advance. About 9pm Fairfax sent out a party to make sure the enemy
was not withdrawing from the town. These men, faced with heavy
firing from the royalist outposts, were quickly reinforced. Within
a short time the two armies were completely engaged in a struggle
for possession of Great Torrington. Long into the night the royalists kept up a fierce fight to defend their position, on several
occasions using their horse to drive out the invaders. Continued
reinforcements eventually told against the Cornishmen who, under cover of night and with their cavalry as a rearguard, made
good their retreat over the river Torridge. No sooner had the
parliamentarians taken possession of the town, than the place was

rocked by the explosion of almost 50 barrels of gunpowder stored in the parish church. The explosion killed 200 royalists imprisoned there, as well as their guards, and very nearly caused the death of Sir Thomas Fairfax.[62] A royalist counter-attack was attempted in the growing confusion, but the Cornish foot took this opportunity to escape into the countryside and were soon outdistanced by their own horse.[63]

Lord Hopton was quick to blame the Cornishmen for the defeat of his army, but parliamentary sources were just as ready to praise them for brave and valiant conduct on the battlefield. All accounts of the fighting remark on the fierocity of the hand-to-hand combat that went on for hours before the parliamentarians finally broke into the town. Even at this late stage of the war, the courage and steadfastness of the Cornish in support of the royal cause had not completely faltered. The superiority of the parliamentary foot, in numbers and in discipline, as opposed to the ill-trained Cornish levies, was bound to carry the day in any pitched battle. At the same time, Hopton himself commented upon the independent nature of his horse, as opposed to the tight discipline of Cromwell's 'Ironsides'.[64] Notwithstanding the reasons, the royalist defeat at the battle of Great Torrington was disastrous for their cause, and in effect brought about its downfall. The cavalier infantry had been decimated and could never be regrouped to anything like its former strength. Morale was struck a fatal blow. And, by falling back on Cornwall, the horse which Goring had commanded found themselves the hated representatives of a dying crusade, quartered on a county which was ill-prepared to maintain them. Besides, Fairfax's New Model Army would eventually drive the royalists into a corner, and they knew it. The events at Great Torrington had destroyed the last effective royalist army in England, and its defeat meant the end of the first Civil War. This occurred notwithstanding the fact that the royalists could still muster more than 4,000 horse, a body which had not been defeated but had hung like a leech on the counties of Devon and Cornwall for months, effecting nothing but discord and raising hostility wherever it went.

Once in Cornwall Hopton received initial orders to defend the borders around Stratton, but was soon convinced that he should collect what men he could and continue further west, nourishing the hope of help from France.[65] Meanwhile, having rested his men and reinforced the troops blockading both Exeter and Barnstaple, Fairfax determined to advance into Cornwall in pursuit of the remnants of Hopton's troops. Intercepted news of possible troops from France, as well as the realisation that the Devon garrisons would surrender more quickly if all hope of relief were denied them, made this strategy necessary.[66]

By 23 February the New Model Army was on the move once again. The advance units pressed the royalists out of west Devon and into Cornwall, taking great care to avoid antagonising the civilian population. The lord general was anxious that all provisions obtained and quarter received be paid for in full, that discipline be strictly maintained, and that looting be avoided. Fairfax was careful to ask parliament for sufficient funds to carry out this policy, and to bring with him many of the county's parliamentary leaders so as to use their influence to re-establish control.[67] Further, the fact that he had sent home all Cornish prisoners with two shillings (10p) in their pockets after Torrington, as he had done after taking Dartmouth, was expected to convince many that parliamentary order was infinitely preferable to royalist tyranny. Early in March, the popularity of the parliamentary cause was enhanced in the eyes of many West Countrymen with news from captured letters that, notwithstanding all peace negotiations then in progress, Charles was actively working to bring in Irishmen to help subdue the kingdom.[68]

By such means as these, Fairfax was eventually successful in subduing Cornwall to his control. Having blocked the enemy from any means of escape into Devonshire, the lord general pursued Hopton's ever-dwindling army from Stratton to Launceston to Truro.[69] Every day more and more Cornishmen submitted to parliament's authority, either offering active support against the royalists, or merely acquiescing in a wave of victory they were powerless to halt.

Unable to recruit men, Hopton was finally obliged, especially after the departure of the Prince of Wales, to permit negotiations with the enemy, while retreating with his foot to Pendennis.[70] Fairfax's comments to Speaker Lenthall summarized the general amazement over the easy success in the West Country:

> Truly, Sir, this must needs be acknowledged for an admirable mercy from the same gracious hand of Providence that hath hitherto gone along with you, that so considerable a force as this should be so

baffled, first at Torrington, and afterwards should put themselves, as it were, into a net; whereby they were necessitated to take terms, to the utter ruin of so great a body of cavalry; which, according to all our information, and the confession of our enemies, was not less at the time of the treaty [ie, 14 March] than 4 or 5,000 horse.[71]

If the royalist horse had attempted either to engage the enemy at any time during their long months in Devon, or to break through to join the Oxford horse, the war might well have been prolonged and the outcome altered. Their failure to do either proved fatal to the king's cause. No wonder then that this success in the West was for Sprigg 'the subject of greatest admiration and thankfulness'.[72]

Leaving behind sufficient force to threaten the isolated royalist strongholds which still held out, Fairfax immediately ordered the bulk of his army to return into Devon.[73] On 25 March Fairfax, Cromwell, and some of the principal officers made a triumphant entry into Plymouth to receive the congratulations of the citizens and troops that had been trapped there for three years. Resting in Plymouth until Friday, the lord general then moved on to Okehampton where he joined his army, and advanced with them to Crediton on 29 March. The major parliamentary objective now was the conquest of Exeter which, without the hope of any relief, was extremely vulnerable, as were the other royalist strongholds in the county. Moving swiftly, the New Model was tightly drawn up around Exeter, sealing off any possibility of adverse enemy activity.[74]

On the last day of March Fairfax summoned Sir John Berkeley to surrender his charge into the hands of the parliamentary forces. The general pointed out that there could be no reasonable expectation of relief for his garrison and, to prevent bloodshed, it would be best to surrender immediately. Following a conference held between his own council of war and the representatives of the Exeter Chamber, Berkeley replied on 1 April that he was ready to negotiate with the parliamentarians in order to obtain 'just and honourable terms', and nominated ten men to act as commissioners for the royalist side. On Thursday Fairfax replied that the number of commissioners suggested was too large, and recommended that each side appoint only six men. This settled, safe-conducts were issued, and the commissioners began their work at Poltimore House, three miles outside the city, on Friday, 3 April.[75]

Originally hoping for a quick settlement of terms, the parliamentarians found themselves negotiating until Wednesday, 8 April. A great deal of time was spent attempting to reduce the royalist demands, particularly with regard to the security of the cathedral and its personnel, and those who were especially notorious in their support of the king.[76] Notwithstanding many in the city who opposed surrender even at this late date, most of the inhabitants were weary of the senseless struggle and the royalist commissioners were forced to listen to reason. Terms of surrender were finally agreed upon, and were signed by both Fairfax and Berkeley on 9 April. Once hostages and places of security had been exchanged, the lord general left for Barnstaple, leaving Cromwell behind to accept the surrender of the city on Monday, 13 April.[77]

The articles agreed upon for the surrender of Exeter were generous indeed. Although the entire city, castle, and fortifications, along with all provisions, supplies, and weapons were to be turned over to the parliamentarians, all officers, soldiers, and civilians who desired to do so were permitted to leave the city on 13 April to go to their own homes or retire out of England, having taken an oath not to fight against parliament. As recipients of the benefits of these articles, all those who had supported the king were to be allowed to compound with parliament for their transgressions, Fairfax proposing a compensation reckoned at two years' value of their estates. Those who remained in Exeter were guaranteed protection against plundering, and the cathedral, churches, and clergy were granted a special pledge of security. To assuage any apprehension of the citizens, all charters, privileges, and property previously held and enjoyed by any individual or corporation were to be safeguarded for the future. Further, the Princess Henrietta, together with her household, was to be at liberty to leave the city and go wherever her governess and the king should decide.[78] Fairfax could afford to be generous; he had taken the major enemy stronghold in the West without a shot being fired.

The capitulation of Exeter was soon followed by the surrender of Barnstaple, as had been expected. Fairfax summoned the town on Friday, 10 April, and received an immediate reply that the governor was willing to negotiate. Saturday and Sunday were spent in agreeing on conditions of capitulation which, in the event, were quite similar to those recently granted to Exeter.[79] Thus, on 14 April the town and castle of Barnstaple were sur-

The Pourtraicture of his Excellency S: Thomas Farfax Generall of all the English forces for the Seruice of ye two houses of Parliament.

Gull. Faithorne Sculp.

Sir Thomas Fairfax

Sir Edward Hyde

rendered by Sir Allen Apsley, and six days later the fort, with its extensive magazine, was also turned over. Fairfax did not wait to take part in the formalities, but attempted to return to Exeter to accept the surrender of that city. Rain prevented his returning on time, but from the 14th until the 17th he remained in the county town and took care for its future government. Saturday, 18 April, the lord general led the New Model out of Exeter and began the march eastward, now to take up the siege of Oxford as the last remaining obstacle to parliamentary supremacy in England. Colonel Robert Hammand, with a regiment of Devonian recruits, was left to secure Exeter and Devon for parliament.[80]

Except for Fort Charles at Salcombe, all of Devonshire was once again in the hands of parliament. On 9 May, with the surrender of Fort Charles, the county was completely within the control of the conquering parliamentarians.[81] And, on 18 August, with the signing of the articles for the surrender of Pendennis Castle in Cornwall, the entire West Country was freed from royalist control. The House of Commons lost no time in securing their domination over this area, having in February issued instructions to western MPs to return to their homes and begin the work which was to launch Devon on a fourteen-year path of non-monarchical government.[82]

The reorganised New Model Army had achieved wonders, often against superior odds in a hostile and unfamiliar country, and under conditions of horrible weather, rough terrain, and widespread disease. But, disciplined and regularly paid, they had prevailed against a gallant, but disorderly force which had incessantly quarrelled amongst themselves, refused to fulfill obligations or carry out orders, and had completely alienated their most faithful supporters and necessary adherents. If the royalists had been able to learn from the enemy in time to achieve greater internal unity, or if substantial help had been received from abroad, the end of the war might have been prolonged. Certainly Devon and Cornwall could not be expected to carry the burden alone, not against the rest of England, and not without sweeping changes in the attitude and organisation of the royalist party.

Notes to this chapter are on page 224

Epilogue

From the outset of the First Civil War it was necessary for king and parliament to control Devon and Exeter if they were to dominate the West Country, with its ports, populace and wealth. Whichever side controlled Devon controlled the fate of the entire peninsula, and thus an important portion of England. The king had to have Devon if he expected to make full advantage of the well of sympathy in Cornwall; the parliament had to make sure that the Cornishmen remained isolated. The royalists increasingly needed Devonian wealth and men to build armies, to capture London, and to carry on the war. The opposition could not allow Devonian strength to be added to Cornish zeal, nor permit Plymouth to be removed as the thorn in the royal side. Charles felt it imperative to maintain an avenue to the continent and Ireland for eventual fulfillment of his plans for foreign relief; while Pym and parliament could not allow such a route to exist nor such an important area of the country to escape their authority. However one approached the subject, it appeared that neither side could do without Devon and its county town of Exeter without thus sustaining grievous harm to the success of its cause.

Throughout the early period of the conflict, and to an important degree throughout the entire war, there is evidence of a great and continuing desire on the part of most Devonians to stop civil strife before it became endemic in the country, to isolate and neutralise their area, or to remain personally aloof if these methods did not work. Although civil war had been slower in spreading to the West Country than to the more populous areas close to London, a few leading Devonians were swift to take sides and eager to take action. In the main, the larger towns and boroughs came to support the parliamentarian position, although Exeter, Barnstaple, and Dartmouth contained large royalist minorities. The county gentry generally favoured the king, and in the South Hams, especially around Dartmouth, cavalier strength was great.

Parliamentarian influence (outside the towns) was soon centred in northern and eastern Devon.

Once engaged, the people of Devon and Exeter contributed as much as any when forced, first to the parliamentary side, and then to the royalist, often giving what was demanded but sometimes vainly attempting to go their own way. But it is important to emphasise that the majority of the people in these counties did not want civil war, had no selfish purpose in promoting such a war, and were anxious to bring it to an end as soon as possible. The early petitions and actions of the two counties show this, and the continued sufferings of the besieged cities, the plundered towns, the over-taxed populace, and the ejected clergy, as well as the shifting of loyalties from one side to the other, all point to this desire for peace and an uninterrupted existence, which neither party could permit. Any irritation or grievance felt as a result of the eleven years of 'Personal Rule' became easily overshadowed by the continued horrors and tragedies of a war which few wanted but in which the many became involved.

Although the parliamentarian faction gained a solid head-start in the struggle for control of the county and its urban centres, including Exeter, the royalists were able to make a sufficiently strong come-back to maintain their authority in the area from late 1643 until the spring of 1646. This period of dominance mirrors some of the greatest royalist mistakes. Their failure to organise the financial or military strength of the county, to settle quarrels amongst their own leaders, and to reconstruct an efficient administrative machinery all point to severe weaknesses generally inherent within the royalist party throughout England. For it was parliament's ability to master the financial and organisational problems of this war which brought it ultimate success. Plymouth, moreover, was never in royalist hands, and this factor was of great significance because of the vital position of that town, and its importance in hindering the royalist cause. Not only did its blockade tie up men and supplies, and cause endless friction among royalist commanders, but the fact that it held out afforded a major distraction to Cornishmen and Devonians who refused to travel far from their homes with this sore-spot yet uncaptured. While Plymouth was in enemy hands, royalist sea traffic was limited, if not impossible.

There is no doubt that those who led in the struggle in the

1640s did so out of deep-seated feelings which went well beyond the fairly superficial level of grievances suffered over the past years. Grievances had existed in the past and had been endured. But Devon MPs—such as John Pym, Oliver St John, John Maynard, Edmund Prideaux—saw and grasped the opportunity provided them to destroy the potential royal despotism *before* it was fairly well established, or before circumstances readily permitted its continuation. The order which they aimed to establish was by no means clearly outlined in their own minds as they drifted slowly, but inevitably, into conflict with their sovereign during the early days of the Long Parliament, and dragged the rest of England along with them.

By 1642 thinking men, and men of conscience, in Devon as elsewhere in England, were cruelly torn in the face of a decision which had to be made. On the one side were those motivated by a profound devotion to the royal dispensation, to an Episcopal Church as a necessary foundation for social order, and to the ancient constitution of the realm as viewed from a traditional standpoint. On the other side were those activated by a no less profound loyalty to a parliament which came to be considered the repository of, and safeguard for, the liberties and freedom of the English people, to be supported by a reformed puritan church. Although in 1640 many from both sides saw the old patterns shifting, by 1642 the men of Devon and Exeter—along with those of the rest of the country—had to decide which view of the past they would support, and ultimately whether they would find themselves reaching backward, or into the future.

But for many ordinary Devonians, those without personal influence or authority, it had seemed that events and circumstances were dragging them ever deeper into participation in a conflict which made little sense, and which allowed some men to change loyalties as easily as they would have changed horses. Feeling little but a concern for the everyday necessities of life—often enough interrupted by strange and threatening forces—the masses of people in the two counties spent the years 1640-6 merely going about their ordinary business, participating when impressed, paying when forced, avoiding what they could—always hoping to be left alone. As with men of every generation, Devonians were concerned first and foremost with their own homes, with their communities, and with their county—after that might come concern for king and parliament.

The period from August 1642 to April 1646 was disastrous for the people of Devon and Exeter. Devonshire was criss-crossed by armies time and again, cities were besieged for months, and in the case of Plymouth for years. Inhabitants of the two counties were impressed into the military units of both sides without consideration for their feelings or opinions. Ratepayers and citizens were persistently taxed and plundered; they had property confiscated, stolen, and destroyed. Months of free quarter and free provisions reduced Devon's produce and Exeter's trade, and limited the ability of many to maintain themselves at anything but subsistence level. These factors were not unique for Devon and Exeter, but that did not mitigate the suffering endured.

By the spring of 1646 parliament had won the civil war. Nonetheless, many parliamentarians had sustained heavy loss from aid given freely to the cause, confiscations by the enemy or their own navy, loss of public office and income from estates long kept in royalist hands. Plymouth probably suffered more than any other stronghold, but Exeter, Barnstaple, Dartmouth, and other towns were also subjected to the hardships of siege and the expense of fortifications. The cavaliers, having enjoyed a dominant position in the two counties for the majority of the war, in their turn would now suffer civil disabilities through loss of office and privileges as citizens, loss of property through sequestration and confiscation, and heavy fines through compounding with parliament for their past political sins. Old grudges would now be settled as the power shift within county and county town replaced royalist sympathisers with those who had long suffered under cavalier control. Prolonged law suits would get underway, and complex negotiations would be the order of the day as the rancorous and the revengeful would seek to strike back at those who had caused them dislocation or humiliation, and from whom they now could obtain profit.

Both sides, however, felt the effects of the 1646 plague, and cavalier and roundhead alike would face years of change, repressive military rule, and taxation of unprecedented stringency. Although tired of military occupation, the citizens of Exeter would have to endure further years of garrison. As their city was regarded as central to the maintenance of control in the West, it would continue to be strongly fortified, thus making impossible any serious royalist uprisings in the region. With the outbreak of the Second Civil War in 1648 in Wales and elsewhere, additional troops were rushed to Devon to ensure the security of the West Country. Although resentful at the additional burden, Devon and Exeter remained peaceful under this rule, with no serious outbreaks occurring despite continuous rumblings and mutterings on the part of royalist sympathisers. Many within the two counties were obviously unhappy with the vigour of puritan administration, the interference in private lives and pleasures, and the increased expense of garrison support, but the region would ride out this period of renewed civil strife without major incident. Their important part in national history had been played in the 1642-6 war, and it would now be a matter of waiting and hoping for better days and a return to constitutional government.

Appendices

A

Extracts from the Exeter Sessions, 1642

The following extracts have been taken from ERO, Sessions of the Peace, Book 64. These entries from October to December 1642 reveal some of the internal problems faced by the parliamentary authorities in the city during the period of the Cornish threat:

19 OCTOBER 1642 (f17)   Richard Rosser of this City, yeoman, being charged yesterday before Mr Alderman Bennett by one Mr Willes of Saltash for speaking divers seditious words yesterday . . . to the said Mr Willes at the house of Richard Kelly of this City, Innkeeper, tending to the great danger of this City; viz, that he would go this day to Launceston to the Cavaliers there; and that he knew three several places in this City where they might enter . . . [He being examined] confessed he said that he thought they might more easily enter the City at the Eastgate, Westgate, or Northgate of the said City than at the Castle. And that in the speaking thereof he meant no hurt to the City, but in regard that those words are conceived of such ill consequence as may occasion too much freedom in others to further the surprisal of this place, he is ordered to be committed to his Majesty's prison.

2 NOVEMBER (f18)   Robert Sprague, one of the Constables of the East quarter . . . of this City, informed that he being at the East gate of this City this afternoon when divers of Captain Pym's Company were at the said Gate to come into this City, the said Gate was shut. And there being order given by Mr Mayor and some other of the Deputy Lieutenants of this City for the said Captain Pym's Company to come into the said City, this inform-ant saw Emanuell Vigures, haberdasher, then one of the

watchman of the Gate, to keep the said Gate fast whereby the said company were not admitted entrance notwithstanding the foresaid order; for which cause he is
ordered by the said Justices to be committed to the Gaol.

John White of the said City, Merchant, informed that
he was also present at the time and place aforesaid, and
saw one William Dowrich, sadler, one other of the said
watchmen at the said Gate to lay his hands upon the said
Gate to put it fast contrary to the order given . . . ; for
which cause it is also ordered by the said Mayor and
Justices that he shall be likewise committed to the Gaol.

And it is also ordered by the said Mayor and Justices
that both the houses of the said Vigures and Dowrich
shall be searched and their arms to be seized according to
the Ordinance of Parliament lately made in that behalf,
and the same to be put in safety.

Nicholas Carwithie of the City of Exeter, grocer, informed that he coming to the house of the said Emanuell
Vigures with the Constables to seize his arms, according
to the order of the aforesaid Justices, John Vigures, cord-
wainer, his son, having a birding piece in his hand
charged with powder and a bullet, presented the same
against Captain Lovering who, putting the same from
him, the said John Vigures thrust the said piece against
this Informant's breast to his great fear and terror; for
which cause it is likewise ordered that he be likewise
committed to his Majesty's prison.

16 NOVEMBER (f20)   Henry Brayne of this City, yeoman, informed that about the 7th day of this instant
November, he supped at the house of Nicholas Coombe
within the County of this City in the company of
Thomas Warner, worstedcomber, and others, at which
time and place this Informant heard the said Warner to
say: That he did think that all those that had made
those works in Exeter for the defence of the City to keep
out the King and his company would be hanged for
their labour, and he did hope so, as the Minister or
Mayor of Bambury was.

William Fill of this City, fuller, informed that he casually meeting with the said Thomas Warner yesterday in
the morning without the Westgate of this City, the said
Warner told this Informant that he had been to drink a
health to the King and his Cavaliers. . .

Sam Clarke of this City, fuller, informed that he also yesterday in the morning met with the said Thomas Warner, who then told this informant that he had been to drink a health to the King and the Cavaliers, and to the confusion or condemnation of the Roundheads and the volunteers; for which several offences of the said Thomas Warner shall be committed to his Majesty's prison.

Edmond Pafford and Philip Richards of this City, worstedcombers, inform that they being at the house of Edward Cheeke of this City, Brewer, they heard one Philip Job an apprentice of the said Edward Cheeke there to say: That the Parliament's Laws were not worth a turd; for which the said Philip Job is ordered by the aforesaid Justices to be committed to his Majesty's Gaol.

19 NOVEMBER (f21) William Hopping of this City, Locksmith, informed that there being an order given by the Deputy Lieutenants ... to seize the arms of several persons within this City, he was required by Captain Evans to go to the house of William Tayler ... in assistance to the Constables in the seizing of the said Tayler's arms. And that Richard Mountstephyn, one of the said Constables, being come to the said Tayler's house for that purpose and the said Tayler being in his shop, the said Mountstephyn went into the said shop unto him, and by virtue of a warrant granted unto him ... required the said Tayler to deliver his arms to him, which the said Tayler refused to do and required the said Mountstephyn to depart out of his shop, and took up a boot staff in his hand and offered to strike the said Mountstephyn therewith, and throwing that staff on the ground took up an iron hammer in his hand and by his threatenings and the assistance of a servant ... forced the said Constable out of the ... shop. And then the said Tayler took up a dresser in his hand and swore by God's blood that he would throw the same to the said Constable's head, and said often they were a Company of Roundheads and Counterfits...

Adam Bennett the younger, Merchant, informed that he being casually in the Churchyard of St Peter's Church this present day and seeing the Constables and others endeavouring to convent the foresaid Tayler before the Deputy Lieutenants of this City at the Guildhall, the Constables were much opposed. Whereupon Mr Gould,

the Sheriff of this City, being then also present required
this informant to assist the said Constables, which this
Informant endeavouring to perform the same and willing the said Tayler's wife to forebear to lay any violent
hands on the Constables, the said Tayler's wife did spit
in this Informant's face, and called him Traitor, and said
he was against the King, and that she did not doubt but
one time or other to meet with this informant and fit him
a penny worth, and did scorn that her son should be an
excommunicated Rogue, as this Informant was. . .

29 NOVEMBER (f22)   John Brookes of Uffculme in the
County of Devon, Carpenter, and Gyles Brooke of the
same parish, husbandman, inform that they with others
now soldiers under Captain Weare, coming this morning
to the house of George Edmunds in this City to buy a
pair of stockings, the said Edmunds demanded of them
where they were bound. Unto whom these informants
answered they knew not. Then he asked them whether
they were going against the Cornish, these informants
said they thought they were. Whereunto the said Edmunds replied that he wished these informants to return
home again to their wives for the Cornish would set
wildfires in their tails. Whereupon one Robert Gill another of these informants' company said he thought there
were but 1,500 of them, but the said Edmunds said they
should find ten thousand of them when they came there.

8 DECEMBER (f24)   Allan Penny suspected to be an ill-
affected person to the peace of this City and endeavouring to labour others to do the same . . . [committed to
gaol].

Roger Treble, Fuller, being a wardsman this day
appointed at the Castle, is complained of by William
Spillar, Richard Mountstephyn, and others for cutting
down the rails and fortifications at the Castle, is ordered
also to be committed to his Majesty's said prison also.

24 DECEMBER (f27) . . . George Stone of the parish of
St Edmunds within the County of the City of Exeter,
Brewer, being complained of for sending of beer and ale
into the Country unto those places that give entertain-
ment to the Cavaliers and their adherents whereby they
are encouraged to persist in those ways, which is conceived by the Mayor and Deputy Lieutenants of the said
City to be of ill consequence to the said City.

B

Members of Parliament for Devon and Exeter, 1640-6

Twenty members were returned for Devon and Exeter as a result of the original elections held for the November Parliament in 1640. But within weeks of the first meeting of what was to become the Long Parliament, six further MPs were added to the number representing Devon constituencies as Ashburton, Honiton, and Okehampton were 'restored' the privilege of parliamentary representation.[1] Of the 26 members originally seated following the settlement of election disputes and double returns, sixteen Devon MPs had held seats or been elected to the earlier parliament of that year, fifteen of them being chosen to serve for their old constituency once again.[2] Eight of the original 26 had served in parliaments well before the period of 'Personal Rule', and these men significantly enough included John Pym and William Strode, two of the 'Five Members' whom Charles I would attempt to arrest in his invasion of the House of Commons on 4 January 1642.

The wealth of parliamentary experience enjoyed by the original group of MPs was soon enhanced by the election of Sir Samuel Rolle and Samuel Browne in by-elections to replace two members for Devon constituencies who died by the end of 1641.[3] Before the Civil War had begun, three more by-elections were held to fill the seats of Robert Trelawney and Hugh Pollard who were expelled from parliament, and that vacated by William Lord Russell on the occasion of his elevation to the peerage. But in the case of the MPs selected to replace these three men, members were chosen who had never before served in Commons. John Pym's son, Charles, was named for the Bere Alston seat occupied by Pollard, Sir John Yonge took Trelawney's seat for Plymouth, and John Russell joined John Pym as MP for Tavistock. Inexperience, however, was not confined to these three men. Between the years from

November 1640 to July 1645, during which time Devon and Exeter were represented by a total of thirty-one MPs, eleven had never before sat in parliament.[4] Nineteen members had had previous experience in earlier parliaments.

Of this group of thirty-one members active in the Long Parliament up to the days of 'recruitment', it would appear that the great majority had connections with Devon or Exeter, usually as resident landowners or merchants. Only six MPs could be said to be completely foreign to the county (ie, neither owning land there nor having been born there), while neither William Lord Russell, nor his brother John, could be considered natives, except for the fact that they belonged to a family with extensive landholdings in Devonshire. Of those who were not Devonian by birth, selection for a Devon borough came as a result of marriage or business ties with influential elements within the county. The Russells, of course, could rely on their own family borough of Tavistock, whose second MP, John Pym, had represented the borough continuously since 1625 and was closely connected with the Earl of Bedford through the Providence Island Company.[5]

The Russell influence was also effective in obtaining a seat for their relative, Oliver St John, at Totnes.[6] Charles Pym, on the other hand, although not related to that family, was presumably elected as a result of pressure applied on the local electors of Bere Alston by friends of his father.[7] Among these could be counted the Russells, in addition to the sympathetic gentry who had worked with the elder Pym in parliament, or who had the previous year supported the opposition leader William Strode for that same seat.

Lawrence Whitaker, a clerk of the council, and Edward Thomas were both returned for the restored borough of Okehampton at the nomination of another local magnate, Lord Mohun, Baron of Okehampton and lord of the manor.[8] Keeler suspects the patronage of the Earl of Bedford as the motive force behind the election of Sir Edmund Fowell and Sir John Northcote, Devon gentry and active oppositionists, for the restored borough of Ashburton.[9] As for the third borough to be restored in Devon, Honiton was also represented by neighbouring gentlemen, Walter Yonge and William Pole, both of whose families, along with the Courtenays of Powderham, exercised continuous influence in that borough for years to come.[10] The other 'foreigner', Samuel Browne, was a Bedfordshire man. Browne presumably obtained the Dartmouth seat vacated by John Upton's death through the influence of his cousin, Oliver St John, and that gentleman's wide network of contacts.[11]

Of the remaining MPs who represented Devon and Exeter, all can be seen to have gained seats through influence which they or their families could bring to bear in the competitive whirl of local politics. Prominent men such as Edward Seymour of Berry Pomeroy and Thomas Wise of Sydenham had no difficulty in capturing the county seats.[12] Locally influential gentry such as Walter Yonge of Colyton and Sir Thomas Hele of Flete near Holbeton were ultimately successful in winning places in parliament, often against the vigorous attempts of equally zealous neighbours to be returned. In the larger towns, and in the city of Exeter, there was no question of outside influence. The corporation in each case returned those who had risen in their ranks through the time-honoured process of oligarchic service, selecting men of proven worth who were locally prominent, such as Richard Ferris and George Peard for Barnstaple, John Upton and Roger Matthew for Dartmouth, Trelawney and John Waddon for Plymouth, and Simon Snow and Robert Walker at Exeter.[13]

In terms of occupational background, Devon and Exeter were represented by eight lawyers, seven merchants, thirteen landed gentlemen, and one man of letters (Lawrence Whitaker), in addition to the aristocratic Russells. The average age of the total group of MPs first elected in 1640 was 42 years, at least 17 of these being elder sons, or eventual heirs, only five being younger sons. As a consequence, it is evident that as a group these men constituted an impressive array of economic wealth, and in terms of background, training, and experience, a remarkable reservoir of legal, constitutional, and commercial knowledge to be drawn on in the critical days ahead. This is to say nothing about the size of the group as a significant factor in itself.

These were the men who, as a body, represented the two counties during much of the period from 1640 to 1646. Twelve new names were added to this list in late 1645 and 1646—'recruiters' as they were called—men who, to a large degree, were remarkably similar to those elected in 1640.[14] Except for Philip Skippon of Norfolk, the majority of the Devon 'recruiters' came from old gentry families, long established in the county, such as Francis Drake of Buckland Abbey, Sir Nicholas Martyn of Oxton in Kenton, Robert Shapcote of Bradninch, or from the well-entrenched town families, like John Doddridge of Barnstaple and Samuel Clarke and Charles Vaughan, both of Exeter. There was no radical departure from the sentiments previously expressed by the Devon electors, nor any revolutionary change in county politics or leadership as a result of the war, except for the obvious absence of royalist candidates.

In addition to those who actually represented Devon constituencies, there were at least twelve Devonians who sat in the Long
Parliament as members for boroughs outside their native county.
All but three, Sir John Clotworthy, John Rolle, and Richard
Long, still made their residence in Devon and even these three
continued to maintain family ties there.[15] Again, all but three
represented constituencies in the neighbouring county of Corn-
wall; Clotworthy (whose residence was in Ireland) sat for Malden,
Essex; Edmund Prideaux for Lyme Regis in Dorset; and Richard
Long for Bristol.

Thus, Devon's direct and indirect representation in the Long
Parliament was a large and powerful one indeed. From 1640 to
1646 forty-three MPs either came from and occupied Devon and
Exeter seats; or were native Devonians sitting for non-Devon, but
neighbouring, constituencies; or were complete 'foreigners' occu-
pying a local seat.[16] Considering that this group was fairly closely
united in terms of background, family connections, and friendships,[17] and that such men as John Pym, St John, Maynard, and
Strode were among their number, it is obvious that Devon and
Exeter would have an extraordinary lobby within the House of
Commons and a sizeable voice in the making of revolution and in
the running of the Civil War then about to explode.

Although all those who were going to do so had not necessarily
broken their ties with the parliament at Westminster by 22 August 1642, a general statement with regard to the loyalties of the
Devon and Exeter MPs can be made by that time. Of the 28 members still sitting for the two counties at the formal outbreak of the
war, 17 can be regarded as 'parliamentarian' and as taking a more
or less active part in the war against the king. The remaining 11
are to be considered 'royalists',[18] and 5 of them are known to
have attended the royalist parliament at Oxford.[19] Of those who
eventually came to the support of the king, 5 were merchants
representing large borough or town constituencies,[20] and 5 were
gentry representing somewhat smaller boroughs, and the county
of Devon.[21] John Russell, member for Tavistock, also seems to
have immediately taken up the royal cause, notwithstanding the
fact that his older brother gave initial support to the parliament.
Of those who supported the parliament, 7 were gentry, 7 lawyers,
only 2 were merchants, and 1 a clerk of the council.

Notes to this appendix are on page 227

C

Devon MPs in the Short Parliament, 13 April-5 May, 1640

CONSTITUENCY	MPS	REMARKS
Devonshire	Seymour, Edward Wise, Thomas	
Barnstaple	Peard, George Matthew, Thomas	
Bere Alston	Harris, John Strode, William	Disputes arising from this election can be traced in: JHC, 2: 14; and J. J. Alexander, 'Bere Alston . . .', RTDA, 41.158
Dartmouth	Upton, John Voysey, Andrew	
Exeter	Walker, Robert Snow, Simon	See: JHC, 2: 3. Snow replaced James Tucker
Plymouth	Waddon, John Trelawney, Robert	
Plympton Earle	Slanning, Sir Nicholas Hele, Sir Thomas	Sir Richard Strode returned his own name. JHC, 2: 7
Tavistock	Pym, John William Lord Russell	
Tiverton	Sainthill, Peter Balle, Peter	
Totnes	St John, Oliver Maynard, John	

D

Devon MPs in the Long Parliament, 1640-60

Key: Following each name is the approximate date of that MP's retirement or expulsion from the House of Commons. Where a member died it is indicated by 'dec', where expelled by 'exp', disabled by 'dis', and secluded at the Purge, 'sec'.

'P' = Parliamentarian

'R' = Royalist

** = MPs who are included in the *Dictionary of National Biography*

1 = Members who sat as the result of an originally undisputed election in autumn 1640

2 = Members who sat as the result of a disputed election

3 = MPs who sat after a double return

4 = MPs who sat after a member chosen for two seats preferred another

5 = Members elected before the outbreak of Civil War to replace other legitimately elected MPs

6 = Recruiters elected between August 1645 and December 1646

Devonshire
1 Thomas Wise (3/41 dec)   Edward Seymour (1/43 dis) R
5 Sir Samuel Rolle (12/47 dec) P
6 Sir Nicholas Martyn (12/48 sec) P

Ashburton
—restored November 26, 1640
1 Sir Edmund Fowell   Sir John Northcote **
  (12/48 sec) P   (12/48 sec) P

Barnstaple
1 George Peard ** (?/44 dec) P
2 Richard Ferris (1/44 dis) R
  (replaced Thomas Matthew
  who was elected but not re-

turned by the Mayor)
6 Philip Skippon John Doddridge (12/48 sec)
Bere Alston
1 William Strode ** (9/45 dec) P
4 Hugh Pollard ** (12/41 exp) R
5 Charles Pym (12/48 sec) P
6 Sir Francis Drake (12/48 sec)
Dartmouth
1 John Upton (9/41 dec) Roger Matthew (2/44 dis) R
5 Samuel Browne ** (12/48 sec) P
6 Thomas Boone
Exeter
1 Robert Walker (3/43 dis) R Simon Snow (12/48 sec) P
6 Samuel Clarke (12/48)
Honiton
—restored in November 1640
1 William Poole (6/43 dis) R Walter Yonge ** (12/48) P
6 Charles Vaughan (12/48)
Okehampton
—restored in November 1640
1 Edward Thomas (12/48 sec) P Lawrence Whitaker P
Plymouth
1 Robert Trelawney (3/42 exp) R John Waddon (12/48 sec) P
5 Sir John Yonge (12/48 sec) P
Plympton Earle
4 Sir Thomas Hele (1/44 dis) R Hugh Potter (12/48 sec) P
6 Christopher Martyn
Tavistock
1 William Lord Russell ** (5/41 John Pym ** (12/43 dec) P
   Peer) P
5 John Russell (1/44 dis) R
6 Elisha Crimes (12/48 sec) Edward Fowell (12/48 sec)
**Tiverton*
1 Peter Sainthill (1/44 dis) R George Hartnoll (1/44 dis) R
6 John Elford (12/48) Robert Shapcote (12/48 sec)
Totnes
1 Oliver St John ** P John Maynard (12/48 sec) P
*Representation restored in 1615.

NATIVE DEVONIANS WHO SAT FOR OTHER CONSTITUENCIES IN THE
LONG PARLIAMENT (1640-5)

NAME	HOME ORIGINALLY	CONSTITUENCY
Nicholas Gould	Plymouth	Fowey, Cornwall
Gregory Clement	Plymouth	Fowey, Cornwall
John Harris	Radford, nr Plymouth	Liskeard, Cornwall
Edmund Prideaux	Ottery St Mary	Lyme Regis, Dorset
John Bampfield	Poltimore	Penryn, Cornwall
Sir Nicholas Slanning	Maristow	Penryn, Cornwall
John Rolle	Devonshire	Truro, Cornwall
Sir John Clotworthy	Devonshire	Maldon, Essex
John Harris	Hayne	Launceston, Cornwall
George Parry	Exeter	St Mawes, Cornwall
Sir Ralph Sydenham	Youlston	Bossiney, Cornwall
Richard Long	Axminster	Bristol, Somerset

List of Abbreviations

ACTS PC	Acts of the Privy Council
BM	British Museum
BIHR	Bulletin of the Institute of Historical Research
CCC	Calendar of the Proceedings of the Committee of Compounding, etc. 1643-60 ..., (ed) Green, M. A. E., 1889-92
CCSP	Calendar of the Clarendon State Papers preserved in the Bodleian Library. 1, (ed) Ogle, O. & Bliss, W. H. 1872: 2 & 3, (ed) Macray, W. D. 1869 and 1876
CSPD	Calendar of State Papers, Domestic Series
DCNG	*Devon and Cornwall Notes and Gleanings*
DCNQ	*Devon and Cornwall Notes and Queries*
DCRO	Devon County Record Office
DL	Deputy Lieutenant
DNB	*Dictionary of National Biography*
ERO	Exeter City Record Office
EHR	*The English Historical Review*
HMC	Historical Manuscripts Commission
JHC	*Journal of the House of Commons*
JHL	*Journal of the House of Lords*
JP	Justice of the Peace
MP	Member of Parliament
PC	Privy Council
PRO	Public Record Office
QSOB	Quarter Sessions Order Book
RTDA	*Report and Transactions of The Devonshire Association*
RTPI	*Report and Transactions of The Plymouth Institution*

Notes to the Text

Prologue and Chapter 1. Structure of the County and City by 1640. Pages 12-23

1 Blake, William J. 'Hooker's Synopsis Chorographical of Devonshire', RTDA, 47, 335-8
2 Hoskins, William George. *Devon* (1954), 11, 12 & 172; MacCaffrey, W. T. *Exeter, 1540-1640 : The Growth of an English County Town* (Cambridge 1958), 7
3 Hoskins (ed), *Exeter in the 17th Century : Tax and Rate Assessments 1602-1699*, Devon and Cornwall Record Society, New Series, 2 (Torquay 1957), ix & xii; Stephens, W. B. *Seventeenth Century Exeter : A Study of Industrial and Commercial Development, 1625-1688* (Exeter 1958), 40
4 Hoskins, *Devon*, 114
5 Ibid, 63-4
6 Ibid, 74
7 Pole, Sir William. *Collections towards a Description of the County of Devon* (1791), 78
8 Blake, 'Synopsis', 347; Hoskins, *Devon*, 132 & 140
9 Ibid, 213
10 Stephens, W. B. 'The West-Country Ports and the Struggle for the Newfoundland Fisheries in the 17th Century', RTDA 88 (Torquay 1956), 91
11 Russell, P. *Dartmouth : A History of the Port and Town* (1950), 82, 87 and 108
12 Stephens, 'West-Country Ports', 95
13 Stephens, *Exeter*, 3, 4
14 Ibid. During the 1620s and 1630s local specialisation within the woollen industry became evident to an extraordinary degree as indicated in MacCaffrey, *Exeter*, 161-2. 'Crediton continued to produce ordinary kerseys while Ottery St Mary made a coloured type of the same cloth. Totnes specialised in coarse cloths, called narrow pin-white, while Barnstaple and Torrington were the home of baize, Pilton the home of 'cottons' used for lining. Cullompton turned out kerseys, but was also a centre for stocking manufacture. More specialised still were the bone-lace of Honiton and Bradninch and the shoemakers' thread of Combe Martin. According to Hoskins, *Devon*, 128: 'The principal spinning districts were to be found around Barnstaple and Bideford, the receiving ports for Irish wool; between Dartmoor and Bodmin Moor . . . ; and on the eastern side of Dartmoor around Ashburton. The manufacturing area proper (weaving, fulling, and dyeing) lay to the north, northeast, and west of Exeter, in a belt extending from Taunton across to North Tawton.'

15 Ibid, 66. See: Lipson, *History of the English Woollen and Worsted Industries*, 21-6. For a description of the processes of cloth production in the Exeter district, see Blake, 'Synopsis', 346-7
16 Stephens, *Exeter*, 6
17 Ibid, xix-xxi; and MacCaffrey, *Exeter*, 162
18 Ibid, 12
19 Stephens, W. B. 'The Officials of the French Company of Exeter in the Early Seventeenth Century', DCNQ 27 (1958), 113
20 Russell, *Dartmouth*, 82
21 Cotton, R. W. *Barnstaple and the Northern Part of Devonshire during the Great Civil War, 1642-1646* (Chilworth & London 1889), 3 and 6
22 Russell, P. *The Good Town of Totnes* (Torquay 1963), 64. Under the 1596 charter, the government of Totnes resided in the hands of the Mayor and fourteen Aldermen who filled vacancies in their ranks through their own initiative. Although the charter required the appointment of twenty Councillors to be elected to aid in the administration of the town properties and other matters, this was seldom done
23 In 1623, and for years to come, Francis Lord Russell (later Earl of Bedford) was lord lieutenant of Devon and Exeter, often in conjunction with his son William. ERO, 'Commissions', 85
24 Blake, 'Synopsis', 340-1
25 Stephens, *Exeter*, 41 & 43. See also: HMC, 12th Rept, App, Pt 1, 'Coke MSS' (1888), 213
26 MacCaffrey, *Exeter*, 276 & 279. In the borough '. . . status was measured not by birth but by commercial success. Here rapid ascent from humble to exalted social position was not only an acceptable but a common phenomenon'. And this was nowhere so evident as in Exeter
27 Ibid
28 Vivian, J. L. (ed). *The Visitations of the County of Devon, Comprising the Heralds' Visitations of 1531, 1564, and 1620* (Exeter 1895) 221, passim. Younger sons and daughters moved easily from one class to another. A young lady with a small dowry in a family of 15 to 25 children might have to settle for someone beneath her station. A young man with little to offer in the way of a landed estate, or engaged in commerce or law or the Church, would have to aim for a younger daughter of a good family.
29 MacCaffrey, *Exeter*, 279
30 Blake, 'Synopsis', 339. Hoskins, W. G. & Finberg, H.P.R. *Devonshire Studies* (1952), 334. Hoskins puts the number of Devon gentry at between 360 and 400 by 1640
31 Ibid, 337
32 Ibid, 351 & 353. A further characteristic of the Caroline gentry in Devon was their heavy indebtedness, especially through mortgages and loans, in the years before the Civil War
33 Although it does not appear to have been the habit to send elder sons to university, it does appear that many younger sons of Devon gentry found their way to Exeter College, Oxford. St Leger-Gordon, D. F. *Devonshire* (1950), 155. See also: ERO, Letter Book 60c, Letters 167, 172, 184, 185. W. K. Willcocks shows that at Inner Temple alone there were more than 150 Devonians registered during the years 1590 to 1646. Willcocks, 'Devonshire Men at the Inner Temple, 1547-1660', RTDA 17 (Plymouth 1885), 257-64
34 Vivian, *Visitations*, 86 & passim

35 Hoskins, *Studies*, 346-7; and Hoskins, 'Devonshire Gentry in Carolean Times', DCNQ 22 (Exeter 1946), 358
36 Blake, 'Synopsis', 341
37 Hoskins, *Devon*, 90
38 Blake, 'Synopsis', 341
39 Hoskins, *Devon*, 90
40 Hoskins & Finberg, *Studies*, 419
41 Hoskins, *Devon*, 96

Chapter 2. Years of Growing Discontent, 1625-40. Pages 24-41

1 Hamilton, A. H. A. *Quarter Sessions from Queen Elizabeth to Queen Anne* (1878), 100, passim
2 Ibid, 105-6
3 HMC, 'Coke MSS', 213 & 249
4 Stephens, *Exeter*, 14. Thornton, W. H. DCNQ 6 pt 1 (1911), 198-9
5 Hamilton, *Quarter Sessions*, 105-6
6 HMC, 10th Rept, App, Pt 4 (1885), 'Borough of Plymouth MSS', 542
7 Eliot-Drake, Lady. *The Family and Heirs of Sir Francis Drake* (1911), I:214. ERO, Letter Book 60D, Letters 285 & 291; Hamilton, *Quarter Sessions*, 107
8 Eliot-Drake, *Drake*, I:214-15
9 James Bagg, one of Buckingham's minions, had been instrumental in obtaining men, supplies, and munitions for this expedition. On 18 April 1625 he wrote from Fowey to Sir John Coke, a Master of Requests, stating: 'I had help of Sir Edward Seymour, Sir George Chudleigh, Sir William Strode, the Mayors of Exeter, Plymouth, and Dartmouth, Sir Edward Giles and my cousin Drake. Opposition of Sir John Eliot'. 'Coke MSS', 190. Eliot was not alone in opposing Buckingham's scheme nor the shoddy methods employed by men such as Bagg to obtain profit from sale of poor goods. According to C. W. Bracken: 'Too well did Eliot know who had furnished the crazy hulks, the meat that stank, and the clothes that rotted, and into whose pockets the gold had gone which should have furnished the sinews of war'. Bracken, *A History of Plymouth and Her Neighbours* (Plymouth 1931), 127
10 Eliot-Drake, *Drake*, 215 & 216
11 Ibid, 216-18
12 Ibid, 218-20
13 Hamilton, *Quarter Sessions*, 108
14 ERO, Letter Book 60D, L 300
15 Ibid, L 301
16 Ibid, L 303 & 304
17 Hamilton, *Quarter Sessions*, 107-9; Eliot-Drake, *Drake*, 220
18 Thomas Barnes has examined this point with regard to the JPs who

were also DLs in Somerset: See: *Somerset 1625-1640 : A County's Government during the 'Personal Rule'* (1961), passim

19 Hamilton, *Quarter Sessions,* 109
20 Ibid, 109-10
21 ERO, Letter Book 60D, L 305 & 307
22 Ibid, L 308 & 309
23 Eliot-Drake, *Drake,* 220
24 The correspondence between the Devon JPs and the PC in the autumn of 1627 indicates that the press-gangs had taken an especially heavy toll of seamen and farm labourers. The apprentices and craftsmen of Exeter appear to have been spared on several occasions. See also: ERO, Letter Book 60D, L 296 & 297
25 Granville, R. *The History of the Granville Family* (Exeter 1895), 162
26 Devon paid £5,960.10.8 (£5 960.53) and Exeter £96.18.0 (£96.90) on the basis of this legal parliamentary grant. Worth, R. N. (ed) *The Buller Papers* (privately printed 1895), 36
27 PRO, SP 16/6, no 70. Those who contributed are listed in PRO, E 401/2586
28 PRO, SP 16/31, nos 30-1
29 ERO, 'Misc Papers', Box 6
30 ERO, 'Commissions', 95
31 ERO, Letter Book 60D, L 293 & 294
32 Ibid, L 295 & 299
33 Stephens, *Exeter,* 15. A valuable discussion of Exeter's commercial policy before the civil wars is found in W. B. Stephens, 'Merchant Companies and Commercial Policy in Exeter, 1625-1688', RTDA 86 (Torquay 1954), 137-45
34 Stephens, *Exeter,* 16. For the year 1625 alone more than 1,000 men were reportedly captured from West Country ships
35 Ibid. Not only was Devon expected to pay £5,000 more than London itself, but the figure set was £7,000 more than any other county in the kingdom
36 Russell, P. *Dartmouth : A History of the Port and Town* (1950), 90
37 Cornish, W. H. 'Sir John Gayer—Merchant Adventurer (1584-1649)', RTPI 21 (Plymouth 1949), 174
38 Russell puts it frankly: 'There is so much sorrowing and sighing in the letters sent out by the Mayors of Dartmouth and other places that it leaves the impression that the merchants were rather too fond of their money bags. They had the resources themselves to clear the Moors off their coasts, if only they would keep a few ships back from trade; but they would neither pay nor fight'. *Dartmouth,* 92
39 ERO, DD 61979, 62056/B, 61981/A, and 62067 in 'Misc Papers'
40 Granville, *Granville,* 136
41 In 1619 the Government launched an unsuccessful expedition against the pirates, for which Exeter saw fit to contribute only half of the £1,000 assessed on it. ERO, 'Deeds', no 1750, Receipt of the Pells dated 10 December 1630, but referring to the contribution of 5 July 1620. Also: Acts of PC, 3, 218-19; 4, 360, 414, 421; 5, 62; and CSPD, 1619-23, vol 107, no 45, p 26
42 ERO, Letter Book 60E, L 327 & 328
43 CSPD, 1629-31, vol 164, no 39, p 232; vol 165, no 15, p 241; 1631-33, vol 189, no 84, p 28
44 HMC, 9th Rept, App, Pt 1 'Corporation of Plymouth MSS' (1883), 269-70. See: Worth, R. N. *Calendar of the Plymouth Municipal Records*

(Plymouth 1893), 219, no 360; and Chanter, J. R. & Wainwright, T. *Reprint of the Barnstaple Records* 2 (Barnstaple 1900) 63

45 HMC, 'Corp. of Plymouth MSS', 270. The signatories to the Six Resolutions reveal the importance of the support given to this motion as all were very substantial men.

46 Ibid, 271

47 ERO, Letter Book 60E, L 357

48 Granville, *Granville*, 136-7

49 ERO, DD 62677; MacCaffrey, *Exeter*, 154

50 ERO, Letter Book 60D, L 292; Cotton, *Barnstaple*, 9. According to Hamilton, (120), Devon was required to provide £17,400 for ship money in 1628, but T. N. Brushfield indicates that the order was revoked due to 'general murmurs of discontent'. Brushfield, 'The Financial Diary of a Citizen of Exeter, 1631-1643', RTDA 33 (Plymouth 1901), 263. This statement is substantiated by Walter Yonge's *Diary*, Camden Society, (1848), 93, where Yonge comments that '. . . our county refused to meddle therein'

51 Under the first ship money writ of 1634, Devon was required to provide a ship of 400 tons. For this purpose, Plymouth was assessed £185.0.8 (£185·04), Plympton St Mary £184.16.0 (£184·80), Barnstaple £252.4.8 (£252·24), Hartland £121.11.4 (£121·57), Braunton £132.10.8 (£132·54), South Molton £116.8.0 (£116·40), Tawstock £100.2.0 (£100·10), Torrington £124.16.4 (£124·82), Tiverton £206, Swymbridge £116.3.4 (£116·67). (Chanter and Wainwright, *Barnstaple Records*, 2, 138). Okehampton was assessed £30. (E. H. Young, 'Okehampton during the Civil War, 1642-46', RTDA 60 (Plymouth 1928), 278.) For funds collected under writs issued from 1635 to 1639 see: M. D. Gordon, 'The Collection of Ship Money in the Reign of Charles I', in *Trans. of the Royal Historical Society, 3rd series*, 4 (1910), 157

52 The writ of 4 August 1635 directed to thirteen specific towns and villages in Devon, in addition to Exeter, began: 'Because we are given to understand that certain pirates, Mohometans [sic] and others, collected together have carried away the ships, goods, etc of our own subjects and of the subjects of our friends, in the sea which has usually been defended by the English race, robbing them at their pleasure, and selling the men in them into capitivity, and since we have seen them day after day preparing to molest our merchants and oppress our realm . . .', this money is needed to equip a fleet sufficient to deal with this menace. Totnes Guildhall, Totnes MSS, Box 104

53 See: HMC. 'Various Collections', Add MSS of Sir Hervey J. L. Bruce 7 (1914), 410

54 Cotton, *Barnstaple*, 12

55 The five commissioners were also DLs of the county: Sir William Strode, Sir Edward Giles, Sir Edward Seymour, Sir Francis Drake, and Sir George Chudleigh

56 Eliot-Drake, *Drake*, 240-1; Hamilton, *Quarter Sessions*, 120. Sir Edward Giles was excused because of age. Lady Eliot-Drake felt that more was intended by the PC than the mild chastisement of these obstinent baronets. See: *Drake*, 242-3

57 According to the 1635 writ Plymouth was rated £190, Exeter £350, and Barnstaple £150. Worth, R. N. *History of Plymouth from the Earliest Period to the Present Time* (Plymouth 1890), 321; Gordon, 'Ship Money', 157. The inclusion of a number of inland communities to those seaports

traditionally liable to pay ship money reduced the burden of payment drastically on such towns as Barnstaple and Plympton. The tax assessed for Plymouth, however, increased

58 At the general meeting of representatives from those communities affected, Totnes was assessed £120, fifth after Exeter (£350), Plymouth, Barnstaple, and Tiverton. (Totnes Guildhall, Totnes MSS, Box 104; and Russell, P. *The Good Town of Totnes*, (Torquay 1963), 61.) In 1636 and 1637 Devon was again required to provide a 900 ton ship. (Chanter & Wainwright, *Barnstaple Records*, 2:64.)

59 Young, 'Okehampton', 278-9. Throughout the ship money controversy petitions were still being sent to the PC requesting protection for western shipping. See: Edward Windeatt, 'Totnes: Its Mayor and Mayoralties, 1627-76', RTDA 32 (Plymouth 1900), 118

60 Eliot-Drake, *Drake*, 253

61 Gordon, 'Ship Money', 157

62 Young, 'Okehampton', 278-9

63 Keeler, M. F. *The Long Parliament, 1640-1641 : A Biographical Study of its Members* (Philadelphia 1954), 398. Also: CSPD, 1639-40, vol 435, no 33

64 Eliot-Drake, *Drake*, 254. Also: Hamilton, *Quarter Sessions*, 120-1, for instances of corruption on the part of several constables. Cf CSPD, 1639-40, vol 432, no 78, pp 105-6; vol 435, no 33, p 147

65 CSPD, 1639, vol 427, no 5, pp 428-9; Windeatt, 'Totnes: Its Mayors', 120

66 In the last ship money collected, Exeter was short some £250, having contributed only £100. PRO, Acts of PC, PC2/51, Pt 2, vol 17, f 590

67 CSPD, 1639-40 vol 444, no 73, p 443

68 Ibid, 1640, vol 458, no 42, p 352. See also: Brushfield, *Diary*, 265-6. The writ issued to Devon in December 1639 called for a ship of 720 tons to be provided, costing some £9,000. While Exeter and the incorporated towns were to provide £1,280, the remaining part was to be raised in the countryside. By the end of March 1640, £3,303.16.8 (£3,303·84) had been turned in following a great deal of effort, with 'some hundreds and parishes' refusing to pay at all. See: CSPD, 1639-40, vol 446, no 50, p 498. By August the county escheator was being added to the group of officials attempting to collect ship money in Devon, but by that time the county had returned two-thirds of the sum required of it for 1639-40. Ibid, 1640, vol 463, no 53, p 563

69 Hoskins, *Devon*, 64-6

70 Hamilton, *Quarter Sessions*, 104-5

71 Ibid, 101-3 & 115-16

72 Devon was third amongst the counties of England to send emigrants to the New World, most of whom came from coastal communities, especially in South Devon, where the tradition of the sea was very strong. See: Brown, 'Devonians and New England settlement before 1650', RTDA 95 (Torquay 1963), 220-1

73 James, F. B. 'A Devonian Emigrant', DCNG 1 (Exeter 1888), 49

74 Brown, 'Devonians', 228

75 Ibid, 222 & 228. Cf 'Captain Francis Champernowne', DCNG, 4:118-22

76 Stephens, *Exeter*, 21, 26-8. Also: HMC, 11th Rept, App, Pt 3 (1887), 'Town of Southampton MSS', 132; and ERO, Letter Book 60E, L 380

77 Customs duties on exports and increased prices resulting from monopoly grants also had their effect on trade. Stephens, *Exeter*, 33, 34; Eliot-Drake, *Drake*, 224

78 Hamilton, *Quarter Sessions*, 110 & 114; Eliot-Drake, *Drake*, 244-5

79 CSPD, 1939, vol 418, no 67, pp 85-6
80 DCRO, Quarter Sessions Records, 1633-40, JPs to PC, 3 October 1639
81 Stephens, *Exeter*, 47 & 49
82 Worth, R. N. 'Puritanism in Devon, and the Exeter Assembly', RTDA 9 (Plymouth 1877), 253ff. By 1640 only a few wealthy and well-established families continued in the old persuasion. See: Hoskins, *Devon*, 236; Oliver's *Collections Illustrating the History of the Catholic Families in Devon and Cornwall* (1857), passim
83 Americanus (anonymous author), 'Puritanism in East Devon and the New England Emigrants (1625-30)', DCNQ 18 (1935), 87-8. The author points to the efforts on the part of reformers to obtain control of advowsons, to institute moderate lecturers and preachers, and to reform quietly the Devon Church from within
84 Finberg, *Studies*, 369
85 Worth, 'Puritanism', 263-4. Worth wrote: 'Was it the recognition of the growing strength of the popular feeling that caused the larger communities to be thus passed by? Assuredly it was not because they were not Puritan; for they were its very heart and life'.
86 Ibid, 267. According to Worth: ' . . . the most Puritan class was the middle class, whether in town or country, . . .'.
87 Granville, R. *The History of Bideford* (Bideford 1883), 51-2; Chanter & Wainwright, *Barnstaple Records*, 2:101
88 Cotton, *Barnstaple*, 29 & 30
89 Finberg, *Studies*, 383 & 384
90 Worth, *Plymouth*, 243 & 248. Also: DCNQ, vol 6, Pt 1 (1911), 200-2.
91 It appeared that the strength of the Devon puritan community could only be enhanced under the auspices of a man like Bishop Hall, '. . . that earnest Puritan occupant of the See of Exeter, . . .'. (Mrs Francis B. Troup, 'Biographical Sketch of the Rev Christopher Jelinger, MA', RTDA 32 (Plymouth 1900), 251.)
   That the scholarly bishop was in fact not a puritan, but a mild-mannered and moderate cleric can be seen from his lengthy correspondence with Laud throughout 1639-early 1640. Cf CSPD, 1639-40, vol 430, nos 50 & 51, pp 20-1; vol 431, nos 2 & 65, pp 30. 54; vol 432, no 63, p 100; vol 436, no 45, p 186; vol 442, no 35, pp 349-50
92 ERO, Letter Book 60E, L 381
93 Ibid
94 Cotton and Woolcombe make the point that for years up to the Scots' revolt, although a difference in religious sentiment existed between members of the Exeter Corporation, these diverse views had not been sufficient to split the city fathers nor to dissuade them from carrying out their municipal duties. Cotton, W. and Woollcombe H.; *Gleanings from the Municipal and Cathedral Records relative to the History of the City of Exeter* (Exeter 1877), 76-7
95 Ibid, 77-8. See: Rev Evans, H. R. 'Broadhempston', RTDA 90 (Torquay 1958), 62-126
96 CSPD, 1640, vol 460, no 28, p 485
97 HMC, 12th Rept, App, Pt 4, 'Duke of Rutland MSS' (1888), 522
98 CSPD, 1640, vol 460, no 52, pp 494-5; vol 460, no 56, pp 496-7; vol 464, no 55, p 613; and vol 465, no 39, pp 645-6. Also: PRO, SP 16/460, no 5
99 HMC, 'Rutland MSS', 522. See: CSPD, 1640-1, vol 467, no 17, p 44; and vol 469, no 54, pp 148-9
100 Worth, *Buller Papers*, 27

Chapter 3. Devon on the Eve of Conflict, november 1640-august 1642. Pages 42-54

1 Eliot-Drake, *Drake*, 277-8
2 The struggle raging between Laudians and puritans is outlined in W. Howell's letter of 20 February 1641 to Thomas Wise, MP. Howell related the abuses of Mr Robert Dove, vicar of Ilsington, who was known to be guilty of switching the communion table altar-wise on three occasions, of threatening the congregation, and of other offences. 'He hath bestirred himself to get hands to uphold Episcopacy and the government of bishops, . . .' *Buller Papers*, 33-4; Rushworth, John. *Historical Collections*, 4 (1721-2), 152
3 Francis Earl of Bedford was particularly active, especially in the promotion of petitions to the crown. See: CSPD, 1640, vol 465, no 16, pp 639-40 & 652; Keeler, *Long Parliament*, 9
4 See Wise's notebook, *Buller Papers*, 135-7. This petition is signed by thirty-eight of the leading gentlemen of the county, many of whom were JPs, apparently predisposed toward the opposition party and later supporters of parliament. Ibid, 137-8
5 In a letter of 10 November 1640 written from Inner Temple, William Davy wrote his uncle Willoughby concerning the trouble of getting the latter's name off the list of possible shrieval candidates. Speaking of current parliamentary affairs Davy wrote: 'Many grievances are stirred, and likely to be redressed; if you have any in Devon, put them forward.' Trevelyan, Walter C. & Charles, E. (eds) *Trevelyan Papers*, Pt 3, Camden Society (1872), 196-7
6 Keeler, *Long Parliament*, 41
7 Coate, Mary. *Cornwall in the Great Civil War and Interregnum 1642-1660* (Oxford 1933), 26; CSPD, 1640-1, vol 471, no 69, p 262; JHC, 2, 57, 58, 194. There had been a scare in 1640 regarding the growing military strength of the Roman Catholics in the county, and Quarter Sessions took steps to disarm 'recusants'. (Hamilton, *Quarter Sessions*, 121-2; Cotton, *Barnstaple*, 33; JHC, 2, 58.) January 1641 saw the beginning of a widespread and systematic destruction of anything that smacked of popery in parish churches. Cf Brushfield, 'Diary', 261-2
8 *Buller Papers*, 138. The privileges of the stannaries were the subject of a petition in July 1641. See: HMC, 4th Rept, App, 'House of Lords MSS', 88; JHL, 4, 187
9 Ibid, 139-40
10 JHC, 2, 49
11 HMC, 'House of Lords MSS', 45
12 JHC, 2, 102. For other Devon and Exeter petitions, see: HMC, 10th Rept, App, Pt 6 (1887) 'Lord Braye's MSS', 140; JHC, 2, 89, 144
13 HMC, 'House of Lords MSS', 114
14 Ibid
15 HMC, 5th Rept, 'House of Lords MSS' (1876), 5
16 Ibid
17 DCRO, QSOB (1640-51), 68. The Order Book has been given artificial pagination. See: JHC, 2, 391; JHL, 4, 536; and Cotton, *Barnstaple*, 45
18 BM. 'Thomason Tracts', 669 f4 (52)

19 Ibid
20 ERO, Chamber Act Book 8, p 258
21 JHL, 4,536; HMC, 5th Rept, 'House of Lords MSS', 4-5
22 See: JHL, 4, 536-7; BM, 669 f4 (50); and DCNQ, 2 (1903), 141-2, entry by Edward Windeatt
23 Ibid, 2, 142
24 Young, 'Okehampton', 281; Cecil Torr (complier), *Index* (Cambridge 1913), 2, passim. The Protestation Returns of 1642 are kept in the House of Lords Record Office, Victoria Tower, and have been listed by parish in HMC, 5th Rept, App, Pt 1 (1876), 120-34. For a copy of the Protestation, see: JHL, 4, 234
25 Economic conditions improved somewhat in 1641 and the money thus made available helped to pay the tax levied that summer for disbanding the army. (See: ERO, Box of Assessments for Subsidies, nos 2 & 3; JHC, 2, 269; Hoskins, 'Tax and Rate', xiv-xv.) But a severe decline in trade made it necessary for the Commons to consider a bill 'for the easing of the Counties of Devon, Norfolk, Surrey, . . . by abating of the several charges imposed upon them by the bill of £400,000'. The relief bill, however, was rejected at first reading. JHC, 2, 517; DCRO, QSOB (1640-51). A renewal of the plague, an irregular increase in customs rates, and the pressure of pirates all tended to irritate a progressively worsening political and economic situation. (See: Stephens, *Exeter*, 59; CSPD, 1641-3, vol 489, no 81, p 298; JHC, 2, 683.)
26 *Trevelyan Papers*, Pt 3, 214-16, 219-21
27 On 17 May 1642 the House took notice of the fact that Exeter had contributed some £800 for Irish relief, £150 of which was returned to that city to help care for 'distressed Protestants'. (JHC, 2, 574.) On 7 June Mr Snow reported to the House that the Corporation of Exeter had subscribed £11,273 as at 31 May, while private citizens had contributed a further £4,581. A letter of thanks was to be sent to Exeter 'to take notice of their forwardness to the public service. . .' This money was to be spent to suppress the Irish rebellion. (Ibid, 2, 634.) Devon eventually gave more than £3,000 for Irish relief, and 'whereas divers distressed persons, Protestants, are come out of Ireland into several parts of that County', £500 was to be kept back to be spent for the immediate relief of those refugees. (Ibid, 2, 574.)
28 JHC, 2, 491, 502, 541. On 25 January 1642 the House gave encouragement to the raising of 500 men in Devon and Cornwall for military service in Ireland. (Ibid, 2, 394-5.) By December 1642 further efforts were being made to obtain supplies from Devon and Exeter in order to supply the army in Ireland. (Ibid, 2, 873.)
29 Ibid, 2, 506, 529. On 10 February 1642 the Earl of Bedford had been nominated by the House as the parliamentary lord lieutenant for Devon and Exeter. (Ibid, 2, 424.)
30 Ibid, 2, 404
31 Ibid, 2, 420, 787; DCRO, Quarter Sessions Rolls; HMC, 5th Rept, 'House of Lords MSS', 24
32 JHC, 2, 430-1, 448, 505, 642-3
33 See: CSPD, 'Ireland Adventurers', 1642-59, viii-x and xiv-xv for an explanation of these Acts of Parliament; Cotton, W. 'The Exeter Corporation and Cromwell's Land Settlement', DCNG, 1 (1888), 6; ERO, 'Misc Deeds', DD 62712, and 'Misc Papers', DD 62700A
34 *Trevelyan Papers*, Pt 3, 192-5, 197, 199-200, passim through p 228

35 See: Ibid, 206-8. HMC, 15th Rept, App, Pt 7, 'Somerset MSS' (1898), 64
36 *Trevelyan Papers*, Pt 3, 208-9, 217
37 Ibid, 211-2
38 Ibid, 210
39 See: DCRO, QSOB, 74, 97
40 JHC, 2, 536; BM, 'A Catalogue of the Names of the Divines . . .', E 144 (23)
41 JHC, 2, 579
42 DCRO, Quarter Sessions Rolls (1642-3). These opinions were given in the 'information of Thomas Rosemond . . . against John Austen of Sydmouth . . .'
43 Also see Somerset's petition in *Trevelyan Papers*, Pt 3, 225-6
44 Hamilton, *Quarter Sessions*, 122
45 QSOB, 99
46 Ibid, 100-1
47 Ibid

Chapter 4. Parliamentary Control of Devon, august-september 1642. Pages 55-69

1 Eliot-Drake, *Drake*, 288-9
2 JHC, 2, 494. See: Windeatt, Edward. 'Notes on Totnes Trained Bands and Volunteers', RTDA, 32 (Plymouth 1900), 95; HMC, 9th Rept, App, Pt 1, 'Borough of Barnstaple MSS' (1883), 215; HMC, 'Lord Montague of Beaulieu MSS' (1900), 80-1; and Cotton, *Barnstaple*, 15 & 17
3 BM, 669 f3 (43 & 44). On 17 March 1642 the list of DLs for Devon was approved by the House of Commons, with the exception of Henry Ashford, replaced by Arthur Ashford. On 28 May Sir John Bampfield was also approved as a DL. JHC, 2, 483 & 591
4 Fortescue's comments are enlightening: 'The scramble was supremely ridiculous, since it was all for a prize not worth the snatching'. 'It was to the party that first made an army, not to that which preferred the sounder claim to regulate the militia, that victory was to belong'. Fortescue, J. *A History of the British Army*, 1 (1899), 198-9
5 On 20 May parliament ordered the 'magazines of the several counties' placed under the control of the lords lieutenant. BM, 'T. Tracts' 669 f5 (28)
6 BM, 669 f5 (36)
7 Chadwyck-Healey, C. E. H. (ed). *Bellum Civile*, Somersetshire Record Society, 18 (1902), xxi. Also: JHC, 2, 635
8 Ibid, 2, 605, 629 & 633. Also: BM, 669 f5 (43)
9 JHC, 2, 651. On 1 August William Bartlett and Edward Anthony were appointed to receive the money, plate, and horses which should be subscribed in Exeter and, presumably, in Devon. (JHC, 2, 699.) They were further instructed on 9 August to pay out £5,000 to Chudleigh, supposedly for military purposes. (Ibid, 710.)
10 BM, 669 f5 (31)

11 Wedgwood, V. *The King's War, 1641-1647* (New York 1959), 114; Fortescue, *Army*, 1, 197
12 *Bellum Civile*, xxi
13 Ibid, 104-7, for a copy of the Devon Commission; and Clarendon, Edward Hyde, earl of. *The History of the Rebellion and Civil Wars in England...* 5 (Oxford 1888), 385
14 The commission had been attempted in North Devon in 1640 to raise troops to put down the Scots' rebellion. See: Cotton, *Barnstaple*, 64
15 *Bellum Civile*, xxii, 104. For the legal dispute between commission and ordinance, see Rushworth, *Collections*, 5:655ff
16 The introduction to this petition is interesting: 'We of the Grand Inquest for this County of Devon, considering by too too many, the present and imminent calamities of this kingdom, are not laid to heart; yea, that in some there appears unto us a disposition of hastening rather than preventing them, . . .'. DCRO, Seymour Papers, no 1392, 'Three Petitions . . .', 5
17 Ibid, 7-8
18 Ibid, 3-4. Other grievances were the absence of a large number of MPs from service in their respective Houses, the reduction of the number of JPs appointed for the county, and the necessity for immediate aid to Ireland as well as the consistent application of the laws against nonconformists and papists. This document was signed by future royalists and parliamentarians alike
19 CSPD, 1641-3, vol 491, p 375
20 Coate, M. (ed). 'An Original Diary of Colonel Robert Bennett of Hexworthy (1642-3)', DCNQ, 18 (1935), 252. Also: Cotton, *Barnstaple*, 58
21 HMC, 13th Rept, Pt 1, 'Duke of Portland MSS' (1891), 54
22 PRO, SP 16/491 no 116
23 The 12 August petition of the constables was markedly different from that presented to Foster by the constables of Somerset. In Somerset the judge was asked to rule on the legality of the commission of array, while in Devon he was asked to declare it illegal. CSPD, 1641-3, p 370
24 'To preserve the peace' was crossed out in the original report. (Ibid, 376.) Sir Robert continued:

> The truth is, the countries are much possessed with the illegality of the Commissions of Array, and the unlimited power, as is alleged, in the Commissioners, and by reason thereof infinitely averse thereunto; .... And, for anything I could perceive, the general desire of the countries is [that] both the Commissions of Array and Militia be laid down, and some way to be established by Act of Parliament for the quiet settling of the militia of the Kingdom. And truly the several contradictory commands make so great distraction (as they say) amongs them, . . . , and is likely to cause a great deal of public and private mischief if not quickly settled.

25 HMC, 4th Rept, App, 'De la Warr MSS' (1874), 308. Those named in the commission may be regarded as the original core of the royalist party within the county
26 Exeter City Library, Reference Room, 'A Declaration made by the Rt. Hon. the Earl of Bath . . .'. (London, September, 1642), I. Cotton, *Barnstaple*, 66-9, claims that it was the Earl's failure at South Molton which preceded, and led to, his Declaration to the county. John Cock, *Records of ye Antient Borough of South Molton in ye County of Devon* (Exeter 1893), 35ff, declares that once the Declaration had been made, then the

Earl moved into South Molton. Since the entire group of documents was printed on 29 September 1642, it is impossible to determine which version is correct, although the second appears to be more reasonable

27 'Declaration', 1-4. Fear of civil war had once again (5 August) produced a petition to the two Houses, this time from the 'Gentlemen, ministers, freeholders, and Inhabitants of Co. Devon'. HMC, 'De la Warr MSS', 307

28 BM, 'A Perfect Diurnall', E 202 (36), 5

29 HMC, 'De la Warr MSS', 307

30 While obeying parliament's orders to disarm recusants, the MPs in Devon also saw to the confiscation of weapons which might fall to the royalists, and took money and plate while they were at it. 'A Perfect Diurnall', E 202 (41), 5

31 Ibid

32 Cotton, Barnstaple, 63-4. Granville, Roger. The History of the Granville Family (Exeter 1895), 230, indicates that Sir Ralph Sydenham raised 500 horse for the royalist cause. He and Sir Bevil Grenville were most active in North Devon

33 Cotton, Barnstaple, 71. See: BM, 'A Letter from Belfast . . .', E 112 (23)

34 BM, 'Certain Information from Devon . . .', E 114 (24)

35 Ibid

36 BM, 'His Majesties Instructions . . .', E 117 (18), 5; and Bellum Civile, 103-4

37 JHC, 2, 744. Also: Buller Papers, 55 & 58; and BM, 'Letter From Belfast', E 112 (23), 7-8. In instructions sent to the DLs of each county on 15 September, additional authority was granted for purposes of controlling county militia and taking steps for further defence. BM, 'Instructions Agreed Upon by the Lords and Commons . . .', E 117 (5)

38 Exeter City Library, 'Declaration', 5

39 Ibid

40 Cotton, Barnstaple, 72. See: HMC, 'De la Warr MSS', 308

41 Ibid. The parliamentarians had been more successful earlier that month in getting men to march into Somerset to aid in the siege of Hertford's forces at Sherborne Castle. (Cf Fisher, 'The Apologie of Col. John Were', DCNQ, 4 (1907), 157.) Other references remark on the 'very courageous and stout-hearted soldiers' recruited from Devon under the command of Chudleigh and Northcote. See also: BM, 'Special Passages and Certain Informations . . .', E 116 (41); Bellum Civile, 11

42 HMC, 'De la Warr MSS', 308

43 Ibid, 304, 308 & 309

44 JHC, 2, 674, 683. See: Cotton, Barnstaple, 34

45 JHC, 2, 713, 770, 783. It is significant to note the acts of indemnity and support which parliament passed during this period, in addition to sending letters of thanks so as to lend authority to their growing party of sympathisers and at the same time to remove from local actions any taint of treason

46 Dunsford, M. Historical Memoirs of the Town and Parish of Tiverton, in the County of Devon (Exeter 1790), 49; ERO, Davidson MSS, 662-3; Russell, Totnes, 66

47 Wedgwood, King's War, 132

48 Cf Stephens, 'Roger Mallock, Merchant and Royalist', RTDA, 92 (Torquay 1960), 279ff

49 Bellum Civile, 24

50 DCNQ, 15 (1929), 33

51 Fortescue, Thomas, Lord Clermont. *A History of the Family of Fortescue in all its Branches* (1880), 30; Hoskins, *Devon*, 195
52 Champernowne, C. E. *The Champernowne Family* (1954), 248
53 Eliot-Drake, *Drake*, 212 & 276

Chapter 5. Outbreak of Civil Strife: Royalist Offensive in Devon, august 1642-june 1643. Pages 70-88

1 *Bellum Civile*, 1; BM, 'Thomason Tracts', E 109 (24); JHC, 2, 711
2 *Bellum Civile*, xxiii & 18; BM, 'Some late Occurrences in Shropshire and Devonshire', E 121 (4), 6. Worth, *Buller Papers*, 59
3 *Bellum Civile*, 18. Cf BM, 'The latest Remarkable Truths . . .', E 240 (23)
4 Cotton, *Barnstaple*, 76
5 BM, 'Latest Remarkable Truths'. It was in chasing Hopton toward South Molton that Bedford's troopers were successful in capturing the unsuspecting Pollard and Sydenham on 26 and 27 September, and then the Earl of Bath at Tawstock. With Hertford's forces dispersed and the leading Devon royalists arrested, Bedford felt the West Country secure enough to join Essex's army. 'Some late Occurrences', 6-7
6 Worth, *Buller Papers*, 59-60
7 Ibid, 73-5
8 'By no other means could Hopton have raised such a force so quickly', than by the legal methods thus employed. *Bellum Civile*, xxiv
9 Clarendon, *History*, 6, 241. See also: *Buller Papers*, 79, 80-4
10 Plymouth was thus to see the beginning of a continuous stream of parliamentarian sympathizers flocking to her gates. BM, 'New Newes from Cornwall . . .', E 124 (20), 5-6
11 Clarendon, *History*, 6, 242; and *Bellum Civile*, 22
12 Ibid, 22 & 23. A royal commission was obtained to insure the legality of the situation
13 JHC, 2, 803, 804
14 Ibid, 829; BM, 'Weekly Intelligence . . .', E 121 (34), 7. This newsbook already reports the 'great hindrance of trade and loss of time' resulting from these measures of defence
15 BM, 'Special Passages and certain Informations . . .', E 124 (14), 95-6; and JHC, 2, 811. On 17 October the House of Commons ordered £2,000 to be made available to Sir John Bampfield and Mr Waddon for the defence of Devon and Cornwall
16 Ibid, 2, 812, 813. On 18 October the House approved the following names of prominent Devonians to be nominated as DLs for that county: Sir Edmund Fowell, Edmund Parker Esq, Sir Shilston Calmady, Robert Savery Esq, Hugh Fortescue Esq, of Weare, John Courtenay Esq, of Melham, Sir Thomas Drew, Henry Walrond Esq, and William Fry Esq, senior
17 Ibid. The small number of troops authorised would seem to indicate that parliament did not yet appreciate fully the threat which Hopton constituted. By 1 November a quarrel over the command of these troops

brought a resolution from Commons providing for a joint command by the DLs of Devon and Exeter, Ibid, 2, 830

18 Ibid, 814, 815. Agreed to by both Houses on 19 October

19 Trevelyan, *Trevelyan Papers*, Pt 3, 228-9

20 Sir Peter Prideaux of Netherton, Sir John Pole of Shute, Sir Samuel Rolle of Heanton, Sir Nicholas Martyn of Oxton, and Sir John Bampfield of Poltimore. These men, in addition to Chudleigh, Northcote, Drake, Sir John Davy, and the DLs named above, constituted the core of the Devon committee and the heart of the parliamentary cause in the county

21 Merivale, J. H. 'Memorials of the Civil War in the County of Devon', *Retrospective Review*, 12 (1825), Pt 2, 180-2

22 Seven members of the Cornish committee, headed by Alexander Carew and Francis Buller, addressed a letter to the House of Lords, dated 29 October from Exeter, once again requesting aid from parliament, and indicating their efforts to obtain what help they could from Devon and the neighbouring counties. However: 'The Gentlemen of this County [ie, Devon] profess much willingness; but withal they protest they want money and arms'. (JHL, 5, 428.) It was this kind of activity which promoted rumours that the western counties were joining forces to halt Hopton's attempt to march to the king's army. (BM, 'God on the Mount', E 73 (4), 207-8.) The Cornishmen were forced to report to parliament shortly after: 'Devon pretends but little, and will act less'. (HMC, 10th Rept, App, Pt 6 (1887), 'Bouverie MSS', 93.)

23 JHC, 2, 818. Cf Ibid, 828, 829

24 BM, 'Thomason Tracts', 669 f5 (99). Accompanying the royal proclamation was an order to the mayor of Exeter demanding the arrest of those putting the militia into execution against royal authority. 'Portland MSS', 1, 68

25 HMC, 15th Rept, Pt 7 (1898), 'Somerset MSS', 64

26 BM, 'True and Remarkable Passages . . .', E 126 (35), 8. The author indicated that the city walls had been repaired, outworks erected, the magazine replenished, and trained men called up to protect Exeter

27 Wedgwood, *King's War*, 210; Granville, *Granville*, 246. Rumour had the number of these forces up to '5 or 6,000 well-armed, and plentifully furnished with money . . .'. 'Bouverie MSS', 93

28 *Bellum Civile*, 23-4

29 Ibid, 24. See also: BM, 'Special Passages', E 128 (28), 135. Ruthven was the new parliamentary commander of the Plymouth garrison

30 BM, 'A Perfect Diurnall of the Passages of Parliament', E 242 (27); 'The English Intelligencer . . .', E 127 (26), 8

31 'A Perfect Diurnall'. Neither Exeter nor Plymouth, for instance, were willing to send men very far from their town walls, each fearing royalist uprisings within their communities, in addition to facing overwhelming (as they believed) numbers of cavaliers in the field. See: Ibid, E 242 (26)

32 No mention of this first siege of Exeter is made in Hopton's *Bellum Civile*. The only evidence for the events of 18-21 November comes from BM, 'True and Joyfull Newes from Exeter', E 128 (11); although reference is made to it in Clarendon, *History*, 6, 246, and the urgency of parliamentary actions suggests such an emergency. On 25 November the parliament authorised the mayor and DLs of Exeter to garrison the castle, to keep continuous watch for enemy forces, and to maintain 200 trained men and volunteers from the county of Devon within easy distance for immediate aid to the city. More significant was the authority granted to the city

N

fathers to levy a general tax upon the inhabitants in order to pay for defence measures. (See: JHC, 2, 864; BM, 'A True and Perfect Relation of a Great and Happy Victory . . .', E 130 (25), 1.) At the same time, steps were taken to rush the Earl of Pembroke into the West. (JHC, 2, 865.)

33 'True and Joyfull Newes', 3-5. Exeter was reported to have some 8,000 men in arms to repel the cavalier threat. See Appendix A for instances of internal situations facing the hard-pressed city authorities at this time

34 Ibid, 4-6

35 Ibid, 6-8; BM, 'Thomason Tracts', E 242 (35). It seems probable that it was during this period that a petition went up to parliament from Devon which called for the strict enforcement of the laws against papist recusants, and particularly against foreign priests moving freely into England. BM, 'The Petition of the Knights, Gentlemen, and Yeomanry of the County of Devonshire', E 181 (27). Also: BM, 'A Remonstrance or Declaration . . .', E 124 (29), 8

36 BM, 'Special Passages', E 129 (5), 144. Also: E 129 (7); E 128 (8)

37 BM, 'True and Perfect Relation', 2

38 Ibid, 2-3; Bellum Civile, 25

39 JHC, 2, 876. On 13 December Robartes was suddenly replaced by Denzil Holles

40 JHC, 2, 884, 886, 895; BM, 'A Perfect Diurnall', E 244 (7). It was finally the Earl of Stamford who arrived in Devon with troops from Bristol. BM, 'England's Memorable Accidents', E 244 (34), 133

41 JHC, 2, 878

42 While the royalist sympathizers in this area had been caught unawares and quickly overawed during the summer months, by year's end the feeling was growing that the parliament had gone too far. Besides, Hopton was victorious in Cornwall, and might as easily conquer Devon

43 JHC, 2, 864; BM, 'True and Perfect Relation', 1. Dartmouth's position was made clear in a letter from Mayor Alexander Staplehill and Roger Matthew, MP, to the Speaker on 5 December: '. . . almost all the gentry in these parts are for the Commission of Array . . .', (HMC, 'Portland MSS', 1:77.)

44 MP for Plymouth

45 'Portland MSS', 1:76

46 Ibid, 1:77; Bellum Civile, 25. Hopton originally hoped to raise sufficient foot to continue his siege of Plymouth, but was disappointed to see the poorly armed and ill-disciplined crowd gathered at what appeared to be 'rather like a great fair than a Posse . . .'.

47 BM, 'Remarkable passages newly received . . .', E 130 (16). Totnes had been taken a few days before by part of Grenville's regiment

48 Bellum Civile, 26; BM, 'A Letter from Exeter . . .', E 130 (20), 3, 4. Some of the more important prisoners taken were Sheriff Edmund Fortescue, Colonel Sir Edward Seymour, and his son Edward, MP for the county

49 BM, 'True and Perfect Relation', 3-5. The Devon cavaliers were sent on to Plymouth and then by ship to London. See also: JHC, 2, 903, 961; Clermont, Fortescue, 33; Karkeek, P.Q. 'Sir Edmund Fortescue and the Siege of Fort Charles.' RTDA (1877), 339-40

50 Bellum Civile, 26. During this royalist occupation, the Corporation of Totnes collected more than £250 in money and plate to be loaned on the bond of a number of leading royalists. Windeatt, 'Totnes and the Civil War', RTDA, 45 (Plymouth 1913), 224

51 BM, 'True Newes from Devonshire and Cornwall', E 83 (43)

52 Ibid, 1-2
53 Cotton, *Barnstaple*, 104
54 BM, 'Thomason Tracts', E 244 (30), 8; and E 245 (11), 148. Cf Cotton, *Barnstaple*, 107; and R. N. Cotton, 'North Devon Cavalier', DCNG, 3:69
55 *Bellum Civile*, 26
56 Just about the time of the Modbury surprise, the Corporation of Exeter had firmly bound themselves to the parliamentary cause by the affirmation of a solemn covenant in which they had sworn to defend the city with their lives against the 'rebellious insurrections' brought about by the Cornish invasion. BM, 'A Letter from Exeter', 5-6
57 DCRO, Seymour Papers, 'A famous Victory . . .', 2-3. On 23 December Charles sent a letter to the Dean and Chapter of Exeter requesting a loan of £1,000. On the 29th he wrote again reproving them for their delay in this matter. Just how he expected them to pay when Exeter was in parliamentary hands is unknown. (HMC, 'Various Collections', Dean and Chapter of Exeter, 15:92.) Parliament was attempting to raise funds for Devon's defence, and on 27 December ordered Northcote to return to Devon to promote their cause. (JHC, 2, 903.) At the same time the two Houses issued a declaration extending their particular protection to Northcote, Rolle, Chudleigh, and Martyn. (BM, 'True Newes from Devonshire', 6.)
58 Hopton wrote to Exeter's mayor on three occasions. See: ERO, no 390A
59 BM, 'A Famous Victory obtained before the City of Exeter', E 84 (24), 3-6
60 *Bellum Civile*, 27-8
61 Prof J. Simmons calls Stamford's appointment as parliamentarian commander-in-chief in the west a 'double mistake' as it was based solely on his rank and wealth, and in the face of his military deficiency, ignorance of the West Country, and 'cantankerous' nature. 'Directly he arrived in Devon he made enemies.' Simmons, 'The Civil War in the West', *The West in English History*, (ed) A. L. Rowse (1949), 86
62 *Trevelyan Papers*, Pt 3, 230-1
63 JHL, 5, 544-5
64 'Portland MSS', 1:88, 89
65 *Bellum Civile*, 28-30
66 See: Coate, *Cornwall*, 42ff; Granville, *Granville*, 249; BM, 'Mercurius Aulicus', E 246 (16), 4; *Bellum Civile*, 29ff
67 'Portland MSS', 1:91-2
68 *Bellum Civile*, 30-1
69 Coate, *Cornwall*, 43, 44
70 Clarendon, *History*, 6, 250. The earl and the remainder of his men had withdrawn to the safety of Exeter
71 BM, 'A Perfect Diurnall', E 246 (1); and *Bellum Civile*, 33
72 See: *Buller Papers*, 84-5, 91; JHL, 5, 590
73 Metcalfe, Reginald. 'Sir Francis Basset . . . His Letters and Papers' . . . (1924), 3:4-5. This demand was based on the numerous reports of the internal divisions within the town, as well as its lack of supplies
74 BM, 'A Continuation of certain Special and Remarkable Passages . . .', E 246 (8) and (12). London newsbooks reported Hopton's retreat toward Dartmouth, but it appears unlikely that more than a small force moved in that direction so as not to prejudice the Plymouth siege. See: *Bellum Civile*, 33
75 HMC, 5th Rept (1876), 'House of Lords MSS', 71
76 See: BM, 'Special Passages', E 89 (17), 226; 'A Continuation . . .', E 246

(19) 2-3; 'A Perfect Diurnall', E 246 (20) and (30)
77 Granville, *Granville*, 251
78 'Special Passages', 226
79 *Bellum Civile*, 33; Granville, *Granville*, 251
80 Cotton, *Barnstaple*, 129
81 BM, 'Thomason Tracts', E 91 (25), 3
82 BM, 'A True and Perfect Relation of the Passages in Devonshire the Weeke', E 91 (4), 1
83 Granville, *Granville*, 252
84 The length of the battle of Modbury is variously reported, but it appears to have lasted from 3pm to 4am, by which time most of Slanning's men had withdrawn. 'A Perfect Diurnall', E 246 (37). Cf 'Passages in Devonshire', 2
85 Ibid
86 BM, 'A Continuation', E 246 (33), (37) and (38); 'The Kingdomes Weekly Intelligencer . . .', E 91 (8); and Seymour Papers, 'True Relation', 4
87 Hopton's and Mohun's regiments. See: Ibid, 5; 'The Kingdomes Weekly Intelligencer', 69; Coate, *Cornwall*, 54
88 *Bellum Civile*, 34; 'Passages in Devonshire', 5
89 'Special Passages', E 91 (5), 229. Also: 'Passages in Devonshire', 3
90 'The Kingdomes Weekly Intelligencer', 69-70
91 Clarendon, *History*, 6, 254. Sir George Chudleigh and the other committeemen emphasised the weak nature of their forces, what with desertion, lack of discipline, and limited supplies, in their letter to the Committee of Safety, dated 3 March 1643 from Plymouth. ('Portland MSS', 1:100.) At the same time, Hopton needed time to regroup his men. (*Bellum Civile*, 31-2.)
92 Coate, 'Bennett Diary', DCNQ, 18:257
93 Seymour Papers, 'A view of the Proceedings of the Western Counties for the Pacification of their present troubles' (1643), 4
94 Ibid, 4-5. Hopton claimed that only six commissioners met from each side, 'Gentlemen of fortune and quality' though they were. (*Bellum Civile*, 35.) The tract entitled 'The Protestation taken by the Commissioners of Cornwall and Devon . . .', E 94 (21), 12, lists nine Cornish names and eight Devonian as being appointed, although not always in attendance. Cf Clarendon, *History*, 6, 255
95 'A view of the Proceedings', 5-7; 'The Protestation'. For a chronological outline of the meetings, see: 'Portland MSS', 1:100-1. The Cornish desired that all forces in both counties be disbanded so that no aid could be sent to Somerset or Dorset if required.
96 Grenville's letter to his wife, 9 March, plainly shows his lack of confidence in the enemy's good faith. (Granville, *Granville*, 255.) See: 'Portland MSS', 1:101-2; 'Special Passages', E 93 (7), 255; JHC, 2, 1003 & 3:29; 'A Continuation', E 246 (45), 3; 'Certain Informations', E 94 (11), 76
97 'De la Warr MSS', 308
98 'Portland MSS', 1:102
99 'A view of the Proceedings', 10
100 BM, 'The Kingdomes Weekly Intelligencer', E 93 (19), 93; 'Certain Informations', E 99 (15)
101 JHC, 2, 1000
102 Addressing the leading citizens of Exeter, Prideaux 'made such a pithy speech that gave great content and encouragement . . .', winning over their support for renewed preparations and a continuation of the conflict.

'Certain Informations', 106. See also: 'Mercurius Aulious', E 96 (5), 157; 'The Protestation', 12; 'Portland MSS', 1:103

103 JHC, 3, 7, 57
104 Ibid, 11-2
105 'Portland MSS', 106
106 BM, 'A Full Relation of the great defeat given to the Cornish Cavaliers, by Sergeant Major General Chudley', E 100 (20), 4; 'A Most True Relation', E 100 (12), 1; 'Portland MSS', I:111
107 *Bellum Civile*, 36
108 Ibid, 37. It was only with the timely arrival of reinforcements from Plymouth that the parliamentarians were able to affect a complete withdrawal of men and equipment, losing only twelve dead and thirty to forty wounded. See: Rushworth, *Collections*, 5:268; and BM, 'A Most True Relation', 2-3
109 BM, 'A full Relation', 2
110 BM, 'A Most Miraculous and Happy Victory . . .', E 100 (6)
111 *Bellum Civile*, 38
112 BM, 'A Full Relation', 2. Retreat at that late hour was impossible as the lack of carriages and oxen would have meant abandoning their artillery and much of their ammunition; 'and to stand still had been to be certainly surprised, to lose their artillery, ammunition, themselves, and by probable consequence, the whole county'. ('A Most True Relation', 4.)
113 BM, 'The Kingdomes Weekly Intelligencer', E 100 (19); BM, 'Exploits Discovered . . .', E 100 (16). Also: 'Special Passages', E 100 (17) which gives Chudleigh's account of the Sourton Down engagement. The most complete account of these events is found in Coate, *Cornwall*, 62-4
114 BM, 'A Most True Relation', 4
115 Ibid, 5
116 The Devon foot were too frightened by the Cornish cannon to give support to Chudleigh's horse, and the General had to be satisfied with the disguise of a 1,000 lighted matches stuck in the hedges. 'The Kingdomes Weekly Intelligencer.' Also: Rushworth, *Collections*, 5:268; *Bellum Civile*, 39
117 Ibid, 40; 'A Most True Relation', 6. More important, perhaps, was the collection of correspondence, accounts, and lists of supporters taken by the Devonians. See: BM, 'Most Miraculous and Happy Victory', 4; HMC, 'Portland MSS', 1:112
118 See: *Rump : or An Exact Collection of the Choicest Poems and Songs relating to the Late Times* (1662), pp 134-5
119 *Bellum Civile*, 41
120 BM, 'A true Relation of the proceeding of the Cornish forces under the command of the Lord Mohune and Sir Ralph Hopton', E 102 (17); 'A true Relation of the Prosperous successe . . .', E 104 (11)
121 BM, 'A Perfect Diurnall', E 249 (8)
122 Coate, 'Bennett Diary', 257
123 Cotton, *Barnstaple*, 166-7. See: 'Certain Informations', E 104 (16), 148; *Bellum Civile*, 44
124 Ibid, 42. A complete discussion of the royalist victory at Stratton is given in Coate, *Cornwall*, 66ff; Gardiner, *History of the Great Civil War*, 1:136-8; Clarendon, *History*, 7, 88-9
125 Within ten days Chudleigh indicated his willingness to ask pardon from the king and accept a commission in the royal army. From Okehampton he sent a letter to his father, Sir George, notifying him of his decision and

urging him to do the same. (*Bellum Civile*, 44 & 45.) The son's actions caused the father to withdraw from parliamentary service, issuing a statement to explain his motives for retiring. (BM, 'A Delaration . . .', E 37 (20).) The Earl of Stamford immediately used these conversions as proof of young Chudleigh's treachery at Stratton. (BM, 'A Perfect Diurnall', E 249 (12).)

126 Clarendon, *History*, 7, 92

127 *Bellum Civile*, 46. Although having scornfully rejected the royalist summons, the Exeter committee was anxious about its position finding the trained bands and volunteers quite unreliable. 'For now the hearts of Parliament's friends are down, and many daily drop from us. We can do little for want of arms, which if not speedily sent will do us little good . . .'. BM, 'The Round-Heads Remembrancer . . .', E 105 (13), 5

128 *Bellum Civile*, 46

129 Clarendon, *History*, 7, 96

Chapter 6. Royalist Conquest of Devon and Exeter, june-december 1643. Pages 89-101

1 Carte, T. (ed) *A Collection of Original Letters and Papers* (1739), 1:21: 'The Gentry come in apace, but the commons not so heartily, nor in any considerable number. The true reason is, as they say, my countrymen love their pudding at home better than a musket or pike abroad, and if they could have peace, care not what side had the better.' Cf Cotton, 'North Devon Cavalier', DCNG, 3, 69; *Bellum Civile*, 85, 87. At this point the parliamentarians were still optimistic of uniting with Waller and forcing the withdrawal of the Cornish

2 *Trevelyan Papers*, Pt 3, 237-8

3 *Bellum Civile*, 50. It was necessary to remove Sir James Hamilton's rowdy force from Devon immediately. See: Cotton, *Barnstaple*, 192

4 It was at Lansdown that Sir Bevil Grenville was mortally wounded. Granville, *Granville*, 268

5 Coate, *Cornwall*, 102. According to Gardiner: 'To the men of the West, Plymouth was all that Hull was to the men of the North. . . Hull and Plymouth saved the Parliamentary cause. Charles' original design of advancing on three lines was necessarily postponed till it was too late . . .'. *Civil War*, 1:195. Cf Clarendon, *History*, 7, 151, 152 & 192

6 Ibid, 7, 150-5 & 192. County patriotism in the case of Devon and Cornwall royalists is held principally responsible for the decision to split the royal army. (Coate, *Cornwall*, 102.) It was not unwise for Charles to attempt to eliminate the threats in his rear, but it was foolish to sacrifice so much in the way of time, effort, and resources for the reduction of such places as Gloucester, Plymouth, and Hull. (Gardiner, *Civil War*, 1:197.)

7 ERO, Letter Book 60F, L 391 (Siege Accounts). A total of £4,374.11.3½ (£4,374.57) was spent on fortifications from December 1642 to August 1643

8 Ibid. Records of payment for Ford's company exist from 23 May to 5 August. Cf ERO, Chamber Act Book 8, 294. The £2,000 was collected within a fortnight, a large part of it contributed by the mayor and aldermen of the city. (Letter Book 60F, L 391.) Some £600 was lent to the DLs of Devon for payment of county troops

9 Nesbitt, F. 'Civil War Entries in Exeter Registers', DCNQ, 17 (1933), 221. Also: BM, 'Certain Informations', E 61 (16), 216. 'Mercurius Aulicus' reported a peace conference held during the first week of July, but nothing came of it. E 60 (18), 362, and E 63 (2), 387-8

10 ERO, Letter Book 60F, L 391

11 Ibid. Lists are provided of the number from each company being paid for service that day. L 391 contains further accounts showing the exact nature of the demands made upon the city in order to provide weekly payment to the troops and thus maintain discipline and loyalty. See: BM, 'The Copie of a Letter sent from Exeter . . .', E 65 (2), 1

12 This total figure from December 1642 to September 1643 resulted from: Provisions (£756.14.0) (£756.70), ammunition (£3,769.10.6) (£3,769.53), soldiers pay (£9,442.2.9) (£9,442.14), scouts (£136.13.6) (£136.67), and fortifications (£4,374.11.3½) (£4,374.57). These figures apparently do not include the £2,765.2.0 (£2,765.10) lent to the DLs of Devon for payment of soldiers on 5 September 1643. £14,020.1.1½ (£14,020.06) remained outstanding at the time of the surrender of Exeter. Edward Anthony and William Bartlett, acting as treasurers, collected £4,459.10.11 (£4,459.55) in voluntary subscriptions of money and plate

13 Some of Berkeley's forces were stationed at Columbjohn, while he maintained control also of the prison, church, inn and houses in St Thomas parish. Cotton, R. W. 'Naval Attack on Topsham', DCNQ, 1 : 153

14 BM, 'Copie of a Letter', 2 & 3

15 Ibid, 6

16 *Trevelyan Papers*, Pt 3, p 239

17 BM, 'A Letter from the Earl of Warwick', E 62 (9), 2

18 Cotton, 'Naval Attack', DCNQ, 1 : 154

19 Clarendon, *History*, 7, 193

20 BM, 'Certain Informations', E 60 (17), 204, and E 59 (1

21 Clarendon, *History*, 7, 194

22 Barnstaple records indicate that a force of 400 foot and 70 horse had been sent 'to beat off the enemy in South Molton' for two days around 17 July. Presumably this had been in response to an isolated excursion by part of the royalist force centred around Exeter. Gribble, J. B. *Memorials of Barnstaple* (Barnstaple 1830), 458

23 Ibid. I agree with Cotton, *Barnstaple*, 206, that the 'Summary' must be in error with regard to the date of the Torrington fight. Clarendon (*History*, 7, 194) puts the parliamentarian strength at 1,200 foot and 300 horse. Cotton's estimate of 500 foot and 200 horse is more reasonable. (*Barnstaple*, 196.)

24 Clarendon, *History*, 7, 194, 195. Clarendon claims 200 were killed, more than 200 captured, in addition to many wounded. (7, 196.) 'Mercurius Aulicus' put the figure at 100 killed and 211 prisoners taken, in addition to equipment and ammunition. (BM, Burney Collection, vol 11, no 13.)

25 Gribble, *Memorial*, 459; Cotton, *Barnstaple*, 207-8; Clarendon, *History*, 7, 197. Clarendon claims that Appledore fell within two or three days after Digby's victory at Torrington

26 BM, 'Add MSS', no 18,980, f110. In addition to a free pardon to all those

within the town walls, Maurice promised protection for the persons and goods of the inhabitants, freedom from heavy or unusual taxes, as well as the guarantee that the borough could continue under their former municipal leaders without burden of a garrison

27 Ibid; and Cotton, *Barnstaple*, 216-17, 227, 228. The ease with which the transition was made in the surrender of the three northern ports raised the cry of treachery from parliamentary pamphleteers. See: BM, 'The Weekly Account', E 250 (11), 2-3; HMC, 5th Rept, 'House of Lords MSS' (1876), 110

28 Clarendon, *History*, 7, 198

29 'Add MSS', no 18,980, f110. Also: HMC, 14th Rept, Pt 2, 'Portland MSS', 3 : 126

30 There is disagreement as to the exact date of the surrender of Exeter. Clarendon, writing many years later, claimed that 'that rich and pleasant city was delivered on the 4th of September which was within 14 or 16 days after Prince Maurice came thither . . .'. (*History*, 7, 198.) The Exeter antiquarian, Izacke, put the date at September 3rd, while Cotton and Gardiner agreed with Clarendon. The parish register of St Mary Arches records, however: 'September the 7th, this city was yielded up to the king's army in the year 1643'. (Brushfield, 'Diary', 268.) See also: Seymour Papers, 'Articles of Agreement', 1, for evidence that 7 September was the actual date of surrender. BM, 'Mercurius Aulicus', 8 September, was the only source, however doubtful, that Maurice did indeed attempt to take Exeter by force. See: Burnard, 'News', 216

31 For the complete terms of surrender see: 'Articles of Agreement'. Also: ERO, Chamber Act Book 8; 'Royal Letters', Letter Book 60A, L 13

32 Chamber Act Book 8, 299, 307, 309. Also see: BM, 'The Weekly Account', E 250 (13), 3; Cotton's *Barnstaple*, 229; Cotton, *Cathedral Records*, 94

33 Clarendon claims Maurice's first mistake following the fall of Exeter was the length of time wasted before advancing, '. . . for victorious armies carry great terror with them whilst the memory and fame of the victory is fresh'. (*History*, 7, 290.) Also according to Clarendon, a flood of new recruits swelled the size of Maurice's army to almost 7,000 men, in addition to a large body of horse. Digby supposedly had some 3,000 foot and 600 horse (Ibid, 289.)

34 See: JHC, 3, 227; Clarendon, *History*, 7, 294; Gardiner, *Civil War*, 1 : 207; and Burnard, 'News', 218. Carew had been an early and enthusiastic supporter of the parliamentary cause in the West and had since become disillusioned over the religious turn the struggle was taking

35 Clarendon comments on the 'great distraction' of the people of Plymouth at this time, as well as the 'wonderful consternation amongst them'. *History*, 7, 295 & 296

36 BM, 'Strange, True and Lamentable newes from Exeter . . .', E 70 (13).

37 DCRO, Seymour Papers, Maurice to Seymour and Fortescue, 10 September
At Totnes 500 horse and foot from Torrington joined Maurice

38 The Dartmouth Archives deposited in the ERO give a full account of the funds spent on Dartmouth defence from late 1642 until 5 October 1643. Eventual claims for reimbursement were sent to Parliament for the sum of £9,734.9.3 (£9,734.46). See especially: DD 62692, 62701, 62703, 62705, 62707-8, 62710a, and 62713

39 Clarendon, *History*, 7, 297. Maurice himself became seriously ill in mid-October. See: Warburton, E. *Memoirs of Prince Rupert* (1849), 2 : 307

40 See: Russell, *Dartmouth*, 113; and ERO, DD 62701
41 BM, 'The True Informer', E 70 (28), 31-2, copy of the Dartmouth articles of surrender
42 The port of Dartmouth subsequently became the seat of the small royalist navy outfitted under the Earl of Marlborough, as well as the storehouse for ammunition and supplies gathered from the South Hams. See: DCRO, Seymour Papers, passim; and HMC, 15th Rept, 'Somerset MSS' (1898), Pt 7, 67-8, 82-3. Also: CSPD, 1644, vol 501, p 160
43 The royalist army was on the march from Dartmouth to Plymouth by 17 October. Warburton, *Rupert*, 2:307. Cf Clarendon, *History*, 7, 297
44 See: Bracken, *Plymouth*, 129; Worth, R. N. 'The Siege of Plymouth', RTPI 5 (Plymouth 1876), 259-60; Worth, *Plymouth*, 98, 416
45 Clarendon, *History*, 7, 297. Parliament also moved to send money and powder to aid in Plymouth's defence. JHC, 3, 275, 293
46 Warburton, *Rupert*, 2:307. At the same time the puritan majority in Plymouth was plagued by the activities of a royalist minority. See: Worth, 'Siege of Plymouth', 5:251-2
47 Bracken, *Plymouth*, 128; Rushworth, *Collections*, 5:297. By this time Plymouth had been periodically under siege since November 1642 and had come to be considered by both sides as 'the Key to the West', a key that both desperately wanted
48 DCRO, Seymour Papers, 'A True Narration of the most Observable Passages', 1-2
49 Ibid, 2-5, 7. Also see: BM, 'A Letter from Plymouth . . .', E 74 (22), 1-3; and 'The Copie of a Letter, sent from the Commander-in-Chiefe . . .', E 76 (11), 1. An attempt was made to fortify Haw Start just above Mount Stamford, but without reinforcements from the town this proved impossible. At the same time, the royalists made an attempt on Lipson work, but probably only as a diversion
50 'True Narration', 5-6. The loss of Stamford did help to consolidate the remaining forces and supplies
51 In 'A Letter from Plymouth', 5, reference is made to the fact that the town was then 'at 6 and 7, and we stand unresolved who it is that doth, or can, or should command, and by that means are in a very ill posture'. (October 27.) See: HMC, 13th Rept, 'Portland MSS', 1:150, 152. Also: JHC, 3, 308-9, 312, 319, 328
52 'The Copie of a Letter', 2
53 'True Narration', 6-7
54 Ibid, 18. See: Rushworth, *Collections*, 5:297-8
55 'The Copie of a Letter', 3
56 'True Narration', 7, 8
57 Ibid, 8
58 Rushworth, *Collections*, 5:298; 'True Narration', 16-17
59 Ibid, 8
60 Ibid
61 See: BM, 'The Weekly Account', E 78 (29), 3
62 'True Narration', 8-11, 12. An attempt was also made that day on Pennycomequick. The next two weeks passed quietly for the garrison, marred only by a few skirmishes and raids
63 The cavaliers lost 100 killed, and the parliamentarians about the same number in killed and wounded. Ibid, 12-13
64 Ibid, 13-14, 19-20
65 See: BM, 'Certain Informations', E 77 (6), 351. The royalist party was

working to smooth the way for the return of English troops from Ireland now that Ormande had engineered a truce with the Irish rebels. At the same time, a royal proclamation condemned the recently secured league between Scotland and parliament which threatened severe consequences for the king's cause. See: Gardiner, *Civil War*, 1:245, 247, 336; BM, 'The Parliament Scout', E 67 (34), 97; 'The True Informer', E 78 (9), 91-2; Cotton, *Barnstaple*, 234

Chapter 7. Royalist War-time Administration of Devon and Exeter, 1643-6. Pages 102-108

1 The membership of the parliamentary committees for Exeter and Devon throughout the First Civil War can be found on a typescript list of Acts and Ordinances affecting these counties located in the ERO. Also see: JHC, passim; Firth, C. H., and Rait, R. S. *Acts and Ordinances*, 1:passim

2 Bedford House was originally used until royal visits became so frequent

3 These previously routine matters of repair took on increasing importance as the constant movement of troops and equipment gutted the highways and destroyed avenues of escape against enemy use. The JPs were forced to send off repeated orders to local officials to see to their repair

4 DCRO, QSOB, passim

5 No record exists of the Quarter Sessions for the Epiphany and Pasche terms of 1646. It appears almost certain that these pages were deliberately torn from the Order Book

6 The constables for each hundred were appointed annually by the two or three JPs living closest to the hundred concerned. See: Exeter City Library, Reference Room, 'Plain Directions to Church-Wardens and Constables', 4-5

7 See: DCRO, QSOB, 188, 197, 212. As the war continued an ever larger sum was required for payments such as that to 'William Gibb of Bradninch a maymed soldier' who received 40 shillings (£2.00), and Daniel Heard of Halberton who obtained 20 shillings (£1.00) from the Treasurer of Maymed Soldiers. Ibid, 137, 138

8 Ibid, 134, 121

9 See: Ibid, 139, 142, 144, 185, 194

10 Ibid, 186, 194

11 Ibid, 134, 144, 179. Late in 1643 a seven-man committee of JPs was appointed to look into the complaints over martial rate payments in Tiverton hundred, while at other times justices were called upon to consider the various assessments for other sections of the county

12 Ibid, 132, 182, 187

13 The same is true with regard to the royalist committees established in each of the major boroughs once a cavalier takeover had been accomplished

14 QSOB, 147, 182. See: Hamilton, *Quarter Sessions*, 130-1

15 QSOB, 164, for evidence of the structure of power in Devon

16 This sum was substantially higher than the £1,800 required weekly of Devon and the £50.10.0 (£50.50) from Exeter according to the Parliamentary Ordinance of 24 February 1643

17 Once the Western Association was formed, the Grand Committee took decisions for the entire region

18 County MP for Devon who was disabled from sitting in the Commons in June 1643

19 It took £194.4.6 (£194.23) to pay the garrison each week. Numerous receipts exist amongst the Seymour Papers for this weekly expenditure. £30 came from Dartmouth and Kingswear, the rest from the county commissioners. Even with reasonably steady contributions from Stanborough and Coleridge, the Dartmouth garrison was never entirely self-sufficient

20 DCRO, 'Seymour Papers'. On 23 February 1644 the commissioners agreed to allow Devonians to deduct sums spent on billeting from their weekly rates. 'Somerset MSS', 69

21 'Seymour Papers', passim

22 By the end of his year as Mayor of Totnes (1645-6), the corporation still owed Ley £128.19.0 (£128.95) for such expenses

23 Totnes Guildhall, 'Ley MSS', Box 17G

24 See: 'Seymour Papers', passim

25 ERO, DD 34816, 34817a-i, 34818, 34820, 34822

26 Coate, *Cornwall*, 110-17

Chapter 8. Consolidation of Royalist Control, january-september 1644. Pages 109-122

1 Exeter City Library, Reference Room, 'The Association, Agreement and Protestation of the Counties of Cornwall and Devon', 8

2 Ibid, passim. By June an association of the four counties and Exeter had been created. See: Metcalfe, 'Basset', 3:29:30; Cotton, *Barnstaple*, 237

3 See: DCRO, 'Seymour Papers', Sir Hugh Pollard to Seymour; 'The Association', 6-7

4 'Somerset MSS', 82, 83

5 'Add MSS', 18,981, f47

6 HMC, 7th Rept, App, 'Sackville MSS', 259; Cotton, *Barnstaple*, 239, 243

7 Also see: ERO, 'Davidson's Axminster MS', 663-5; HMC, 10th Rept, Pt 6, 'Lord Braye MS' (1887), 151; Arthur Fisher (ed), 'The Apologie of Colonel John Were . . .', DCNQ, 4:173; BM, 'A Perfect Diurnall', E 252 (25), 272

8 Clarendon, *History*, 8, 1. This parliamentary success was unfortunate in tempting Essex to march into Devon and Cornwall rather than concern himself with the capture of the king at Oxford

9 'Somerset MSS', 72

10 Lt Colonel Pryce at Cullompton related the difficulty in raising men for his regiment as the people 'generally cry out of the pressure and abuses of

the French horse and other troopers now in these parts . . .'. *Trevelyan Papers*, Pt 3, 248-9

11 Metcalfe, *Basset*, 3 : 18, 24-5. Also: 'Seymour Papers', Digby to Seymour, 22 April, and Grenville to Seymour, 24 April

12 ERO, 'Axminster MSS', 665; BM, 'Mercurius Aulicus', E 47 (14), 955

13 Clarendon, *History*, 8, 21

14 Long, C. E. (ed). *Diary of the Marches of the Royal Army during the Great Civil War; kept by Richard Symonds, Camden Society* (Westminster 1859), 3

15 On 2 May the Exeter Chamber agreed that £200 'shall be presented to the Queen's Majesty from this house as a testimony of the respect of this house unto her Majesty now in this City . . .'. ERO, Act Book 8, 315

16 JHC, 3, 488; Paul Q. Karkeek, 'Queen Henrietta Maria in Exeter . . .', RTDA (1876), 468. Also: Green, M. A. E. *Letters of Queen Henrietta Maria* (1857), 243

17 Rushworth, *Collections*, 5 : 684; Mary Coate, 'Exeter in the Civil War and Interregnum', DCNQ, 18 (1935), 347, a copy of an extract from St Edmund Parish register. In a letter to the Earl of Bath, Sir Ralph Sydenham wrote: '. . . a guard brought the news to the Preacher; he mistook, and gave thanks for a son; after dinner it proved a girl . . .'. 'De la Warr MSS', 296

18 Cotton, *Gleanings*, 98; Cotton, 'Misc', *Notes and Gleanings*, 1 : 46, 99-100; CSPD, 1644, vol 502, p 314

19 PRO, SP 21/16, ff20, 21. See: CSPD, 1644, vol 502, p 211

20 Ibid, 190, 240, 241

21 It was not the intention of the House that Essex go pesonally to relieve Lyme, but merely send such troops as he could spare. PRO, SP 21/18, ff99, 100. See: CSPD, 1644, vol 501, 181-2; 'A Perfect Diurnall', E 252 (50), 379. By mid-June a further delegation of 'Western Gentlemen' was in London pressing for the continuation of Essex's army in that area. JHC, 3, 488, 542

22 CSPD, 1644, vol 502, pp 232, 233. Cf JHL, 6, 603

23 Ibid, 616

24 CSPD, 1644, vol 502, pp 226, 228, & 241. See: Gardiner, *Civil War*, 1 : 356

25 Rushworth, *Collections*, 5 : 683-4

26 Symond, *Diary*, 98. Colonel John Were had hopes of crushing Maurice's army by swift cavalry action, but Essex moved in a slow and determined manner. CSPD, 'Addenda', vol 539, Pt 2, no 230, p 667; Fisher, 'Were', 166-8

27 Clarendon, *History*, 8, 60; CSPD, vol 502, p 240. Henry Jermyn put the figure at 3,000 in a letter to Rupert, 14 June. (Warburton, *Memoirs*, 2 : 422-3.) Wedgwood (*King's War*, 326) claims that in addition to the time wasted by Maurice at Lyme, some 1,000 men had been killed, large quantities of supples and ammunition used, and his reputation severely damaged

28 'Somerset MSS', 73

29 CSPD, 1644, vol 502, p 251

30 DCRO, 'Seymour Papers', Ames Amerideth to Seymour. Cf Warburton, *Rupert*, 2 : 422. On 29 June Richard Grenville wrote to warn Seymour of a plot within Dartmouth to overwhelm the garrison with the aid of forces from Plymouth

31 'Somerset MSS', 73-4

32 DCRO, 'Seymour Papers', 26 June. See: Letter from W. Grant, 24 June, from Exeter

33 Green, *Letters*, 247-9
34 Symond, *Diary*, 97. Essex had gone from Axminster to Honiton (1 July) to Cullompton (2 July) to Tiverton (3 July). Maurice's army was around Okehampton during this three-week period. Young, 'Okehampton', 287
35 Essex had refused the queen a safe conduct to Bath. Green, *Letters*, 246; CSPD, 1644, vol 502, 318. The Princess Henrietta was left with Lady Anne Dalkeith who saw to her safety until after the surrender of Exeter in 1646. See: *Notes and Gleanings*, 2:99-100; Rushworth, *Collections*, 6:318
36 Young, 'Okehampton', 287. Sir Francis Basset wrote to his wife on 3 July, presumably from Launceston: 'Here is the woefullest spectacle my eyes yet ever looked on. The most worn and weakest pitiful creature in the world, the poor Queen, shifting for an hour's life longer'. Metcalfe, *Basset*, 3:34. Also: Roberts' *Memorial Book*, RTDA, 10:325; Karkeek, 'Henrietta Maria', 474
37 Green, *Letters*, 249-50. Although chased by ships under the command of Vice-Admiral Batten, the queen arrived safely in France on 15 July. Karkeek, 'Henrietta Maria', 479
38 A letter from Colonel John Luttrell to Captain Bennett (25 June from Barnstaple) indicates that plans had been in the making for an uprising for some time. Cotton, *Barnstaple*, 255-7
39 'De la Warr MSS', 304; Rushworth, *Collections*, 5:684
40 Chanter, *Barnstaple Records*, 2:247; BM, 'Mercurius Britanicus...', E 54 (6), 331. Also: Cotton, *Barnstaple*, 263-6
41 CSPD, 1644, vol 503, 303
42 Gribble, *Memorial of Barnstaple*, 458, 459. Robartes' three companies, plus the forces Luttrell had raised, were quartered on the town from the first week in July until the surrender on 17 September. This alone cost £1,120.18.0 (£1,120.90)
43 Cotton, *Barnstaple*, 277-8. See: Coate, 'Bennett's Diary', DCNQ (1935), 18:258-9
44 Cotton, *Barnstaple*, 298-9. Sir Allen Apsley was sent to lift this siege on 17 August. See: 'Somerset MSS', 79. At the same time Sir Francis Dodington, by-passing Barnstaple, set siege to Ilfracombe. (Cotton, *Barnstaple*, 307, 309.)
45 CSPD, 1644, vol 502, pp 304 & 335. Symond's diary indicates that some 3,205 officers and men were mustered at Tiverton in July. (p 73)
46 CSPD, 1644, vol 502, pp 304:335. Cf JHL, 6, 616-17. On 10 July the House of Commons ordered any western MP who belonged to a county committee to return to his respective county 'to advance the service of the Parliament'. (JHC, 3, 556.) On the same day Lord Robartes was appointed Lord Lieutenant of Devon and Exeter, and on 15 July John Luttrell became High Sheriff of Devon. (Ibid, 556, 561.)
47 CSPD, 1644, vol 502, p 335
48 'Somerset MSS', 75, 76-7, 81-2
49 BM, 'Perfect Occurrences', E 252 (53); CSPD, 1644, vol 502, p 342. See: Ibid, p 356; & 'Somerset MSS', 75-6
50 'Seymour Papers', Maurice to Seymour, 11 July; 'Somerset MSS', 74, 75-6, 77
51 CSPD, 1644, vol 502, pp 350-1
52 Rushworth, *Collections*, 5:686
53 In early July the prince had concentrated his forces at Okehampton, recalling the men sent to Barnstaple and drawing off others from before Plymouth. ('Seymour Papers', Grenville to Seymour, 19 July.) Once the

queen was safely in Cornwall, he had returned via Okehampton to Crediton, and then to Heavitree, narrowly missing contact with Essex's army in doing so. See: Cotton, *Barnstaple*, 283-4, 287; 'Somerset MSS', 76; Warburton, *Rupert*, 3:2; 'A Perfect Diurnall', E 254 (7), 416

54 CSPD, 1644, vol 502, pp 358-9. On 16 July the committee warned Essex of the king's advance into the West, and that Waller had only 2,500 horse and 1,500 foot. (Ibid, 354.) Even this figure was too optimistic

55 Clarendon, *History*, 8, 91 92, Waller's appearance was expected at any time and this would hopefully place the king's army at the disadvantage if Essex were to turn eastward. (Rushworth, *Collections*, 5:690.)

56 Symond, *Diary*, 98. See: Young, 'Okehampton', 288. Essex reached Horsebridge by 26 July

57 See: 'Seymour Papers', Edmund Fortescue to Seymour, 24 July

58 'The True Informer', E 4 (11), 299, and (32), 307; 'Perfect Occurrences', E 254 (9); Rushworth, *Collections*, 5:691

59 CSPD, 1644, vol 502, p 379

60 'The True Informer', E 4 (32), 308

61 See: Cotton, *Barnstaple*, 294

62 Clarendon, *History*, 8, 71. Also: Carte, *Original Letters*, 1:59

63 Warburton, *Rupert*, 3:3

64 This venture proved unsuccessful, but was repeated in November, with the same sad results. 'Axminster MSS', 667-9

65 Ibid, p 666; 'A Perfect Diurnall', E 254 (12), 241

66 Symond, *Diary*, 38

67 Chamber Act Book 8, 316 & 317. In order to raise this money the Chamber had had to sell the city's plate

68 Symond, *Diary*, 2

69 Chamber Act Book 8, 318

70 Ibid. Warrants were sent out from Exeter to muster the Devon trained bands, but few came in

71 Symond, *Diary*, 39; Warburton, *Rupert*, 3:3. Miss Coate (*Cornwall*, 138) puts the number of Maurice's army at almost 9,000 men. This appears rather high as contemporary accounts put the prince's force at 7,500 and the king's at about 8,000

72 Symond, *Diary*, 39, 41 & 42. The king's army quartered on Sunday night at Newton St Cyres. Symond reports the plundering and sacrilege done by the parliamentary forces in the Crediton region just the week before. At Bow, Charles slept in an alehouse, while his army quartered at Spreyton, some three miles from town. See: Warburton, *Rupert*, 3:4

73 Symond, *Diary*, 44 & 45. Also: 'De la Warr MSS', 308. Symond puts the size of Grenville's army at 8,000 men; the DNB puts the figure at 2,400. (DNB, vol 23, p 125.)

74 Symond, *Diary*, 98

75 Warwick wrote to the Committee of Both Kingdoms on 18 August from Plymouth: 'The wind has been long at west, and blown so hard that we could send no relief to the Lord General's army, which receives all its provisions from this town, and will soon exhaust them if not still supplied'. CSPD, 1644, vol 502, p 436

76 Charles wrote to Essex on 6 August asking him to treat for peace, but the parliamentary commander had not responded. Thus, on 8 August the king had a letter sent from his leading officers, again entreating negotiations for peace. Essex returned a flat refusal on 10 August. 'Seymour Papers'. See also: CSPD, 1644, vol 502, pp 433-4

77 Ibid, p 398; and 'Mercurius Civicus', E 8 (12), 634. Essex's letter to the committee on 16 August reveals a steadily worsening situation as he was completely hemmed in and 'in great want of victuals, . . .'. The narrow passages made movement extremely difficult. 'For aught I can perceive the enemy's intention is to starve us out, . . .', while the Cornish were proving to be 'more bloody than the enemy'. CSPD, vol 502, pp 433-4

78 Ibid, 398-9. Essex wrote on 16 August: 'If any [of the Parliament's] forces had followed the King, as we expected, when we came into these parts, in all probability this war would have had a quick termination'. Ibid, 434

79 Ibid, 420. Essex apparently did not receive this letter, as the committee repeated themselves on 19 August. Ibid, 437-8

80 For this Cornish phase, see: Coate, Cornwall, 139-51

81 CSPD, vol 502, pp 439-40 & 446. Waller was to follow soon thereafter with additional forces. See: JHC, 3, 601, 602, 603 & 605

82 Clarendon, History, 8, 114

83 JHC, 3, 615; BM, 'The Parliament Scout', E 8 (11), 505

84 Symond, Diary, 62. Local forces had to be raised by Colonel Seymour during mid-August to suppress disturbances in the South Hams. See: 'Somerset MSS', 78; 'Seymour Papers', Sir Edmund Fortescue to Seymour, 23 August from Lostwithiel

85 BM, 'Add MSS', no 18,981, f241; Clarendon, History, 8, 14

86 CSPD, 1644, vol 502, p 456

87 With Lord Wilmot's arrest, George Goring had taken command of the royalist horse. Clarendon, History, 8, 116. See: 'Somerset MSS', 79

88 BM, 'The Parliament Scout', E 8 (34), 510; 'The Kingdomes Weekly Intelligencer', E 12 (14), 601-2; 'Add MSS', no 18,981, f239. At Crediton the parliamentary horse had split, one part moving toward Lyme Regis, and the other to Barnstaple. (Cotton, Barnstaple, 315.)

89 'De la Warr MSS', 308

90 Warburton, Rupert, 1:519. Goring settled his forces at Okehampton; Berkeley's at Tiverton. (Cotton, Barnstaple, 314, 315.) Grenville's delay in reaching Goring added to the latter's insistance that he could do little without a strong body of foot. (Clarendon, History, 8, 131.)

91 Coate, Cornwall, 149

92 On 3 September Essex wrote to both Houses disclaiming all blame for himself and his officers for this disaster: 'I shall only add this, that if relief had come in time, by the Grace of God the war had been ended, . . .'. HMC, 6th Rept, 'H. of Lords MSS' (1877), 25

93 For a description of the harsh treatment accorded the foot soldiers on their march to Portsmouth, see: 'The Parliament Scout', 511; Fisher, 'Were's Apologie', 159-63; Coate, Cornwall, 152; Young, 'Okehampton', 289

94 Clarendon, History, 8, 131 & 133. By making an attempt on Plymouth immediately the king could be assured of the continued service of the Cornish levies who were anxious for such an enterprise. See: HMC, 15th Rept, App, Pt 2, 'Hodgkin MSS' (1897), 99-100. This delay, however, dissipated the force which a victorious army might have had in striking quickly at London. See: Coate, Cornwall, 156

95 Symond, Diary, 78; Warburton, Rupert, 3:4

96 Strenuous efforts were still being made to halt the parliamentarian horse escaping through Devon. Berkeley was ordered to take all available force of horse and musketeers from the Exeter garrison in pursuit of the enemy, and Sir Richard Cary was to follow with 2,000 additional musketeers. ERO, 'Letters and Papers', No 56999, nos 7 & 8

97 HMC, 'Hodgkin MSS', 100-101 & 106; ERO, 'Letters and Papers', No 56999, nos 5, 6, 9, 10 & 11. Clarendon remarks on the rapid wasting away of the royalist armies, but has high praise for the 'diligence and activity' of the Devon commissioners for their ready provision of £2000 in cash, 300 suits of clothes, besides shoes and stockings. *History*, 8, 145

98 BM, 'Mercurius Civicus', E 10 (11), 656; Symond, *Diary*, 80 & 81. Clarendon attributed the stubborness of the place to the fact that Lord Robartes was now governor of Plymouth: '. . . one who must be overcome before he would believe that he could be so'. *History*, 8, 133

99 See: Cotton, *Barnstaple*, 317, 318 & 325

100 'De la Warr MSS', 308. See: 'Mercurius Civicus', E 13 (9), 1174; 'The True Informer', E 10 (17), 348-9. Ilfracombe surrendered to the cavaliers at the same time

101 Cotton, *Barnstaple*, 350; Granville, *Granville*, 311-12

102 Clarendon, *History*, 8, 145; Warburton, *Rupert*, 4; Symond, *Diary*, 82-3

103 Cotton, *Gleanings*, 100

104 Sir Francis Dodington was to march his regiment to Taunton, while Exeter troops were to go to Lyme. 'Hodgkin MSS', 101; Clarendon, *History*, 8, 146 & 147

105 ERO, 'Letters and Papers', No 56999, nos 13 & 18. On 21 September an arrangement was also worked out whereby Haytor hundred agreed to support a regiment of 1,000 officers and men to serve under Sir Henry Cary wherever desired, in lieu of payment of all regular taxes and martial rates. This regiment was to report to Chard by 30 September. (Ibid, no 12.)

106 Symond, *Diary*, 97 & 110; Warburton, *Rupert*, 4

107 See Windeatt, E. 'Totnes and the Civil War', RTDA, 45 (1913), 221-2

108 ERO, 'Letters and Papers', No 56999, no 14

109 For the activities in east Devon on 15 November, and again in mid-December, see: BM, 'Three Several Letters of Great Importance', E 21 (6), 2-3; 'Perfect Passages', E 19 (3), 46-8; 'The True Informer', E 22 (14), 442; DCRO, 'Seymour Papers', commissioners in Exeter to Edward Seymour, 23 December

Chapter 9. The Siege of Plymouth, 1644-january 1646. Pages 123-134

1 BM, 'A Continuation of the true Narration', E 47 (1), 2

2 HMC, 6th Rept, 'House of Lords MSS' (1877), 3; 14th Rept, 'Portland MSS, 3 : 120. For the controversy which developed over the command in late January-early February, see: BM, 'The Military Scribe', E 35 (21), 9-11

3 Rumours were again widespread in April when it was discovered that a Plymouth woman was corresponding with the enemy, providing them with information about the strength and morale of the garrison, and actually supplying clothes for the fugitive Collins. BM, 'A Continuation', 9

4 Clarendon, *History*, 9, 62, 63
5 'Somerset MSS', 71-2
6 Granville, *Granville*, 285-6
7 Ibid, 3-4. With Gould's death, the military command was put into commission, authority being shared by the mayor and Colonels Crocker and Martin, while Captain Henry Hatsell commanded the Island and Captain Samuel Birch the Fort. On 16 April Martin obtained sole command
8 Ibid, 5, 6; 'Portland MSS', 121
9 BM, 'A Relation of the Great Victories . . . ,' E 59 (10), 1-3, 5-6; 'A Perfect Diurnall', E 252 (38), 349
10 Ibid, E 252 (47), 376
11 'House of Lords MSS', 12, JHC, 3, 488; 'A Perfect Diurnall', E 252 (32), 326. Also JHL, 6, 545; C. E. Welch, DCNQ (1964), 29 : 146-7
12 CSPD, 1644, vol 502, pp 390, 436
13 'House of Lords MSS', 25
14 PRO, SP 21/7, 184 & 188; CSPD, 1644, vol 503, pp 482, 485-6 & 496. Colonel William Strode was ordered to send 500 to 600 foot to Plymouth, but it soon became clear that he had no such force to send. Ibid, 487 & 502
15 JHC, 3, 621
16 CSPD, 1644, vol 503, pp 482 & 485
17 Ibid, 486. Of the many troops ordered to Plymouth it is not clear just how many actually arrived in addition to the 700 men with Colonel Birch. (Ibid, 526, 534.) Essex had left Colonel Harvey's regiment of horse there, with sufficient supplies and money. (pp 493-4. See also: pp 498, 503, 504, 515.) Essex felt that men and money were most severely needed in Plymouth, not provisions
18 Ibid, pp 515-16
19 In the last royalist assault, the parliamentarian seamen played a key role in the defence of the town, giving much-needed support to the dispirited inhabitants who 'have laid aside their way of trade and commerce, and wholly betake themselves for defence of the Town, . . .'. BM, 'The Weekly Account', E 10 (6), 441-2; CSPD, 1644, vol 503, p 515
20 See: Ibid, pp 522 & 536
21 Ibid, 515 & 536. Grenville thought the time suitable to attempt to bribe Colonel Searle into betraying the place. Captain Joseph Grenville was captured and hung as a spy when the plot was discovered, something Sir Richard did not forget. (See: 'Mercurius Civicus', E 10 (30), 666; JHC, 3, 667) Symptomatic of the internal quarrels was the series of letters published in November 1644 stating the accusations and counter-accusations of Charles Vaughan and Philip Francis, late mayor of Plymouth, charging one another with malfeasance in office, misappropriation of funds, and even treason. See: BM, 'Some of Mr Philip Francis misdeameanours . . . , E 257 (10); 'The Misdemeanours of a Traytor . . .', E 258 (13); 'The Most True and Unanswerable Answer of Charles Vaughan . . .', E 258 (29)
22 BM, 'A Diary, or an Exact Journal', E 16 (13), 188
23 Clarendon, *History*, 9, 22
24 'Seymour Papers', passim; Clarendon, *History*, 9, 54
25 See: 'Somerset MSS', 81
26 CSPD, 1644-5, vol 503, p 12. See: 'Mercurius Civicus', E 13 (6), 681-2; 'A Diary or an Exact Journal', E 256 (22), 169; 'The Kingdomes Weekly Intelligencer', E 12 (23), 613; JHC, 3 : 662
27 'Mercurius Aulicus', E 16 (24), 1211
28 'A Diary, or an Exact Journal', E 16 (13). Cf 'Mercurius Aulicus', 1212;

'Mercurius Civicus', 686; 'Perfect Passages', E 14 (14), 9; CSPD, 1644-5, vol 503, p 36

29 'The True Informer', E 19 (9), 422
30 'Three Several Letters of Great Importance', E 21 (6), 3
31 13th Rept, 'Portland MSS', 1 : 193
32 'Perfect Occurrences', E 258 (9)
33 'The True Informer', 422 & 424; 'Portland MSS', 1 : 194
34 'Perfect Occurrences'
35 Portland MSS', 1 : 194
36 'Perfect Occurrences'
37 JHC, 4, 2
38 Several London newsbooks carried stories of Grenville's cruel and oppressive behaviour during these winter months as he attempted to raise a sufficient force with which to attack Plymouth, as well as to maintain control of the countryside. See: 'Perfect Passages', E 258 for March 5-11 and 12-19
39 BM, 'Mercurius Britanicus', E 25 (10), 526; 'Perfect Occurrences', E 258 (14)
40 'A Perfect Diurnall', E 258 (15), 611. Also: CSPD 1644-5, vol 506, pp 251-2
41 CSPD, 'Addenda', vol 539, pt II, no 253, p 673
42 'A Perfect Diurnall', 612; 'Perfect Occurrences'
43 'Seymour Papers', passim. Grenville was acting under authority granted by a royal commission to draw on Devon and Cornish forces to carry on the siege of Plymouth. He was also high sheriff of Devon. Also: 'Somerset MSS', pt 7, p 84
44 BM, 'A True Relation of a Brave Defeat . . . ', E 271 (3), 1-2
45 'Mercurius Civicus', E 270 (29), 835; 'A Perfect Diurnall', E 258 (31), 556. Also: JHL, 7, 255
46 BM, 'God appearing for the Parliament . . .', E 271 (22), 4. See: True Relation of a Brave Defeat', 4; and JHL, 7, 256
47 The accounts of this committee have been reproduced by Worth, R. N. in 'The Siege Accounts of Plymouth', RTDA, 17 (Plymouth 1885), 216-39. The earliest mention of committee action dates from September 1644, but the regular accounts exist only from February 1645
48 Replaced by Robert Gubbes on 25 March
49 Sir John Bampfield, Colonel James Kerr, John Beare, Philip Francis and Colonel John Crocker were also recorded as members of the committee during 1645. Henry Rexford acted as clerk. See: Worth, 'Siege Accounts', 219-20, where Robartes is seen as making the appointments to the committee by virtue of his position on the parliamentary Committee of the West, and as governor of Plymouth. Once Robartes was forced to give up his command, Colonel Kerr appears to have taken charge, with Bampfield in authority on the Island. Also: Granville, Roger. *The King's General in the West*, opposite p 60
50 Alsop had retained control of the bulk of the £2,511 sent down from parliament by February 1645. £511 was granted to Bampfield for payment to his men. Worth, 'Siege Accounts', 216, passim
51 See: JHC, 4, 72 & 79
52 See: Worth, *History of Plymouth*, 128
53 Worth, 'Siege Accounts', 238; Worth, 'The Siege of Plymouth. A Chapter of Plymouth History Re-Written', RTPI, 5 (Plymouth 1876), 303-4
54 Worth, 'Siege Accounts', 239
55 Carte, *Letters*, 1 : 79. Cf 'Somerset MSS', 84

56 'Perfect Passages', E 260 (3), 174
57 'The Weekly Account', E 277 (9)
58 'A Diary or an Exact Journal', E 284 (8)
59 Ibid; and JHC, 4, 137
60 'House of Lords MSS', p 58
61 JHC, 4, 136-7; BM, 'The Moderate Intelligencer', E 284 (6), 85; 'A Perfect Diurnall', E 260 (35), 741
62 JHC, 4, 157; 'A Diary, or an Exact Journal', E 286 (27)
63 CSPD, 1644-5, vol 507, p 524
64 Worth, *Plymouth*, 128
65 'The City Scout', E 298 (28), 2-3
66 DCNQ, 12 (1923), 30
67 JHC, 4, 279 & 293. Kerr appears to have remained in command until January 1646 however. (See: JHL, 8, 6; JHC, 4, 375 & 394; Worth, *Plymouth*, 129.) On 29 September Arthur Upton was nominated to be governor of the Fort and Island (JHC, 14, 293), while Captain William Batten had already been selected to command at Batten's Tower and Mount (Ibid, 4,261.)
68 DCNQ, 12:30; 'Perfect Passages', E 266 (16), 439, emphasised the help given Plymouth by nearby parliamentarian port towns and others friendly to the cause without which 'they might have been distressed ere this; . . .'. See: 13th Rept, 'Portland MSS', 1:313. £1,000 a week was now required for payment of troops
69 JHC, 4, 355
70 JHL, 8, 8
71 Ibid, 6-7
72 JHC, 4, 355
73 BM, 'Sir John Digby's Letter . . . ', E 314 (10), 3, 4, 6, 7
74 See: 'Seymour Papers', 'Parliaments Victories', 3-4, 6; 'Portland MSS', 1:330; 'Perfect Passages', E 314 (20), 497, 498. Also: Worth, 'Siege', RTPI, 5:296-7
75 Worth, *Plymouth*, 130
76 'Perfect Diurnall', 17 January 1646, as found in R. Burnard, 'News from the West, 1643-1646', RTDA, 11 (1889), 227
77 Worth, *Plymouth*, 131, 132

Chapter 10. The Prince of Wales in the West, january 1645-april 1646. Pages 135-151

1 Metcalfe, *Basset*, 3:31. Also: Warburton, *Rupert*, 2:412-13; 'Add MSS' 18, 981, f184; Roy, Ian. 'The Royalist Council of War, 1642-6. BIHR (1962) 35:165
2 See: Gardiner, *Civil War*, 2:180; Clarendon, *History*, 8, 256 & 257
3 HMC, 15th Rept, Pt 2, 'Hodgkin MSS' 106. See: Clarendon, *History*, 8, 258
4 Ibid, 179-80, 253, 279, and 9, 6 & 7. See also, 8, 286, footnote no 2. Prince Charles was to act on the advice of a council whose membership included

the Lords Capel, Hopton, and Colepeper, Sir Edward Hyde, and the Earl of Berkshire

5 Ibid, 9, 10

6 CCSP, 1:259, no 1834. Goring anticipated the immediate arrival of 1,500 horse and foot from Exeter. See: Clarendon, *History*, 9, 8 & 9

7 Gardiner, *Civil War*, 2:182. Berkeley apparently agreed to supply 1,000 foot and 500 horse. See: CCSP, 1:259 & 260

8 Clarendon, *History*, 9, 11-13. See Coate, *Cornwall*, 169

9 Carte, *Letters*, 1:97

10 Clarendon, *History*, 9, 12, 13, 14; CCSP, 1:261, nos 1850 & 1852

11 Carte, *Letters*, 1:77. 'Here will be no good done, the enemy being so powerful and the Gentlemen of the Country so divided, that it is of equal difficulty to vanquish the one, as to compose the other'.

12 CSPD, 1644-5, vol 507, p 426

13 Clarendon, *History*, 9, 15. Clarendon indicates that Grenville actually told his men to refuse obedience to Berkeley. See: Carte, *Letters*, 1:97-8

14 CCSP, 1:263, nos 1866 & 1868

15 Clarendon, *History*, 9, 16 & 17; Warburton, *Rupert*, 3:79-80

16 See: Chanter, *Barnstaple Records*, no lxxxi

17 See: Clarendon, *History*, 9, 20, 25 & 26

18 Ibid, 22. The commissioners complained that Grenville took most of the letter and subscription money contributed in Devon and refused to recognise their authority to settle confiscated estates, and collect excise and other taxes in the hundreds under his control

19 Clarendon, *History*, 9, 23, 24-5 & 26

20 Ibid, 27. Grenville never did accept this new financial arrangement. See: Ibid, 52-3; 'Seymour Papers', Grenville to Seymour from Exeter, 25 May 1645

21 Carte, *Letters*, 1:98

22 Clarendon, *History*, 9, 31 & 43. Berkeley was confirmed in his new command before Plymouth

23 CSPD, 1644-5, vol 507, no 58, p 480. Colepeper described their hope of having an army of 9,000 foot and 5,000 horse if all went well. (Ibid, 479.) On 22 May Colepeper again wrote an encouraging letter to George Lord Digby to remark on the 'extraordinary willingness' of the Devon commissioners, and Berkeley, in raising new recruits. (Ibid, 512.) The council also wrote to remark on the excess of authority granted to Goring, but not until mid-June did the king respond to say that he had had no intention of limiting the prince's authority by his letter of 20 May. (CCSP, 1:266, 267, nos 1890 & 1895.)

24 13th Rept, 'Portland MSS', 1:224-5. Cf Clarendon, *History*, 9, 44

25 Ibid, 47. The prince's council had little choice but to support Goring in his refusal to leave the West, as they had no forces with which to replace his. Although Hyde had been optimistic in his letter of 2 May to Rupert (Warburton, *Rupert*, 3:95-6), in that of 24 May the councillors declared that the entire West would fall if Goring's army marched to the king's assistance. (Lister, T. H. *Life and Administration of Edward, First Earl of Clarendon* (1837), 3:11-12.)

26 Carte, *Letters*, 1:98

27 'Seymour Papers', Grenville to Seymour, 11 May; Henry Ashford, Peter Sainthill, and John Were to Seymour, 11 June

28 Carte, *Letters*, 1:98

29 CCSP, 1:267, no 1892

30 Warburton, *Rupert*,3 : 92-3. See: Chanter, J. P. 'Charles, Prince of Wales, at Barnstaple, and His Hostess', RTDA, 49 (Plymouth 1917), 389-96

31 Carte, *Letters*, 1 : 98

32 CCSP, 1 : 267, 268 & 269, nos 1897, 1898 & 1909. See: 'Portland MSS', 1 : 230 & 232; Lister, *Clarendon*, 3 : 22

33 Quite possibly because Goring objected to Grenville having the rank of of field marshal which would be superior to that of Goring's second-in-command, Lord Wentworth. CCSP, 1 : 269, no 1909

34 Carte, *Letters*, 1 : 99-100. Cf Clarendon, *History*, 9, 54 & 56

35 'Seymour Papers'

36 Clarendon, *History*, 9, 59; 'Somerset MSS', 85. See: Warburton, *Rupert*, 3 : 125

37 CCSP, 1 : 269-70, nos 1910 & 1911. Grenville apparently felt that Berkeley was behind the charges made against him, and accused the council of favouring the governor of Exeter. Clarendon, *History*, 9, 60

38 Carte, *Letters*, 1 : 100-1

39 Clarendon, *History*, 9, 64, 65, 75 & 76. The Prince of Wales was scheduled to leave for Cornwall on Friday, 11 July. (Warburton, *Rupert*, 3 : 134)

40 See: Clarendon, *History*, 9, 48, for a description of Goring's attitude and demands during the June meeting with the prince's agents.

41 'Portland MSS', 1 : 227-8

42 Clarendon, *History*, 9, 54: Chanter, 'Charles, Prince of Wales', 391

43 CCSP, 1 : 269. See: ERO, DD 34817h. On 23 June, and as a direct result of his stunning defeat at Naseby, King Charles wrote privately to his son, then at Barnstaple: '. . . if I should at any time be taken prisoner by the rebels, I command you (upon my blessing) never to yield to any conditions that are dishonourable, unsafe for your person, or derogatory to regal authority, upon any consideration whatsoever, though it were for the saving of my life; which in such a case, I am most confident, is in greatest security by your constant resolution, and not a whit the more in danger for their threatening, unless thereby you should yield to their desires'. (See: Clarendon, *History*, 10, 4, for the complete letter.)

44 Lister, *Clarendon*, 3 : 19-21, gives the entire letter. Also: CCSP, 1 : 268-9, no 1904

45 BM, 'A Continuation of the Proceedings of the Army . . .', E 293 (33), 1

46 Warburton, *Rupert*, 3 : 138-9 & 142-3

47 Clarendon, *History*, 9, 58; Warburton, *Rupert*, 3 : 153

48 'Perfect Passages', E 262 (38); 'Perfect Occurrences', E 262 (36), (29), and (40); 'The Moderate Intelligencer', E 293 (23), 167. It was generally reported that the 'clubmen', instead of joining with Goring, were actively harrassing his forces, especially in North Devon. See: 'A Diary, or an Exact Journal', E 262 (31). Clubmen were generally the middle sort of farmer and yeomen who had originally attempted to remain neutral but were now finding that things had gone beyond what they would endure. At first they were not *for* any group but <u>against</u> whichever army entered their area. By late 1645 they were definitely pro-parliamentarian

49 'Perfect Passages', E 262 (27). 311. Clarendon reported that Goring's horse committed 'such intolerable insolences and disorders that [they] alienated the hearts of those who were best affected to the King's service'. (*History*, 9, 58.)

50 Lister, *Clarendon*, 3 : 23 & 25. By 27 July Goring claimed to have only 1,300 foot left. CCSP, 1 : 271

51 Ibid, 1 : 270-1; Clarendon, *History*, 9, 58. Hyde confirmed the frustration

of the council in his letter to Digby of 6 August: '. . . it is evident the whole design is to put all the contempt upon us that is possible, and for aught I know to take away the Prince's person from us, . . .'. (CSPD, 1645-7, vol 510, p 46.)

52 Half of the weekly martial rates, plus £5,000 in arrears, was required for the support of this army. CCSP, 1:272; CSPD, 1645-7, vol 510, pp 46 & 47. See: Clarendon, *History*, 9, 76

53 Goring's troopers had such a bad reputation that efforts were made to keep them out of Cornwall entirely. 'Perfect Passages', E 262 (42), 336.

54 'Perfect Occurrences', E 262 (48); 'The Moderate Intelligencer', E 297 (12), 193; 'The True Informer', E 296 (29), 133. Also: 'Seymour Papers', Berkeley to Seymour, 3 September

55 'The Moderate Intelligencer', 196; 'The Scottish Dove', E 298 (2), 758; 'Perfect Passages', E 262 (51), 347

56 Ibid, 348

57 CCSP, 1:273 & 274

58 Clarendon makes clear the intolerable situation of 'insolences and out-rages' suffered by the people of north and central Devon at the hands of Goring's ill-disciplined and rowdy troopers, taking what they wanted without compensation, while their general enjoyed himself in Exeter. *History*, 9, 80. Cf 'The Scottish Dove', E 298 (9), 763. It was as a result of this behaviour that groups of clubmen became active in North Devon. See: 'Mercurius Britanicus', E 301 (9), 871, and E 302 (15), 879; 'The Weekly Account', E 302 (21); 'Perfect Passages', E 303 (28), 390

59 'Portland MSS', 1:262; 'The Moderate Intelligencer', E 299 (8), 214 & 216; and 'The True Informer', E 300 (2), 158. It seems that Goring was still manoeuvering for complete control of the western army before he would march. (Clarendon, *History*, 9, 83.)

60 'Portland MSS', 1:262. The City of Exeter granted the prince £100 as a reflection of their loyalty. (ERO, Chamber Act Book 8, p 335.)

61 Clarendon, *History*, 9, 82

62 'Perfect Passages', E 303 (28), 387. Fairfax sent the request to Westminster, but it came to nothing

63 'Portland MSS', 1:274. CCSP, 1:277-8. Grenville was to command the trained bandsmen raised in Cornwall, as well as his former regiments, while General Digby was to return to the command of the forces before Plymouth. (Clarendon, *History*, 9, 92 & 93.)

64 Ibid, 9, 84

65 'Portland MSS', 1:278; CCSP, 1:279

66 Lister, *Clarendon*, 3:26-7. See: 'Portland MSS', 1:270; 'Perfect Occur-rences', E 264 (21); 'The Scottish Dove', E 304 (18), 810; 'A Diary, or an Exact Journal', E 303 (29), 7

67 CCSP, 1:279, 280; Clarendon, *History*, 9, 78; Lister, *Clarendon*, 3:30-2

68 CCSP, 1:280; Cotton, *Barnstaple*, 424-6

69 Clarendon, *History*, 9, 94; CCSP, 1:280 & 281, nos 1982, 1988. See: Cotton, *Gleanings*, 104

70 Clarendon, *History*, 9, 94, 96 & 97; CCSP, 1:279, 280, 281, 282, 283, nos 1983, 1984, 1990, 1991, 1993 and 1997; 'Portland MSS', 1:282. Also: Lister, *Clarendon*, 3:32, 33-4

71 CCSP, 1:283, no 1998; Lister, *Clarendon*, 3:34

72 CCSP, 1:283, no 1999. See: Lister, *Clarendon*, 3:35

73 Cotton, *Gleanings*, 105. The Exeter Chamber rewarded Berkeley's service with a gift of £100 on 18 October. Chamber Act Book 8, p 339

74 'Seymour Papers', Pollard to Seymour, 13 & 28 October; Berkeley to the same, 20 October. Grenville also wrote to Seymour on the 20th urging him and Sir Henry Cary to raise additional levies in their area

75 Clarendon, *History*, 9, 103

76 Ibid, 99; CCSP, 1:288, no 2033. Also: Warburton, *Rupert*, 3:215. Goring warns of the necessity 'to settle a good understanding between the army, garrisons, and the country', and especially to win over the clubmen to the king's side. The best way to accomplish all this, according to Goring, was for the king to go into the West in person

77 Clarendon, *History*, 9, 100 & 101. See: 'Portland MSS', 1:323-4, 328 & 335; Cotton, *Barnstaple*, 440-1. Rumour continuously reported aid from France and Ireland, but very little was forthcoming

78 Clarendon, *History*, 9, 103

79 Rather than remove the prince from the country, and thus deal a fatal blow to their cause, the council had disobeyed the king's order and moved their charge further west

80 Carte, *Letters*, 1:102, 103-6

81 Clarendon, *History*, 9, 104 & 105. In December Grenville suggested that all royalist forces be concentrated behind a fortified line from Newton Bushel to Okehampton to Chulmleigh. This plan was not acceptable either. (Carte, *Letters*, 1:106-7.)

82 Clarendon, *History*, 9, 107-8. See: CCSP, 1:292, no 2056; and CSPD, 1645-7, vol 513, pp lix-lxiii

83 Ibid, vol 511, pp 282-3. See: 'Somerset MSS', 86. The royalist commanders had been sending out warrants to the countryside for some time before the prince's arrival, trying desperately to raise additional men, money, and supplies for a final attempt to drive the enemy from the county. See: 'Perfect Passages', E 314 (20), 503-4

84 Clarendon, *History*, 9, 109. See: Lister, *Clarendon*, 3:36-7; and CCSP, 1:297, no 2085

85 See: Ibid, 1:295 & 297, nos 2081, 2086 & 2087

86 Clarendon, *History*, 9, 117, 133; 'The Scottish Dove', E 316 (2) 926. Also: CSPD, 1645-7 vol 513, pp lxiii-lxiv. Upon this occasion, the blockade of Plymouth was again lifted

87 CCSP, 1:298, no 2090

88 Ibid, no 2091; Clarendon, *History*, 9, 133-5. That this was to be only a temporary situation is seen by the letter of assurance which the prince sent to Lord Goring on 21 January. (CCSP, 1:300, no 2100.)

89 Carte, *Letters*, 1:107; CCSP, 1:299, no 2096; Clarendon, *History*, 9, 137

90 Ibid, 138; CCSP, 1:299, no 2098. See: Carte, *Letters*, 1:107-9. Grenville felt that he had been trapped into losing his command. There is no doubt that the council had already made the decision to appoint Hopton some days before Sir Richard had suggested it. See: Hardacre, P. 'The End of the Civil War in Devon', RTDA, 85 (1935), 97-101

91 See: CCSP, 1:300, no 2101

92 Clarendon, *History*, 9, 139

93 Ibid, 9, 112-16, 146, 149

Chapter *11*. *Royalist Defeat in the West, october 1645-april 1646. Pages 152-169*

1 See: Gardiner, *Civil War*, 2:116-17; Fortescue, *Army*, 1:214-16, 219-20; Sprigg, *Anglia*, 327-30

2 Ibid, 327 & 335. Fairfax's army rested at Chard during the week of 6 October, collecting recruits, waiting for the soldiers' pay to arrive, and mapping out strategy. Care was also taken to ensure that Goring's horse did not escape eastward. See: 'Portland MSS', 1:292; BM, 'General Fairfax's letter . . .', E 307 (5), 3-4; 'The Moderate Intelligencer', E 305 (3), 157 & 170; Sprigg, *Anglia*, 145 & 146

3 CSPD, 1645-7, vol 510, p 153; JHC, 4, 292. Also: 'Perfect Passages', E 302 (24), 379-80; 'The Moderate Intelligencer', E 304 (11), 149

4 Other strongholds included those around Plymouth and Powderham Castle, as well as St Budeaux Church. See: Sprigg, *Anglia*, xi; Karkeek, P. Q. 'Fairfax in the West, 1645-46', RTDA, 8 (1876), 118

5 'The Moderate Intelligencer', E 306 (3), 165

6 BM, 'A Packet of Letters from Sir Thomas Fairfax . . .', E 307 (24), 3

7 'Perfect Occurrences', E 266 (3)

8 'The City Scout', E 305 (16), 5, where in reporting certain desertions the newsbook indicated '. . . that many more wait but for an opportunity to come away . . .'. See: 'The Moderate Intelligencer', 170; 'A Continuation of certain Special and Remarkable passages', E 306 (7), 2

9 The Moderate Intelligencer', 167; Rushworth, *Collections*, 6:94; Sprigg, *Anglia*, 146; 'Fairfax's Letter', 4

10 Sprigg, *Anglia*, 146-7; BM, 'The Taking of Tiverton . . .', E 306 (1), 2-3; 'Portland MSS', 1:292. Sprigg stated bluntly the general parliamentary feeling (and fear) which expected Goring to make some attempt to escape from Devon, when he called it '. . . the best game they had to play, and most disadvantageious to our proceedings'. (p 146) Cromwell's horse had not yet arrived to join the rest of the army

11 Sprigg, *Anglia*, 148; 'Fairfax's Letter', 4-5

12 'Portland MSS', 1:292; 'The Taking of Tiverton', 4-6; 'Fairfax's Letter', 5-6; Sprigg, *Anglia*, 154-6

13 Ibid, 157-8

14 See: 'The City Scout', E 308 (10), 3; 'A Continuation', 8, and E 307 (26), 7-8

15 Sprigg, *Anglia*, 158-9; 'Perfect Occurences', E 266 (10); 'Packet of Letters', 1-2

16 See: 'Perfect Passages', E 266 (13), 427-8; 'The Weekly Account', E 308 (13); 'The Moderate Intelligencer', E 308 (16), 185

17 Sprigg, *Anglia*, 160-1. See: 'The City Scout', 3-4; 'The True Informer', E 308 (3), 220-1; 'Mr Peters Message . . .', E 318 (6), 3

18 'The Moderate Intelligencer', E 309 (11), 189, and (25), 198; 'The City Scout', E 309 (2), 6-7; 'The Weekly Account', E 309 (6); 'Perfect Passages', E 266 (16), 438

19 Sprigg, *Anglia*, 161-3; 'Perfect Passages', E 266 (19), 445-6. See: 'A Continuation', E 310 (10), 3-4; 'The True Informer', E 309 (31) 243; 'The Moderate Intelligencer', E 311 (21), 218-19. Also: Rushworth, *Collections*, 6:95; Sprigg, *Anglia*, 165-7

20 Ibid, 335

P

21 'Perfect Passages', E 266 (26), 468; 'Perfect Occurrences', E 266 (23). See: Bell, *Memorials*, 1:257 & 259

22 Sprigg, *Anglia*, 167; 'The Moderate Intelligencer', 214-15; Bell, *Memorials*, 1:261. See: 'Portland MSS,' 1:307

23 Sprigg, *Anglia*, 169-70; 'The Moderate Intelligencer', E 309 (11), 190; 'Perfect Occurrences', E 266 (17)

24 Portland MSS', 1:322; 'Perfect Occurrences', E 266 (30). See: 'The Kingdomes Scout', E 311 (30), 4-6; 'Perfect Passages', E 266 (35), 489-90 & 494; 'The Moderate Intelligencer', E 313 (21), 231

25 BM, 'A Diary . . .', E 311 (23), 4; 'The Moderate Intelligencer', E 311 (21), 214-15; Bell, *Memorials*, 1:261. Also: JHL, 7, 713

26 Bell, *Memorials*, 1:262-4, 265-6; Sprigg, *Anglia*, 170-3. Cf 'The Moderate Intelligencer', E 313 (3), 226; 'The Scottish Dove', E 314 (2), 909

27 'Perfect Occurrences'; Cotton, R. W. 'Canonteign', *Notes and Gleanings*, 4:104; 'Perfect Passages', 495; Sprig, *Anglia*, 173

28 Bell, *Memorials*, 1:266-8; 'A Continuation', E 314 (9), 6; 'The Moderate Intelligencer', E 314 (4), 240, 243; Sprigg, *Anglia*, 175

29 'Perfect Occurrences', E 266 (34), and (37); 'A Diary', E 314 (5), 4-5

30 Bell, *Memorials*, 1:267 & 268; Sprigg, *Anglia*, 174; 'The Moderate Intelligencer', E 315 (4), 248, 250-1; 'Perfect Passages', E 314 (20), 499-500

31 See: Bell, *Memorials*, 1:269; Rushworth, *Collections*, 6:96

32 Sprigg, *Anglia*, 175

33 'Portland MSS', 1:331; Cotton, *Barnstaple*, 448; 'A Continuation', E 315 (7), 5

34 'A Diary', E 317 (7), 1-3; 'A Perfect Diurnall', E 266 (40). Colepeper was fairly optimistic in his letter of 8 January in which he speaks of an infantry of 4,000 'good men', with almost as many horse, 'which I would call very good ones, if they would fight more and plunder less'. ('Portland MSS', 1:334.)

35 'The Weekly Account', E 315 (8). Cf 'Portland MSS', 1:332; 'Perfect Occurrences', E 506 (1); 'The Moderate Intelligencer', E 316 (7), 259

36 Rushworth, *Collections*, 6:96; Sprigg, *Anglia*, 177. See: BM, 'A True Relation of the Fight at Bovy-Tracy . . .', E 316 (5), 7

37 Carte, *Letters*, 136; 'The Moderate Intelligencer', 262

38 Bell, *Memorials*, 1:274-5; 'Bovy-Tracy', 3-6; 'Perfect Passages', E 316 (27); 'The Moderate Intelligencer', 260

39 Reports reaching London told of the royalists 'then in a flying condition; the Cornish will not come in; most of their quarters were beaten up; the enemy flying some to Tavistock, others further into Cornwall, all much distracted'. 'Perfect Passages'. Cf 'The Scottish Dove', E 317 (4), 937; 'A Diary', 4-5; Sprigg, *Anglia*, 178

40 Rushworth, *Collections*, 6:96; Sprigg, *Anglia*, 179; 'The Moderate Intelligencer', E 317 (10), 267

41 'Perfect Passages', E 319 (8), 522 & 523. Most of the remaining royalist horse rallied in the region around Holsworthy in northwest Devon where they lived off the land for several weeks before being forced further west. Cf Cotton, *Barnstaple*, 458-9

42 'Perfect Passages', E 316 (27); 'Seymour Papers', 'Parliaments Victories' . . . 'Portland MSS', 1:336

43 See: 'A Diary', E 317 (7), 7-8; Bell, *Memorials*, 1:276-7. Also: 'Perfect Passages', 518-19

44 Sprigg, *Anglia*, 179-81; 'Portland MSS', 1:339-40; 'Seymour Papers', 'A Full and Exact Relation . . .', 4-5; Carte, *Letters*, 1:136-8

Q

45 Sprigg, *Anglia*, 183-5; 'Perfect Passages', E 319 (8), 524-5; 'A Continuation', E 317 (12), 8. See: 'Portland MSS', 1:351

46 Letters taken from a captured royalist ship at Dartmouth revealed that plans were still under way to obtain French aid. See: Sprigg, *Anglia*, 188; 'Mercurius Civicus', E 320 (13), 2027-8

47 See: Sprigg, *Anglia*, 185; 'Exact Relation', 6; Rushworth, *Collections*, 6:98

48 See: Dymond, G. P. 'Oliver Cromwell in the West', RTPI, 15 (1918), 244

49 Rushworth, *Collections*, 6:99; Sprigg, *Anglia*, 186; BM, 'Powderham Castle . . .', E 319 (22), 5; 'The Moderate Intelligencer', E 320 (11), 280

50 'Powderham Castle', 3-4; DCRO, Drake Collection 346M/F545, 'Sir Thomas Fairfax's Proceedings . . .', 1-2; 'The Weekly Account', E 322 (14); Sprigg, *Anglia*, 187; Bell, *Memorials*, 1:281

51 'The Moderate Intelligencer', E 319 (16), 276; 'The Kingdomes Weekly Intelligencer', E 320 (17), 5

52 See: HMC, 6th Rept, 'House of Lords MSS', 94

53 'Perfect Occurrences', E 320 (18)

54 'A Continuation', E 320 (21), 2

55 Bell, *Memorials*, 1:282

56 See: Sprigg, *Anglia*, 189 & 191; 'Fairfax's Proceedings', 8-9; 'Perfect Passages', E 322 (15), 542-3; 'The Cities Weekly Post', E 322 (9), 7. Sir Hardress Waller was in charge of the blockade of Exeter. See: HMC (1905) 'Egmont MSS', 1:280; Bell, *Memorials*, 1:282-3; Carte, *Letters*, 1:139

57 'Fairfax's Proceedings', 4-5. See: Sprigg, *Anglia*, 191; 'Egmont MSS', 1:280; CCSP, 1:303, no 2121. Also: Carte, *Letters*, 1:109-10

58 Sprigg, *Anglia*, 198

59 Cotton, *Barnstaple*, 476; Bell, *Memorials*, 1:284

60 Cotton, *Barnstaple*, 474; Sprigg, *Anglia*, 192-4

61 Carte, *Letters*, 1:112

62 Complete accounts of the battle of Great Torrington can be found in the following places. For the parliamentarian side: Sprigg, *Anglia*, 194-204; 'Sir Thomas Fairfax's Letter', E 324 (15); Carte, *Letters*, 1:140-2; Bell, *Memorials*, 1:285; 'A True Relation Concerning the Late Fight at Torrington', E 323 (8), 4-7; HMC, 6th Rept, p 100; 'A Fuller Relation . . .', E 324 (6), 8-11. For the royalist point of view: Carte, *Letters*, 1:110-14; Clarendon, *History*, 9, 143; HMC, 12th Rept, Pt 9 (1891), 'Duke of Beaufort MSS', 43. Also: Coate, *Cornwall*, 203-4; and Karkeek, 'Fairfax', 130-2

63 See: 'A More Full Relation . . .', E 325 (2), 2; 'A Perfect Diurnall', E 506 (13), 1080

64 Carte, *Letters*, 1:111

65 CCSP, 1:303; Carte, *Letters*, 1:114-15, 116

66 Sprigg, *Anglia*, 204-5; 'A Perfect Diurnall', 1080-1 & 1085; 'The Moderate Intelligencer', E 327 (2), 318

67 Sprigg, *Anglia*, 206-7. Also: Bell, *Memorials*, 1:286; 'A Perfect Diurnall', 1086; 'Two Letters . . .', E 325 (17), 7

68 Sprigg, *Anglia*, 213-14; Bell, *Memorials*, 1:286

69 Sprigg, *Anglia*, 207-8

70 See: Clarendon, *History*, 9, 150; Carte, *Letters*, 1:117-24. Also: Bell, *Memorials*, 1:287 & 288; Sprigg, *Anglia*, 225ff

71 Ibid, 228

72 Ibid, 236

73 'A Perfect Diurnall', E 506 (23), 1118; 'Colonel Weldens taking of Inch-House', E 330 (5), 1

74 'Mercurius Civicus', E 332 (4), 2096; Sprigg, *Anglia*, 239-41; 'Sir Thomas Fairfax's Letter . . .', E 330 (20), 1-2

75 Sprigg, *Anglia*, 241-3; ERO, Act Book 8, p 350; Cotton, *Gleanings*, 110-11; Bell, *Memorials*, 1:289. Rushworth mentioned that the parliamentarians had certain knowledge that once Exeter surrendered, Barnstaple would do the same. Also: BM, 'The Agreement . . .', E 333 (7), 4-5; 'The Treatie for the Surrendring of Exeter . . .', E 332 (2)

76 Ibid, 5-6

77 'Perfect Occurrences', E 506 (31); 'A Perfect Diurnall', E 506 (29), 1134; 'Sir Thomas Fairfax's Further Proceedings in the West', E 333 (23), 1 & 4; 'Seymour Papers', 'Several Letters . . .', 4-5; Bell, *Memorials*, 1:290

78 'Seymour Papers', 'The Articles of Exeter . . .', passim

79 Sprigg, *Anglia*, 250; 'Four Strong Castles Taken . . .', E 334 (8), passim; Cotton, *Barnstaple*, 512-15. Also: 'Barnstaple agreed to be Surrendred...', E 333 (13), 3, 6-7

80 Sprigg, *Anglia*, 251-2; 'Fairfax's Further Proceedings', 5; CSPD, 1645-7, vol 514, p 416. See: ERO, Act Book 8, p 351; Cotton, *Gleanings*, 114-17

81 See especially: Karkeek, 'Fortescue', 339-50; 'Seymour Papers', 'The Articles of Agreement . . .'; Clermont, *Fortescue*, 35,7 & 39

82 See: JHC, 4, 440, 456, 492 & 506

Appendix B. Members of Parliament for Devon and Exeter, 1640-6. Pages 179-182

1 See: Lady Evangeline de Villiers, 'Parliamentary Boroughs restored by the House of Commons 1621-41', EHR (1952), 67:175-202

2 Hugh Potter sat for Berwick-on-Tweed previously. Sir Samuel Rolle, who took Wise's place in 1641, sat for a Cornish borough in the Short Parliament. Alexander, J. J. 'Devon County Members of Parliament', RTDA (1916), 48:332

3 Thomas Wise and John Upton

4 Twelve if Simon Snow were counted since there is a question as to whether he did in fact sit in the Short Parliament

5 Brunton, Douglas and Pennington, D. H. *Members of the Long Parliament* (1954), 134; Keeler, Mary Frear. *The Long Parliament, 1640-1641 : A Biographical Study of its Members* (Philadelphia 1954), 318

6 Ibid, 330

7 Ibid, 318

8 Ibid, 43

9 Ibid, 42

10 Wilkin, W. H. 'Notes on the Members for Honiton, 1640-1868', RTDA (1934), 66:253-4

11 Keeler, *Long Parliament*, 119

12 Ibid, 42

13 It is generally true that from these larger towns, and from Exeter, there came as MPs well-to-do merchants; from the smaller boroughs, gentlemen or lawyers; and from the county, the gentry

14 During this period 233 writs were issued for recruiters to reinforce the membership of the Long Parliament. It can be assumed that those elected for Devon were probably chosen during this period as only eleven new writs were issued in February and March of 1647. Kershaw, R. N. 'The Recruiting of the Long Parliament, 1645-7', in *History* (October 1923), 8:177 and 178

15 John Rolle, merchant of London, for instance, was brother to Sir Samuel Rolle, cousin to Sir Thomas Hele, brother-in-law of Alexander Carew, all MPs in the Long Parliament, and was married to the daughter of Sir George Chudleigh of Ashton. Keeler, *Long Parliament*, 327

16 Kershaw, 'Recruiting', 169

17 Keeler, *Long Parliament*, passim

18 Although George Hartnoll was neither a particularly strong nor ardent royalist

19 Those at the Oxford Parliament included: Ferris, Matthew, John Russell, Peter Sainthill, and Robert Walker

20 One each from Exeter, Barnstaple, Tiverton, Dartmouth, and Plymouth

21 Tiverton thus had two royalists as burgesses, and Bere Alston, Plympton Earle, and Honiton one each. The knight of the shire, Edward Seymour, was also a royalist

Bibliography

Primary Sources

A MANUSCRIPTS

1. Unpublished Manuscripts
British Museum. Addition Manuscripts. 18980, 18981, 35297
Devon County Record Office. Book of Geldings Armor and Weapons within the East Division, Devon 1569 MSS
—. Drake Collection 346M/F545
—. Quarter Sessions Records of the County of Devon (1640-1651)
—. Quarter Sessions Rolls
—. Seymour Papers, no 1392
—. Wollocombe MSS, no 198M/
Exeter City Record Office. Account Book of Household Expenses of John Hayne (1631-1643)
—. Dartmouth Corporation Archives
—. Act Books of the Chamber, vols 7 and 8
—. Commissions Pardons Etc
—. Letters and Papers relating to the Civil War in Devon and Cornwall in 1644, no 56999
—. Royal Letters and Other Papers, Letter Books 60A-60G
—. 'Sir Francis Basset, Knt of Tehidy, Cornwall AD 1594 to AD 1645 his Letters and Papers . . .', handwritten compilation by Reginald Metcalfe, 1924
—. Steele-Perkins Papers. The Civil War: Proceedings in Devon and Dorset, nos DD 34815-34822
Public Record Office. State Papers, Domestic Series
Totnes Guildhall. Ley Account
—. Totnes Manuscript

2. Published Collections, Contemporary Memoirs, and Diaries
Bell, Robert (ed). *Memorials of the Civil War : comprising the Correspondence of the Fairfax family . . . ,* (1849)
Blake, William J. 'Hooker's Synopsis Chorographical of Devonshire'. RTDA, 47 (Plymouth 1915), 334-48
Carte, Thomas (ed). *A Collection of Original Letters and Papers, concerning the Affairs of England, from the year 1641 to 1660.* (1739)
Chadwyck-Healey, Charles E. H. (ed). *Bellum Civile. Hopton's Narrative of his campaign in the West (1642-1644) and other papers.* Somersetshire Record Society, 18 (1902)
Coate, Mary. 'An Original Diary of Colonel Robert Bennett of Hexworthy (1642-3)'. DCNQ, 18 (Exeter 1935), 251-59

Cruwys, Margaret C. S. (ed). *A Cruwys Morchard Notebook 1066-1874.* (Exeter and London, 1939)

Fisher, Arthur (ed). 'The Apologie of Colonel John Were in Vindication of His Proceedings since the beginning of this present Parliament'. DCNQ, 4 (Exeter 1907)

Green, Mary Anne Everett (ed). *Letters of Queen Henrietta Maria, including her private correspondence with Charles the First.* (1857)

Historical Manuscript Commission. Reports. (See specific footnes involved.)

Hoker, John Vowell alias. *The Description of the Citie of Excester.* Edited by Walter J. Harte, J. W. Schopp, and H. Tapley-Soper. (Exeter, 1919-1947)

Hyde, Edward, Earl of Clarendon. *The History of the Rebellion and Civil Wars in England begun in the year 1641.* Edited by W. Dunn Macray. Oxford, 1888)

Izacke, Richard and Samuel. *Remarkable Antiquities of the City of Exeter.* (1723)

Karkeek, Paul Q. (ed). 'Extracts from a Memorandum Book belonging to Thomas Roberts and Family, of Stockleigh Pomeroy, 1621 to 1644'. RTDA, 10 (1878)

Long, Charles Edward (ed). *Diary of the Marches of the Royal Army during the Great Civil War; kept by Richard Symonds.* (Camden Society, Westminster, 1859)

Pole, Sir William. *Collections towards a Description of the County of Devon.* (1791)

Risdon, Tristram. *The Chorographical Description or Survey of the County of Devon.* (1811)

Rushworth, John. *Historical Collections.* vols 4-6. (1721-1722)

Sprigg, Joshua. *Anglia Rediviva; England's Recovery : Being the History of the Motions, Actions, and Successes of the Army under the immediate conduct of . . . Sir Thomas Fairfax . . .* (1647)

Trevelyan, Sir Walter C. and Sir Charles Edward (eds). *Trevelyan Papers,* Pt 3, (Camden Society. Westminster, 1872)

Troup, Frances B. (ed). 'A Cavalier's Note-book: continued by his Son'. RTDA, 21 (Plymouth 1889)

Warburton, Eliot. *Memoirs of Prince Rupert, and the Cavaliers.* (1849)

Worth, R. N. (ed). *The Buller Papers.* (Privately printed, 1895)

—. 'The Siege Accounts of Plymouth'. RTDA, 17 (Plymouth 1885)

Yonge, James. 'Plimouth Memoirs . . .' Edited by R. N. Worth. *Transactions of the Plymouth Institution . . . ,* 5 (Plymouth 1876), 509-66

                          B   OFFICIAL RECORDS

Bush, R. J. E. 'The Civil War and Interregnum in Exeter, 1642-1660'. (Taken from Minute Books of the Sessions of the Peace for Exeter, ERO, Book 64.) DCNQ, 29 (Torquay 1964)

Chanter, J. R. and Thomas Wainwright. *Reprint of the Barnstaple Records.* (Barnstaple, 1900)

Cock, John. *Records of ye Antient Borough of South Molton in ye County of Devon.* (Exeter, 1893)

Cotton, W. and Henry Woollcombe. *Gleanings from the Municipal and Cathedral Records Relative to the History of the City of Exeter.* (Exeter, 1877)

Firth, Charles Harding and R. S. Rait. *Acts and Ordinances of the Interregnum, 1642-1660.* (1911)

Fry, Henry A. (ed). *A Calendar of Inquisitories Post Mortem for Cornwall and Devon . . . 1216-1649.* (Devon and Cornwall Record Society, 1906)

Green, Mary Anne Everett (ed). *Calendar of the Proceedings of the Committee for Compounding . . . 1643-1660.* (1889-1892)

Hamilton, A. H. A. *Quarter Sessions from Queen Elizabeth to Queen Anne.* (1878)

Hamilton, William D. (ed). *Calendar of State Papers, Domestic Series, of the Reign of Charles I.* Vols 1625-49, 1641-47. (1887-1891)

Journal of the House of Commons, vols 2-4. (1803)

Journal of the House of Lords, vols 4-8

Mahaffy, Robert P. (ed). *Calendar of the State Papers Relating to Ireland . . . Adventurers for Land. 1642-1659.* (1903)

Moore, Stuart A. (ed). *A Calendar of the Archives of the Borough of Dartmouth.* (1879-1880)

—. *A Calendar of the Records and Muniments belonging to the Corporation of the City of Exeter Preserved in the Record Room of the Guildhall.* (Exeter, 1863-70)

Ogle, O. and Bliss, W. H. (eds). *Calendar of the Clarendon State Papers preserved in the Bodleian Library.* (Oxford, 1872)

Tapley-Soper, H. and Reynell-Upham, W. U. *The Registers of Baptisms, Marriages, and Burials of the City of Exeter.* (1910-1933)

Vivian, J. L. (ed). *The Visitations of the County of Devon, Comprising the Heralds' Visitations of 1531, 1564, and 1620.* (Exeter, 1895)

Worth, R. N. *Calendar of the Plymouth Municipal Records.* (Plymouth, 1893)

C NEWSBOOKS, PAMPHLETS, ETC

The newsbooks, pamphlets, and tracts found in the Thomason Collection in the British Museum constitute one of the most valuable contemporary sources for the study of the civil war period. Although mainly published in London, and therefore prejudiced in tone, these items help to clarify parliamentarian thoughts, reactions, and hopes during years of civil strife. Although all issues of newsbooks, and copies of pamphlets for this period were studied, only those used in this book have been noted in the footnotes

Secondary Sources

A MONOGRAPHIC AND ANTIQUARIAN HISTORIES

Alexander, J. J. and Hooper, W. R. *The History of Great Torrington in the County of Devon.* (Norwich, 1948)

Bracken, C. W. *A History of Plymouth and Her Neighbours.* (Plymouth, 1931)

Brunton, Douglas and Pennington, D. H. *Members of the Long Parliament.* (1954)

Coate, Mary. *Cornwall in the Great Civil War and Interregnum 1642-1660 : A Social and Political Study.* (Oxford, 1933)

Cotton, Richard W. *Barnstaple and the Northern Part of Devonshire during the Great Civil War, 1642-1646.* (Chilworth & London, 1889)

Davidson, James. *A History of the Town and Parish of Axminster, in the County of Devon.* (Manuscript vol in ERO.) Secktor, 1832

Dunsford, Martin. *Historical Memoirs of the Town and Parish of Tiverton, in the County of Devon.* (Exeter, 1790)

Fortescue, J. W. *A History of the British Army.* 2 vols. (1935)

Gidley, John. *Notices of Exeter; comprising A History of Royal Visits to the Ancient and Loyal City, from A.D. 49, to A.D. 1863.* (Exeter, 1863)

Granville, Roger, *The History of Bideford.* (Bideford, 1883)

Gribble, Joseph Besley. *Memorials of Barnstaple.* . . (Barnstaple, 1830)

Hardacre, Paul H. *The Royalists During the Puritan Revolution.* (The Hague, 1956)

Harding, W. *The History of Tiverton in the County of Devon.* (Tiverton, 1845-1847)

Hoskins, William G. *Devon.* (1954)

—, and Finberg, H. P. R. *Devonshire Studies.* (1952)

— (ed). *Exeter in the 17th century : Tax and Rate Assessments 1602-1699.* Devon & Cornwall Record Society, New Series vol 2. (Torquay, 1957)

—. *Two Thousand Years in Exeter.* (Exeter, 1960)

Jenkins, Alexander. *Civil and Ecclesiastical History of the City of Exeter and its Environs.* . . (Exeter, 1841)

Keeler, Mary Frear. *The Long Parliament, 1640-1641 : A Biographical Study of its members.* (Philadelphia, 1954)

MacCaffrey, Wallace T. *Exeter, 1540-1640 : The Growth of an English County Town.* Cambridge, (1958)

Oliver, George. *Collections, Illustrating the History of the Catholic Religion in the Counties of Cornwall, Devon,* . . . (1857)

—. *The History of the City of Exeter.* (Exeter, 1861)

Polwhele, Richard. *The History of Devonshire.* (1797)

Powell, John Rowland. *The Navy in the English Civil War.* (1962)

Rowe, J. Brooking. *A History of the Borough of Plympton Erle.* (Exeter, 1906)

Russell, Percy. *Dartmouth: A History of the Port and Town.* (1950)

—. *The Good Town of Totnes.* (Torquay, 1963)

St Ledger-Gordon, Douglas F. *Devonshire.* (1950)

Stephens, W. B. *Seventeenth-Century Exeter : A Study of Industrial and Commercial Development, 1625-1688.* (Exeter, 1958)

Wedgwood, V. *The King's War, 1641-1647.* (New York, 1959)

Worth, R. N. *A History of Devonshire.* (1895)

—. *History of Plymouth from the Earliest Period to the Present Time.* (Plymouth, 1890)

B   BIOGRAPHICAL AND GENEALOGICAL WORKS

Adams, Maxwell. 'A Brief Account of Ashton Church and of Some of the Chudleighs of Ashton'. RTDA, 1899

Brett, S. Reed. *John Pym 1583-1643 : The Statesman of the Puritan Revolution.* (1940)

Champernowne, Catherine Elizabeth. *The Champernowne Family.* Typescript, 1954

Chichester, Sir Alexander P. B. *History of the Family of Chichester, from A.D. 1086 to 1870.* (1871)

Cleaveland, Ezra. *A Genealogical History of the Noble and Illustrious Family of Courtenay.* (Exeter, 1735)

Drake, Sir William R. *Devonshire Notes and Notelets, Principally Genealogical and Heraldic.* (London, n d)

Eliott-Drake, Lady. *The Family and Heirs of Sir Francis Drake.* (1911)

Fortescue, Hugh 4th Earl. *A Chronicle of Castle Hill, 1454-1918.* (1929)

Fortescue, Thomas, Lord Clermont. *A History of the Family of Fortescue in all its Branches.* (1880)
Granville, Roger. *The History of the Granville Family.* (Exeter, 1895)
—. *The King's General in the West : The Life of Sir Richard Granville, Bart., 1600-1659.* (1908)
Harrison, F. *The Devon Carys.* (New York, 1920)
Hexter, Jack H. *The Reign of King Pym.* (Cambridge, 1941)
Lister, Thomas H. *Life and Administration of Edward, First Earl of Clarendon.* (1837)
Radford, G. H. 'Lady Howard of Fitzford'. RTDA, 22 (1890), 66-110
—. 'The Wyses and Tremaynes of Sydenham'. RTDA, 41 (1909), 131-5
Skinner, A. J. P. 'Pedigree of the Family of Walrond of Bovey in the Parish of Seaton and Beer, County Devon'. RTDA, 39 (1907), 264
Troup, Frances B. 'Biographical Sketch of the Rev Christopher Jelinger, M.A.' RTDA, 32 (1900), 249-70
—. 'The Sainthills of Bradninch, Devon: Being a Pedigree of the Family, with notes thereon, and copies of Documents relating to the Family History'. RTDA, 21 (1889)
Wade, C. E. *John Pym.* (1912)

C ARTICLES

Of the eighty articles consulted in the preparation of this book, those actually

used have been included in the appropriate notes

Acknowledgments

The publication of a first book, particularly one based on a doctoral dissertation, leaves a great deal to be desired. This work is no exception. In its preparation, however, a number of people were both kind and helpful. I would like to express my gratitude to Professor William L. Sachse, University of Wisconsin, for his guidance and comments. Especially co-operative and of great service were Miss Margaret Cash, the then Devon Deputy County Archivist, and her assistants. Also, the staff at the Exeter Record Office and the Exeter City Library were always helpful.

Chapter 7 (Royalist War-Time Administration of Devon and Exeter) and the appendix material (Members of Parliament for Devon and Exeter) were originally published in the *Devon and Cornwall Notes and Queries*.

Travel grants from the University of Wisconsin were helpful during the research stage of this study, and a research grant from the University of Louisville made easier the final preparation of the manuscript.

Index